Advertising and Society

ADVERTISING AND SOCIETY

Controversies and Consequences

Edited by Carol J. Pardun

WILEY-BLACKWELL

A John Wiley & Sons, Ltd., Publication

This edition first published 2009
© 2009 Blackwell Publishing Ltd

Blackwell Publishing was acquired by John Wiley & Sons in February 2007. Blackwell's publishing program has been merged with Wiley's global Scientific, Technical, and Medical business to form Wiley-Blackwell.

Registered Office
John Wiley & Sons Ltd, The Atrium, Southern Gate, Chichester, West Sussex, PO19 8SQ, United Kingdom

Editorial Offices
350 Main Street, Malden, MA 02148-5020, USA
9600 Garsington Road, Oxford, OX4 2DQ, UK
The Atrium, Southern Gate, Chichester, West Sussex, PO19 8SQ, UK

For details of our global editorial offices, for customer services, and for information about how to apply for permission to reuse the copyright material in this book please see our website at www.wiley.com/wiley-blackwell.

The right of Carol J. Pardun to be identified as the author of the editorial material in this work has been asserted in accordance with the Copyright, Designs and Patents Act 1988.

Wiley also publishes its books in a variety of electronic formats. Some content that appears in print may not be available in electronic books.

Designations used by companies to distinguish their products are often claimed as trademarks. All brand names and product names used in this book are trade names, service marks, trademarks or registered trademarks of their respective owners. The publisher is not associated with any product or vendor mentioned in this book. This publication is designed to provide accurate and authoritative information in regard to the subject matter covered. It is sold on the understanding that the publisher is not engaged in rendering professional services. If professional advice or other expert assistance is required, the services of a competent professional should be sought.

Library of Congress Cataloging-in-Publication Data

Advertising and society : controversies and consequences / edited by Carol J. Pardun.
  p. cm.
  Includes bibliographical references and index.
  ISBN 978-1-4051-4409-4 (hardcover : alk. paper)—ISBN 978-1-4051-4410-0 (pbk. : alk. paper)
  1. Advertising—Social aspects—United States.   2. Advertising, Political—United States.
3. Advertising—United States.   I. Pardun, Carol J.

  HF5813.U6A6196 2009
  659.1′0420973—dc22

                                                                    2008040261

A catalogue record for this book is available from the British Library.

Set in 10.5/13pt Minion by Graphicraft Limited, Hong Kong
Printed in Singapore by Utopia Press Pte Ltd

01   2009

Contents

Argument	Counterargument

Argument	Counterargument

Contents

Argument	Counterargument
Companies are wise – and ethical – to use "social responsibility" as a creative strategy 178 *Debra Merskin*	The adoption of social responsibility through cause-related marketing as a business strategy is unethical 187 *Peggy Kreshel*

(All illustrations are reproduced courtesy of Randy Livingston.)

Notes on Contributors

Edd Applegate, Professor of Advertising, School of Journalism, Middle Tennessee State University, Murfreesboro, teaches primarily senior-level courses in advertising, including Advertising Management and Advertising Campaigns. He has edited and/or written several books, including *The Ad Men and Women: A Biographical Dictionary of Advertising, Personalities and Products: A Historical Perspective on Advertising in America, Strategic Copywriting: How to Create Effective Advertising*, and *Cases in Advertising and Marketing Management*.

Beth Barnes, Director of the School of Journalism and Telecommunications, University of Kentucky, teaches in the school's Integrated Strategic Communications program. Her research interests are in integrated communication campaign planning and advertising pedagogy.

Jason Chambers, Associate Professor of Advertising, University of Illinois at Urbana-Champaign, conducts research on advertising history and on advertising to diverse audiences. He is the author of *Madison Avenue and the Color Line: African Americans in the Advertising Industry*.

Kathy Roberts Forde, Assistant Professor of Journalism, University of Minnesota, teaches and conducts research in the area of media history, media law, and literary journalism. She is the author of *Literary Journalism on Trial: Masson v. New Yorker and the First Amendment*.

Jennifer D. Greer, Chair, Department of Journalism, University of Alabama, specializes in the effects of media content and has published research focusing on political advertising, online media, and gender issues.

Marie Hardin, Associate Professor of Journalism, Penn State, is also Associate Director of the Center for Sports Journalism. Her research focuses on ethics and diversity issues in sports media and on the experiences of women in sports journalism.

R. Michael Hoefges, Associate Professor of Advertising and Media Law, University of North Carolina at Chapel Hill, publishes on the topic of advertising law and regulation, and currently serves on the National Advertising Review Board. He was in private law practice for nearly a decade before entering academia.

Keisha L. Hoerrner, is interim Department Chair at Kennesaw State University's Department of First-Year Programs and Associate Professor of Communication. Her specialty research area is the electronic media's effect on children.

C. Ann Hollifield, Thomas C. Dowden Professor of Media Research, Grady College of Journalism and Mass Communication, the University of Georgia, also serves as coordinator of the Michael J. Faherty Broadcast Management Laboratory. Her research focuses on media management and the effects of media on the economy.

Anne Johnston is Associate Dean for Graduate Studies, School of Journalism and Mass Communication, the University of North Carolina at Chapel Hill. Her research interests include political communication, political advertising, women and politics, and diversity issues in the media.

Peggy Kreshel, Associate Professor of Advertising, Grady College of Journalism and Mass Communication and affiliate faculty member in the Institute for Women's Studies at the University of Georgia, conducts research on the professional culture, social issues and ethics, and history of advertising, as well as race and gender issues in the media.

Randy Livingston, Assistant Professor, Media Design, School of Journalism, Middle Tennessee State University, is co-author of *Adobe Illustrator CS3 Wow! Book* and is beginning work on the *Adobe Illustrator CS4 Wow! Book*.

Charles Lubbers, Chair, Department of Contemporary Media and Journalism, University of South Dakota, teaches public relations, advertising, and research methods courses; his major areas of research include public relations pedagogy, travel and tourism, and entertainment promotion.

Jane Marcellus, Associate Professor of Journalism, Middle Tennessee State University, teaches courses in media history, feature writing, qualitative research methods, and cultural studies. Her research, which examines media representation of women in the early twentieth century, has been published in *Journalism & Mass Communication Quarterly*, *American Journalism*, and *Women's Studies – An Inter-disciplinary Journal*.

Kathy Brittain McKee, Associate Provost, Dean of Academic Services and Professor of Communication, Berry College, teaches courses in public relations and journalism. She is a co-author of *Media Ethics Cases and Moral Reasoning* and *Applied Public Relations* and has published research in media ethics, advertising and video imagery, product placement, communication pedagogy, and student–press regulation.

Debra Merskin, Associate Professor, School of Journalism and Communication, University of Oregon, is head of the communication studies sequence. Her research focuses on stereotyping of women and other minorities in mass media representations. Her work appears in *Mass Communication & Society*, *The Howard Journal of Communication*, and *American Behavioral Scientist*, and she is co-editor of *Critical Thinking about Sex, Love, and Romance in the Mass Media*. Her *Minorities, and Media: A Critical Introduction* is due out in 2008.

Carol J. Pardun, Professor and Director, School of Journalism and Mass Communications, University of South Carolina, teaches advertising courses and conducts research on the impact of the media on adolescents. She became president elect of the Association for Journalism and Mass Communication in October 2008 and in 2009 will be the organization's president.

Ivan Preston, Professor Emeritus of Advertising, University of Wisconsin-Madison, headed the advertising sequence in the School of Journalism and Mass Communication for 31 years. He is the author of many books and articles specializing in advertising regulation, including the iconic *The Great American Blowup: Puffery in Advertising and Selling*.

Paula Rausch MAMC, RN, is a doctoral student focusing on science/health communication at the University of Florida College of Journalism and Communications.

Tom Reichert, Associate Professor of Advertising and Public Relations, Grady College of Journalism and Mass Communication, the University of Georgia, teaches advertising courses and conducts research on media and politics, social marketing, and the content and effects of sex in the media. He is the author of *The Erotic History of Advertising* and co-editor of *Sex in Advertising* and *Sex in Consumer Culture*. He also maintains the website <sexinadvertising.com>.

Jef I. Richards, Professor of Advertising, University of Texas at Austin, conducts research that deals with legal and ethical issues related to advertising, which has appeared in numerous books and articles. He holds both a Ph.D. and J.D.

J. Walker Smith, President of Yankelovich, Inc., is a leading expert in marketing and consumer trends and a frequent speaker on marketing issues. He does a weekly commentary about cities and communities for public radio and he is the author of four books on topics ranging from marketing to generations to work/life balance. He holds a Ph.D. in Mass Communication from the University of North Carolina at Chapel Hill.

Debbie Treise, Associate Dean of Graduate Studies, at the College of Journalism and Communications, University of Florida, focuses her research on science and health communications, and advertising public service announcements.

Bruce G. Vanden Bergh, Professor, Department of Advertising, Public Relations, and Retailing, Michigan State University, has written about regulatory, social, cultural, and creative aspects of advertising for over 30 years. He was Chair of the Department of Advertising at MSU from 1986 to 1997, and President of the American Academy of Advertising in 1995.

Lara Zwarun, Assistant Professor, Department of Communication, University of Texas at Arlington, teaches advertising, persuasion, and communication law. Her research has appeared in the *American Journal of Public Health*, the *Journal of Broadcasting and Electronic Media*, and *Mass Communication and Society*, and centers on self-regulation and regulation of advertising for controversial products, such as alcohol, tobacco, and junk food.

1 Introduction

People Don't Hate Advertising

They Hate Bad Advertising

Carol J. Pardun

It's easy to take shots at advertising. After all, it messes with our television programs, it clutters up our newspapers, it destroys the ecological balance on the highways with too many billboards imploring us to "See Rock City!"

But we also love advertising. We talk about our favorite Super Bowl commercials, we incorporate jingles into our everyday language, and we even place them as art in our homes. I have five ads hanging in my office from the early 1900s. I bought them on Ebay after getting into a bidding war with other ad collectors. I had them custom framed. There is no question. These five wall hangings aren't just ads. These are great ads!

Still, a lot about advertising makes us uneasy. We're just not sure why.

Advertising is a strange business. It's everywhere, so people often think they're advertising experts. But, the reality is, many people don't know that much about how ads are made, how much they cost, how they work, and how to figure out whether an ad is appropriate or deceptive – let alone legal.

It's important to think about advertising. From the money that exchanges hands, the messages that bombard us throughout the day, the politicians who fight to regulate the messages that enter our homes, to the technology geniuses who are trying to figure out ways to better count how many advertising messages we see at home, at work, on the way to work, and every other minute in between – the more we can understand about the world of advertising, the better.

One way to learn about advertising is to begin to think critically about it. That's the focus of this book. While you undoubtedly already have some fairly strong opinions about advertising, the people who have written the essays you'll be reading want you to take a hard look at those opinions. They want to challenge your assumptions. They want you to think. You may not change your mind about a topic, but at the very least you'll have the opportunity to examine these issues from more than one perspective.

A Mirror of Society? Or an Agent of Change?

Years ago, Richard Pollay (1986) wrote a scholarly article laying out the argument about the role of advertising. It's a seminal paper and has been quoted by many advertising scholars through the years. Whenever I teach an introduction to advertising class, on the first day of class, I ask my students those two questions. Is advertising a mirror of society? Or an agent of change? The basic premise is something like this: if advertising is a mirror of society, then the advertising industry is not really to blame for all the problems associated with bad advertising. *We're to blame.* If we don't like the ads, stop watching the shows that they're on, or stop buying the products, or tell the advertising agencies that you hate their ads. But if we respond (as we might to sexy ads), then that shows advertising is only going in that direction because it's what we want. It's a reflection of our culture. We look in the mirror and we see (and have no one to blame but) ourselves.

On the other hand, perhaps advertising is an agent of change. This means that advertising can change our perspectives about a particular product and eventually contribute significantly to what we purchase. *So, if that's true, then it's advertising's fault we're the way we are.*

I remember the first time I saw an ad for a coffee bag. Wow, I thought. What a great idea. Fresh-brewed coffee, one mug at a time. I went to the grocery store and looked for the specific brand of coffee I saw in the ad that was selling this new "coffee bag." So, in some regard, this would be an example that advertising is an agent of change. Before seeing the ad I ground my own coffee beans and used a drip coffee maker. Basically, I was a coffee snob. After just one advertisement I was willing to potentially give up my coffee-brewing habit and totally change the way I drank coffee. The only problem was that after one "dunk" I realized that this coffee was not going to taste anything at all like my more labor-intensive coffee. In fact, it wasn't even as good as some instant coffee I had tasted. The advertisement had created false hope. I may have been willing to change, but the product didn't live up to its advertising. So, even if I had been willing to accept that advertising is powerful, I had to at least pause (while taking a sip of my rather mediocre coffee) to consider the limits of advertising.

On the other hand, the first time I saw an ad for a gourmet butternut squash soup, I felt compelled to check it out. Until I saw that ad, I was a die-hard chunky tomato soup eater. I changed. Now I prefer butternut squash. I owe it all to advertising. Well, not quite. The soup is quite good – in fact, perhaps even better than the advertising promises that it is.

These might seem like silly examples, but many people through the years have argued that all sorts of ads have impacted people and persuaded them to change their buying behaviors – and ultimately change their lives – all because of the ads. Some people claim they have friends who drink vodka now simply because of those funky, art-inspired ads. Of course, they never think advertising has impacted them personally. Only others. (This is called Third Person Effect and there are whole books written on this very interesting media theory.) Many people have argued that advertising is to blame for why so many young kids smoke. You'll read more about that in chapter 5. So, there is a lot of evidence that advertising is, indeed, an agent of change.

Now, at this point, you're thinking: the answer's clear. It's both! Advertising must be both a mirror of society *and* an agent of change. That's right, of course. But it's way more interesting – and instructive – to stick to one side or the other. That's what I make my students do. When I ask the questions on the first day of class, they typically start out answering the expected "both." I ask them to explain. The answers are not very interesting. After a few minutes of trying to give an "on the one hand/on the other hand" answer, they give up, shrug their shoulders and say, "Well, it just is. I don't know why."

Then I'll tell them they have to choose a side. Each student must vote one way or the other. I have the "mirror of society" people move to one side of the classroom and the "agent of change" people move to the other side. Then I'll ask them to tell me why they are on the left (or right) side of the room. Finally, the answers start getting interesting. My students are really starting to think. They're starting to get passionate about the issue. They're starting to form an opinion. They're learning.

That's what this book is about. It's about examining the controversies, thinking about the consequences of perspectives, and then choosing a side.

Intuitively we already know that both sides have merits, but we end up learning more about *both* sides if we're willing to argue *one* side. Even if we argue a side we don't actually believe, we can come to appreciate the other side of the argument and learn more about our own convictions.

There are a number of fine books on the market that deal with the impact of advertising on society. What is different about this book is that it is organized by "controversies and consequences." I've asked a number of advertising experts to write essays about a controversial topic – but to write the essay from only one perspective. I found that as I read the essays I would be persuaded by the first argument – and then persuaded by the second argument. With the essays side by side, it becomes easier to see that these topics are complex and not to be dismissed easily.

The idea for this book came out of a class I taught when I was a faculty member at the University of North Carolina-Chapel Hill in 2005. I had my students conduct research and debates about these very topics. I put them into teams without considering what their personal views were about a particular topic. In fact, if I knew they felt one way, I would try to put them on the opposite team. After researching the topic and trying to develop a strong argument, they would begin to see that the "other side" also had a point. Over the course of the semester, they came to understand that there is more than one way to look at just about everything that has to do with advertising – and many other socially oriented subjects.

Some of the authors of these essays feel very strongly about a particular topic. They have written with passion about a topic they feel passionate about. Ivan Preston is a good example of this kind of writer. He has spent his entire academic career writing about the dangers of puffery in advertising. He has re-articulated this compelling argument in the essay found in chapter 11. However, some of the authors climbed out on a limb and decided to try looking at the issue from a perspective that is not what they believe. They did it because I asked them to. But I hope they also did it because it opened up the issue to them in a new way. Jef Richards is a good example of this. He has written extensively about the dangers of regulating tobacco advertising, yet in chapter 5 in this book he was willing to explore the idea that the government has not done enough. As you can imagine, for the writers like Jef and others in this book who were willing to step over to the other side for a bit, this is a gutsy move for an academic. To them, I'd like to say a hearty "Thank you!" for entering into the spirit of the book.

I'd also like to thank my students from that class way back in 2005. It was the very last class I taught at UNC – and the students wholeheartedly embraced the notion of thinking more deeply about controversial issues. In their quest to find answers, they helped me become a student again. Every one of those 40 students helped me to think more critically about advertising. How well did they do? *You decide.*

Ideas to get you thinking . . .

1 Make a list of everything you could change about advertising if you could. How different would the world look if you had the power to adopt every change you wrote down? Would it be a better world? Why or why not?
2 If you could create one law about advertising, what would it be? Why?

If you'd like to read more . . .

Berger, A. (2007). *Ads, fads, and consumer culture: Advertising's impact on American character and society.* Lanham, MD: Rowman & Littlefield.
Sheehan, K. B. (2003). *Controversies in contemporary advertising.* Thousand Oaks, CA: Sage Publications.
Shrum, L. J. (2004). *The psychology of entertainment media: Blurring the lines between entertainment and persuasion.* Mahwah, NJ: Lawrence Erlbaum.

References

Pollay, R. W. (1986). The distorted mirror: Reflections on the unintended consequences of advertising. *Journal of Marketing* 50(April), 18–36.

2

The Economic Impact of Advertising

What's the Controversy?

Some topics in advertising are just plain more interesting than others – or so it might seem. Should cigarette advertising be legal, for example? Is it fair to manipulate children with our advertising? You get the picture. But economics? Who wants to talk about money anyway?

In reality, the topic of the economic impact of advertising is critical – and fascinating! Have you ever thought about what the world would look like without advertising? Sure, the highways might be more natural without billboards, but would we have as many food choices in the grocery store? And, if we did, how would we figure out which brand to buy?

What would happen to our favorite television programs without the commercials in them? Without advertising, would we still have magazines to read? What about the newspaper? We don't often think about the role that advertising plays in letting us consume the different kinds of media that we have come to rely on. Things that we get for free – or nearly free – like the newspaper, magazines, radio, primetime television, are all supported by advertising. Then there are the people who work in advertising, creating the ads, buying and selling the ads, etc. How much does advertising contribute to our economy anyway? What kind of money are we talking about?

You have probably heard about the outrageous costs of a 30-second Super Bowl commercial ($2.6 million, give or take a few hundred thousand!). However, here is an even more interesting factoid. Back in 2005, it was estimated that advertising in general pumped $5.2 trillion into the U.S. economy. In 2006, it was estimated that the world's wealth (all 6-plus billion of us, including Bill Gates, the Queen of England, and Queen Latifah) added up to $44 trillion. Okay, so we understand that there is a lot of money involved in advertising.

Why is the Economic Impact of Advertising an Ethical Issue? What's the Controversy?

This chapter attempts to answer whether advertising ultimately increases the price of products or decreases it. Why should we care anyway? Think of it this way. If advertising actually lowers the price of products, then that would mean that people who might not be able to afford a product without advertising could *with* advertising. It might not be so important whether or not we can buy luxury items, but if a mother can afford to buy healthy food for her children because the prices are held in check thanks to advertising, it's not too much of a stretch to see how this can become an ethical – and controversial – issue. However, what if the above were true, but in the process the advertising created false needs for a mother who can't really afford the particular food? Like pomegranate juice, for example. Plenty of research extols the antioxidant value of drinking pomegranate juice, but it's expensive compared to other juices.

Or, what if the price of the product the mother wanted was, indeed, lower, but a cheaper brand (perhaps the store brand) with the same ingredients was also available? (Tropicana orange juice versus Kroger orange juice, for example.) The price for the Tropicana orange juice might be lower than it would be without advertising, but the mother would actually be spending more money because she chose Tropicana when she should have picked the Kroger brand because the advertising made her think that Tropicana was healthier for her children. Would it be a controversial decision then?

And who says we need all these choices, anyway? When I walk down the grocery store aisle, it's a little stressful to try to figure out exactly what kind of peanut butter I need. The one with honey? The natural one? The one that Choosy Mothers Choose Most?

But, maybe choices are good. I hate to think about walking through the grocery aisles and only having "Value Packs" to choose from. I like to choose between my rainforest-friendly whole-bean coffee and my naturally brewed ground Kona. Besides, the last time I checked, this was a free market economy. People are free to buy – or not.

The authors of these essays, Edd Applegate and C. Ann Hollifield, have written many articles about the business side of advertising. Here they take opposite approaches and each make compelling arguments for their particular side. Does advertising make products cheaper (by increasing competition) or more expensive (passing the ad expense on to the customer)? *You decide.*

Ideas to get you thinking . . .

1 Make a list of all the advertising you encounter in a given day. Besides television, think of billboards you pass on your way to work or school, commercials that pop up on the radio, internet ads that pop out at you without warning. Make a list of all the kinds of people who you imagine might be involved in these ads.
2 Would you be willing to pay for your media use without advertising? How much would you pay? What would happen to the media without advertising?

If you'd like to read more . . .

Ekelund, R. B., and D. S. Saurman (1988). *Advertising and the market process: A modern economic view.* San Francisco: Pacific Research Institute.

Goldfarb, A. (2006). State dependence at internet portals. *Journal of Economics & Management Strategy* 15(2): 317–52.

Kirkpatrick, J. (2007). *In defense of advertising: Arguments from reason, ethical egoism, and laissez-faire capitalism.* Claremont, CA: TLJ Books.

Argument

Advertising makes products more expensive

Edd Applegate

In a study about business executives and advertising, Greyser (1975: 39) writes that just about half of the respondents deny that advertising lowers prices, and the same proportion think that it results in higher prices. Interestingly, executives in consumer goods companies were slightly more likely than others to say that advertising raises prices. Indeed, only 35 (out of 100) claimed that advertising lowered prices while 49 (out of 100) claimed that it increased prices.

The purpose of this essay is to explain that advertising, especially in the U.S., increases prices of goods and services that consumers purchase.

Advertising is prevalent in the U.S. Indeed, compared to other Westernized nations, advertisers in the U.S. spend considerably more dollars per year (see table 2.1.)

We spend almost $900 on advertising to each man, woman, and child living in the U.S. Advertising may be considered by consumers to be helpful, but it is not free. Indeed, practically every medium a consumer watches, reads, or listens to contains advertising. If the medium did not,

Table 2.1 2005 per capita ad spending ($U.S.)

Country	Amount
Canada	207.22
France	240.63
Germany	230.57
Italy	153.19
Japan	397.91
Spain	154.49
U.K.	329.21
U.S.	876.59*

* This amount multiplied by the population equals 2.2 percent of the Gross Domestic Product (GDP). Adapted from Arens and Schaefer (2007: 28).

it probably would not exist, at least not in its current form. Advertisers pay for their persuasive messages to be broadcast or published, then pass along their advertising expenses to consumers by charging them more for the products and services they provide. In short, expenses for advertising become part of the expenses for producing and selling products and services.

Why Advertising Grew

In the essay, "The Economic Aspects of Advertising," Nicholas Kaldor (1960) claims that manufacturers in the 1800s produced products based on orders received from wholesalers. Retailers based their orders on the products offered by wholesalers, and retailers repeated orders to wholesalers based on their consumers' demand for certain products. Kaldor writes,

> It devolved, therefore, on the wholesalers to determine what should be produced and made available to the market and to strike a balance between following consumers' requirements more closely by offering wider assortments and obtaining things more cheaply by ordering larger volumes on the same pattern. (1960: 122)

Kaldor referred to this market system as "wholesalers' domination." In essence, a manufacturer's selling prices had to be kept low in order to compete; otherwise, wholesalers would order products from another manufacturer.

Primarily for the purpose of change, growth, and profit, manufacturers in the late 1800s and early 1900s began to advertise their respective products (brands) to the ultimate consumer. These advertisements differentiated the manufacturers' brands from similar products, which wholesalers could purchase from other companies. As a result, manufacturers were able to "release themselves from dependence on wholesalers' goodwill" (Kaldor, 1960: 125). As Kaldor writes,

> Thus the growth of modern advertising is closely linked up with the manufacturers' attempt to obtain control of the marketing and distributive mechanism; and conversely the growth of "manufacturers' domination" was closely linked up with the discovery of the power of advertising. (1960: 125)

Advertising enabled manufacturers to raise prices of their brands since wholesalers had lost control of which products sold. Furthermore, as manufacturers continued to advertise their brands, some of these brands became the major selling brands in their respective categories. Indeed, through advertising, some manufacturers created monopolies for their products. As a result, these manufacturers were able to charge higher prices.

Some texts in advertising do claim that national advertising enables manufacturers to sell more of their products and consequently enjoy "economies of scale," referring to a manufacturer creating large-scale demand for its products so that the quality of the products is increased. The books argue that this leads to lower costs for producing each unit. Production costs, then, *decrease* because fixed costs are spread over a greater number of units manufactured, thus lowering retail prices. Apparently, these writers have not read Neil Borden's study, *The Economic Effects of Advertising*. Borden (1942) found that one of the acts (lowering costs) mentioned above does not necessarily cause another act (lowering prices) to happen.

Addressing manufacturers' production, Schmalensee writes, "In fact, if all industries exhibited economies of scale in production, advertising could not lower costs in some industries without raising them in others, unless it increased aggregate consumer demand for all goods and services in the economy" (1974: 94). Of course, this is not the case. Some brands sell more than others.

National brands or advertised brands are priced higher than private brands or unadvertised brands. Even Jerry Kirkpatrick, who wrote *In Defense of Advertising: Arguments from Reason, Ethical Egoism, and Laissez-Faire Capitalism*, acknowledged this (1994: 139).

To illustrate the above, let's examine two brands of toothpaste. First, let's consider Colgate Palmolive's Colgate Total, 6-ounce size. It costs about $2.50. Second, let's consider Colgate Palmolive's Ultra Brite Advanced Whitening, 6-ounce size. It costs about $1. Why is this brand less than half the price of Colgate Total? Because Colgate Total, like other brands of toothpaste with "Colgate" in the name, is heavily advertised – indeed, millions of dollars are spent every year – and is one of the best-selling brands in this product category. On the other hand, Ultra Brite is not heavily advertised and is not a best-selling brand. "Economies of scale" notwithstanding, Colgate Palmolive charges more for Colgate Total, even though it is one of the best-selling brands of toothpaste in the country, if not the world.

On a different note, the next time you purchase a new car, look at the list of expenses very carefully. You will probably notice an amount for "advertising fees." Since brands of cars are advertised by the manufacturers as well as dealers, manufacturers pass their advertising expenses on to their dealers and consumers. For instance, if you purchase a new Honda Civic, you will in all likelihood be charged a certain amount based on what the manufacturer has spent on advertising the brand. Of course, the amount you pay is a percentage of the total amount the manufacturer has spent or has allocated. The total amount is spread over the total number of units manufactured and/or sold. Although you were not interested in paying for the advertising about the Honda Civic that you may have seen on television or read in a magazine, you were nonetheless charged for it.

Based on the examples above it is clear that manufacturers' advertising expenditures are passed on to consumers and consequently cause prices to be higher. The examples above are for best-selling brands in their respective product categories. Yet both cost more than other brands in their respective product categories. Advertising certainly is one reason.

References

Arens, W. F., and D. H. Schaefer (2007). *Essentials of contemporary advertising*. New York: McGraw-Hill/Irwin.

Borden, N. H. (1942). *The economic effects of advertising*. Chicago: Richard D. Irwin.

Greyser, S. A. (1975). Businessmen look hard at advertising. In J. E. Littlefield (ed.), *Readings in advertising: Current viewpoints on selected topics* (pp. 32–51). St. Paul: West Publishing.

Kaldor, N. (1960). *Essays on value and distribution*. Glencoe, IL: The Free Press.

Kirkpatrick, J. (1994). *In defense of advertising: Arguments from reason, ethical egoism, and laissez-faire capitalism*. Westport, CT: Quorum Books.

Schmalensee, R. (1974). Advertising and Economic Welfare. In S. F. Divita (ed.), *Advertising and the public interest* (pp. 82–97). Chicago: American Marketing Association.

Counterargument

Advertising lowers prices for consumers
C. Ann Hollifield

One of the positive effects advertising has on society is to save consumers money by lowering prices. Although economists have argued for decades that advertising causes higher prices, there is now a great deal of evidence that, in many cases, the opposite is true.

In fairness to the traditional view, the relationship between advertising and prices is complicated. However, those arguing that advertising raises prices have tended to look only at how advertising by *manufacturers* affects prices. More recent economic models and empirical research suggest that, in fact, advertising has different effects on prices depending on (a) what part of the manufacturing and distribution process you look at and (b) what type of product is being sold. This essay will explore the evidence that advertising can actually lower the prices that consumers pay for goods.

Advertising Increases Demand

So how does advertising act to lower prices? There are several ways. First, advertising increases demand (Leach and Reekie, 1996; Steiner, 1973). In a study of the toy industry, Steiner demonstrated that after the Mattel Company began advertising on *The Mickey Mouse Club* in 1955, demand in the United States for toys in general, and for heavily advertised toys in particular, rose sharply. During the same period, demand for toys remained unchanged in countries where there were not high levels of toy advertising on television and in newspapers.

As demand rises, manufacturers gain what are known as "economies of scale." This means that it costs the manufacturer less to produce each unit of a product that it makes as the total number of units it manufactures rises. These cost savings come about largely because the manufacturer is able to spread overhead costs such as the costs of labor and manufacturing equipment over more units, thereby lowering the production cost of each individual unit. As production costs per unit fall, it becomes possible for the manufacturer to lower the price it charges for the product and still maintain the same level of profit. In industries where there are many manufacturers and, thus, a lot of competition, manufacturers may share some of the benefits of economies of scale with consumers by cutting prices.

But as those who argue that advertising raises prices point out, manufacturers don't always pass such savings on to consumers. Instead, they sometimes use the savings to increase their own profits. But even then, increased demand can still lower prices. As consumer demand for a product rises, retail stores sell more of the product and the products move off stores' shelves faster. Steiner (1973) found that as the sales of advertised products increased, retailers cut prices by reducing *retail* profit margins on the products. The retailers were willing to take less of a markup on each item because they made more money overall as a result of higher sales volumes. Indeed, the idea of selling more for less is the business model behind discount retailing, in general. But that business model depends on high levels of consumer demand for the products being sold.

Critics argue that when advertising focuses consumer demand on a particular brand of a product, the price of that brand may rise as the manufacturer and retailers try to maximize their profits from consumers' brand loyalty. However, even if the prices of the most popular brands increase, if advertising increases overall consumer demand for a product category, the number of manufacturers producing versions of that product will grow. Retailers may begin offering both brand name and private-label versions. As off-brands enter the market and the number of brands battling for market share increases, consumers will have a wider range of product choices. Even more importantly, the average price for the product category will fall, even if the prices of certain name brands remain high (Albion and Farris, 1981; Steiner, 1973).

An example of this would be the rapid decrease in the price of MP3 players in recent years. In 2000 you could get an MP3 player with that would play 100 hours of music for $499. By the end of 2005 you could get an Apple music and video iPOD that would play approximately 750 hours of music or 150 hours of video for $399 (Swett, 2005). In the same period, flat-panel monitors dropped from around $900 to about $200, while HDTV prices plunged from $13,000 to $2,200. While it is not possible to directly attribute the lower prices for such products to advertising, it is clear that as demand for these products increased, prices fell.

Advertising Is Information

Another way advertising lowers prices is by providing consumers with product information. Advertising informs consumers about the range of competing products available and, sometimes, the prices at which those products are being sold. As consumers become more aware of their choices, the level of competition at both the manufacturing and retail levels goes up, which causes the prices for the advertised products to come down. Research has shown that when a producer or retailer advertises a product on the basis of price, competitors often cut their prices for the same or similar products in response.

Advertising is particularly effective in helping lower the prices of "convenience" goods as compared to "non-convenience" goods (Albion and Farris, 1981; Reekie, 1977). Convenience goods are products such as soap, soft drinks, toothpaste, etc., where the price is generally low to begin with, the product is rapidly consumed, the consumer buys it fairly often, and there is little risk to the consumer in making the "wrong" choice.

Advertising puts downward pressure on the price of convenience goods in several ways. First, the prices of convenience goods are so low to begin with that the risk in buying the wrong product is minimal. As a result, consumers are unlikely to invest much time in seeking information about convenience goods beyond what they learn from advertising. For the consumer, the information-search costs of seeking out additional information about competing soft drinks, razor blades, or deodorant brands are higher than the economic return they would get from investing the time. So advertising is consumers' primary source of information about their different product choices among convenience goods.

Second, advertising may make some brands of convenience goods so well known that most retailers will be forced to stock them (Steiner, 1973). In such cases, retailers may begin to cut prices on the name brand convenience products, using them as "loss leaders" to attract customers away from competing retailers.

However, the information function of advertising can help lower the price of even unadvertised products. As individual brands in a product category are advertised, consumers develop a general idea of what products in that product category should cost. This has the effect of creating an invisible "price cap" on most, if not all, products in the category. Manufacturers and retailers hesitate to raise prices above the expected price level out of

concern that consumers will come to believe that everything those manufacturers or retailers offer is overpriced (Steiner, 1973).

Research suggests that advertising has less effect on the price of more
expensive, "non-convenience" goods such as cars, expensive clothing, or
high-end electronics. Non-convenience goods cost more and consumers tend
to own them and use them for longer periods of time. Thus, buying decisions for non-convenience goods carry higher risks than for convenience
goods. While advertising may make consumers aware that a particular non-
convenience product is available, consumers are unlikely to actually buy
the product without doing additional research and talking with the sales
staff at the retailer (Reekie, 1977).

Advertising Improves Operating Efficiencies

A third way advertising may help keep prices low is by improving retailers'
operating efficiency. Advertising informs consumers about the product
choices available and the specific characteristics of individual brands.
Customers who feel able to make product-purchase decisions on the basis
of the information they've gleaned from advertising don't need as much
customer assistance from the retailer. That allows retailers to cut back
on customer-service costs by replacing sales clerks and customer-service
representatives with searchable inventory computers and self-service check-
out devices. Some of the cost savings from these self-service devices are
passed on to consumers through lower prices.

A final way advertising keeps consumer prices low is by helping new competitors gain a foothold in the market. One of the biggest challenges fac-
ing new manufacturers and new retailers is making potential customers aware
that they exist. Advertising creates awareness of the new competitors and
their product offerings. As the number of viable competitors in a market
increases, prices will fall as the competitors compete with each other for
market share.

Conclusion

Despite the arguments and evidence that advertising helps keep consumer
prices low, the debate on the issue is unlikely to be settled any time
soon. For one thing, it is almost impossible to directly test the effect that

advertising has on prices. The problem is that it is difficult, if not imposs-ible, to find consumer products that are not advertised in some way. That makes it hard to study the relationship between advertising and price (Albion and Farris, 1981). Similarly, slight differences in products make it hard to judge whether price variations are caused by differences in advertising or by differences in product quality, product size, or even packaging (Reekie, 1974; Telser, 1964).

Another complicating factor is that research shows that higher-quality and, by extension, higher-priced products are more likely to be advertised than lower-quality and lower-priced products (Albion and Farris, 1981; Reekie, 1974; Telser, 1964). However, it is difficult to tell the direction of the relationship. Are higher-priced products more likely to be advertised in order to increase the likelihood that they will sell? Or does increased advertising create the need for higher prices?

Because of questions like these, we can expect the debate over the effects of advertising on prices to continue. It is likely that the truth lies some-where between the extremes of the argument: the relationship between advert-ising and prices probably varies depending upon the type of product being advertised and the amount of competition among manufacturers and retailers.

What is clear is that the long-standing argument that advertising *raises* prices can no longer go unchallenged. There is substantial evidence that advertising has played an important role in the development of discount retailing and low-cost private-label brands. We can conclude, therefore, that consumers benefit from advertising because advertising *lowers* prices, at least for some of the most commonly used products.

References

Albion, M. S., and P. W. Farris (1981). *The advertising controversy: Evidence on the economic effects of advertising.* Boston, MA: Auburn House.

Leach, D. F., and W. D. Reekie (1996). A natural experiment on the effect of advertising on sales: The SASOL case. *Applied Economics* 28: 1081–91.

Reekie, W. D. (1974). *Advertising: Its place in political and managerial economics.* London: Macmillan.

Reekie, W. D. (1977). The market in advertising. In I. R. C. Hirst and W. D. Reekie (eds.), *The consumer society* (pp. 65–89). London: Tavistock.

Steiner, R. L. (1973). Does advertising lower consumer prices? *Journal of Marketing* 37(October): 19–26.

Swett, C. (2005). Cheaper gadgets spread cheer; remember when? Consumer electronics used to have bigger price tags and smaller memory chips. *Sacramento Bee* D1 (Dec. 23).

Telser, L. G. (1964). Advertising and competition. *The Journal of Political Economy* 72: 537–62.

3

Advertising to Children

Gimme, Gimme, Gimme!!! Do Children Need More Protection from Advertising?

Advertising to children is a topic that creates strong emotion in people. Parent groups want to protect their kids from questionable media and advertisers. Advocacy groups want to protect a vulnerable group they (and the law, for the most part) have decided can't protect itself. And, in the era of doing more with less money, educators find themselves torn between accepting help from media conglomerates willing to fund educational programs, all the while assuring parents that schools are still protected turf.

What's a grownup to do? If we take a "big effects" approach to the media – and especially to advertising – it's a short leap to implore the government to impose stricter guidelines on the advertisers. But as you've already seen in this book, nothing is as easy as it might seem at first.

What are the issues? First, it's easy to blame advertising for all the communication ills of the world – and particularly for children who may have run amok. For one thing, it takes the responsibility away from bad parenting. Yes, it may be nasty to have questionable material imprinted on a second grader's lunch box, but the parent doesn't have to buy the lunch box, the argument goes. Blaming advertisers without looking at the media as a whole is short-sighted at best – and dangerous at worst. As long as grownups are willing to digest hundreds of hours of every gruesome episode of the *CSI* and *Law & Order* franchises, it seems a little hollow to get upset because someone slipped a picture of a Coke can in a Disney movie, doesn't it? Besides, as Walker Smith's essay points out, kids are consumers, too. In some sense, they have earned the right to be treated as a target market.

Or have they? As Keisha Hoerrner points out in her essay, children are vulnerable and don't understand the heavy-hitting tactics that come raining down on them day after day as advertisers try to convince them that they need a certain cereal, a certain brand of jeans, a certain back-to-school notepad. And it's not just about cereal, jeans, and school supplies. The American Psychological Association has called for an outright ban on advertising to children under 8. The recent national interest in obesity and children – and the role of advertising in making kids fat – is fuel for the fire. Lots of laws in the U.S. have been created for the sole purpose of protecting children. No one debates this. Yet just curtailing advertising to children may be easier said than done.

First, hardly anyone would expect children to watch only children-appropriate programming on television. Wildly popular shows like *American Idol* appeal to entire families. It would be impossible (even if everyone agreed this were a good idea) to keep *American Idol* fans under 8 from watching the commercials during the show. Second, if there are no commercials on television programs specifically geared toward children, it wouldn't take long before there were no shows for kids at all. Like it or not, commercial television is a conduit for advertisers. Demographically segmented shows deliver important consumer segments to the companies that pay for the right to advertise. It is impossible to filter out the "media waste" – audience members that the advertisers are not targeting. Third, there is an additional economic issue. While parents may deride the idea of advertising in the classroom, given the lack of adequate funding for public education, who can blame educators who "sell out" for books, audiovisual equipment, and other necessary materials to run a school adequately? As you can see, the issue is rarely as simple as it might seem on the surface.

And, what about programs like the Siemens Competition in Math, Science and Technology, which gives out millions in scholarship money to budding scientists? The corporate name is closely tied to the program. Is that any different than kids being exposed to ads on television? If so, how?

What do we know about the impact of advertising on children? Some researchers have argued that there is a fundamental difference in strategy between advertising to adults and advertising to children. Mason (2004) argued that ads geared toward adults tend to focus on brand loyalty while ads geared toward kids focus on merchandizing tie-ins. (An example of this would be an ad campaign that would encourage kids to go to McDonald's to get their Happy Meal toy based on a current blockbuster movie.)

With the recent interest in the role that advertising plays in childhood obesity, there is renewed discussion on who is to blame. Is it the ads (true, there is lots and lots of non-nutritional advertising aimed straight at kids), or is it the inactivity of children (and poor eating habits) that are largely to blame? Richard Berman, writing in *Advertising Age* (2005), comments that 25 percent of children today get no exercise whatsoever! This is a classic examination of trying to figure out which came first. Do the ads cause obesity? Or do obese children simply watch more television? In research lingo, we call this the debate between causality and association.

Even if the food industry wanted to be helpful, efforts can backfire. As Berman points out, "voluntarily limiting food advertising to children looks like an implicit admission of guilt." What's an advertiser to do? It looks like there are plenty of people on both sides of the issue who have some ideas.

Advertising to children. It's about protecting a vulnerable group that can't protect itself. It's about preserving a free market society. It's about recognizing that a free market comes with responsibility. It's about allowing parents to decide how they want their children to behave. It's about kids being rewarded – and, some would argue, respected – for having opinions. As you can see, this is a complicated issue.

So, what's the right side of the argument? *You decide.*

Ideas to get you thinking . . .

1   Watch an hour of television for a program that you think is geared toward children. (Try the Disney Channel for starters.) Describe all the ads that you see in one show. Now watch an hour of primetime. Describe those ads. What kinds of similarities and differences do you see? Do you think any of the commercials you saw in the children's program are inappropriate?

2   Talk to some young children about the advertisements that they see. What kinds of conclusions could you make based on these conversations?

3   Take a trip to the grocery store and walk around until you find a parent or babysitter with a young child in tow. Without being obnoxious, try to observe the child's behavior

as the shopper walks down the aisle. Is the child asking for particular brands? How is the adult responding?

If you'd like to read more . . .

Clark, E. (2007). *The real toy story: Inside the ruthless battle for America's youngest consumers.* New York: The Free Press.
Gunter, B., C. Oates, and M. Blades (2005). *Advertising to children on TV: Content, impact and regulation.* Mahwah, NJ: Lawrence Erlbaum.
Thomas, S. G. (2007). *Buy, buy baby: How consumer culture manipulates parents and harms young minds.* Boston: Houghton Mifflin.

References

Berman, R. (2005). *Advertising Age* (Midwest region edition) 76(16): 30.
Mason, R. (2004). Advertising children's products. <http://www.cox.smu.edu/article/research/research.do/114>.

Argument

Yes! Children need protection from the bombardments of Sponge Bob Square Pants, Ronald McDonald, and all the big purple dinosaurs

Keisha L. Hoerrner

Just do it. Have it your way. Because I'm worth it. No boundaries. Are these the messages parents strive to teach their children?

They may not learn them from parents, but children certainly learn these messages – and many more – from the advertising industry. The "consumerized childhood" is here, complete with training materials – commercials, billboards, animated cartoon characters making products like cigarettes cool, and catchy slogans – that work to capture the infant, toddler, school-age, tween, and teen audiences.

The numbers make it easy to see why children are an excellent market for advertisers: Children under 14 spend more than $20 billion a year, and teens spend almost eight times that amount ($155 billion) annually (Dominick, 2007; Moses, 2000). Children are also able to influence an additional $180 to $200 billion in purchases by their parents (Alexander and Hoerrner, 2006; Dominick, 2007). Scholars refer to that influence ability as "pester power" (McNeal, 1992). They are big business to advertisers, who currently spend $15 billion a year trying to tap into the child market (Bishop, 2005).

Marketing research has shown that 12-month-old children can make brand associations ("Watch out," 2001), so marketers are striving to literally create "cradle-to-grave" consumers. In March 2000, the International Research Institute, in cooperation with the Parenting Group, held a conference for marketers on children and their parents. Titled "Play-Time, Snack-Time, Tot-Time: Targeting Pre-Schoolers and their Parents," advertisers explored "marketing practices that drive loyalty in the preschool market" and tactics to "find out the desires of toddler-age consumers" ("Watch out," 2001: 12–13).

"Toddler-age consumers"? Do most parents see their 2-year-old as a consumer? As Dominick (2007) asks, would these parents feel comfortable allowing a door-to-door salesperson to come into their living room and hawk a product to their children? Then why are children overwhelmed by advertising messages?

Major Issues

One of the concerns is that these toddlers – and their older pre-teen siblings – clearly do not understand the distinctions of fantasy versus reality and do not have the cognitive skills to discern deceptive and manipulative messages.

The primary reason Action for Children's Television (ACT), and other advocacy groups, implored the Federal Communications Commission (FCC) and Federal Trade Commission (FTC) to either ban ads directed to children or highly regulate them is the concern about manipulation. While ACT no longer exists, other parental groups, including the Motherhood Project of the Institute for American Values, have asked the industry to stop targeting an audience that simply does not understand advertising. The American Psychological Association and the American Academy of Pediatrics have also weighed in on the issue, claiming younger children should not be exposed to advertising because they do not understand its purpose and strategies (American Academy, 1995; Kunkel et al., 2004). Commercial Alert, another advocacy group, proposed a "Parents' Bill of Rights" that includes a requirement for companies to disclose all product placements in movies, books, and video games. Yes, Johnny is not only learning about violent crimes when he plays "True Crime: Streets of L.A." He's also learning that Puma is the foot brand of choice (Dominick, 2007).

Another concern regarding kids and ads is that children who are least likely to understand advertising seem to pay the most attention to it. Young children watch commercials to a greater degree than older children because they do not comprehend the difference between program content and advertisements. It's all enjoyable entertainment, and they learn from ads the same way they learn from program content. "Research suggests that children under age 7 or 8 generally do not realize that ads are intended to persuade them to buy something. Younger children tend to think of ads as informational rather than persuasive" (Alexander and Hoerrner, 2006: 40). By 12, children's viewing habits of commercials are similar to those of adults. They ignore more of the ads and have a more cynical view of those they see than their younger siblings (McNeal, 1999).

Even knowing an ad is intended to sell does not give the child the cognitive capacity to "recognize the bias inherent in persuasive messages and therefore view advertising claims and appeals more skeptically" (Kunkel, 2002).

Children who believe in a six-foot purple dinosaur and assume they can actually visit Mickey Mouse's house when they vacation in Disney World do not perceive subtle advertising effects like bandwagon or strategies like celebrity endorsements. (Since some of those celebrities are actually animated characters, can there truly be truth in those ads?)

Advertisements, indeed, are everywhere, using every character children know and love. Even Children's Television Workshop, the creators of Sesame Street, have sold out. Thanks to a deal with the discount chain, children are learning that an ad for the Sesame Street clothing line is "brought to you by the letter K – for Kmart" (Dominick, 2007: 433).

Characters such as Ronald McDonald, Tony the Tiger, and the lovable Coca-Cola polar bears are helping children make choices about food and drinks. The December 2005 report by the Institute of Medicine, sponsored by the Centers for Disease Control and Prevention, sparked quite a flurry of media attention. Its findings were not new, however. Numerous studies have consistently shown that food advertisements directed toward children encourage a diet of sugar, fat, and empty calories that leads to obesity, diabetes, and other health problems ("Selling junk food," 2006). "Far from following the USDA Food Guide Pyramid, recent data show that TV ads promote a diet of more than 40 percent fats, oil, and sweets but only 6 percent fruits and 6 percent vegetables. The pyramid is basically being turned upside down" (Alexander and Hoerrner, 2006, p. 40). While the Institute for Medicine report recommended that popular children's characters such as SpongeBob Square Pants be used to promote healthy foods rather than junk foods, the advertising industry has been slow to accept this nudge ("Carrots Monster?," 2005).

In addition to 30- and 60-second commercials, children are exposed to advertising disguised as programs. For more than 20 years, toy companies have been working with production companies and networks to create animated cartoons based on their toys (Pecora, 1998). From "He-Man and Masters of the Universe" to "Justice League," cartoons are dedicated to selling toys. These "toy-based programs," as they are called by scholars, have been quite successful in terms of delivering an excited child consumer base to the toy companies while providing television networks with cost-effective animated programming (Pecora, 1998).

Another major concern regarding children and advertising is the "hyper-consumerism" created in children. The American Psychological Association noted that a comprehensive review of the research showed children are learning to be materialistic and to associate their self-worth with what they purchase: "They are what they buy" (Kunkel et al., 2004: 11). Teens are especially materialistic and very concerned with brands. As Moses noted in her book *The $100 Billion Allowance: Accessing the Global Teen Market*, "A brand says a lot about who they [teens] are and where they stand in life" (2000: 8). Teens around the world, not just in the United States, want to achieve the American dream, according to Moses. "The United States has exported the American dream – translated loosely as the freedom to consume . . ." (2000: 10).

Protections for Child Audiences

There are some protections mandated by the government and provided voluntarily by the advertising industry to protect children from the onslaught of advertisements. Most of them are simply window dressing, however, and do little to truly protect this vulnerable market.

Thanks to parental advocacy groups like ACT, the FCC has required "separators" between television programs and ads directed toward children since the mid-1970s. The separators generally say "We'll be back after these messages" and "We now return to our program." The commercials directed toward children also include "disclaimers," statements that are supposed to provide important information to the viewers. The most popular disclaimers are "Products sold separately," "Some assembly required," "Batteries not included," and "Part of a balanced breakfast."

Unfortunately, these do little to protect children from advertising. Research shows that children (especially those aged 8 and younger) do not understand the disclaimers (Kunkel et al., 2004). If the industry really wanted children to grasp the meaning of disclaimers, they would have to be rewritten to use words children comprehend. "You have to put it together" makes more sense to a first-grader than "Some assembly required" (Liebert, Sprafkin, Liebert and Rubinstein, 1977, as cited in Kunkel et al., 2004: 5).

In addition to mandating minor aspects of the advertising content, the FCC also limits the amount of time advertisements can take up within children's programming. The passage of the 1990 Children's Television Act forced broadcast stations to limit the total number of advertising minutes within children's shows to 12 per hour during weekdays and 10.5 per hour on the weekends. These advertising restrictions only apply to programming targeted to an audience of children below the age of 17. There are currently no governmental restrictions on the total number of ads within print media directed toward children or on internet sites targeting child audiences.

The advertising industry says it adheres to voluntary guidelines developed by the Children's Advertising Review Unit of the Better Business Bureau. Its guidelines include statements about exercising care to avoid unfair exploitation of the "imaginative quality of children" and to avoid "social stereotyping" in ads with diverse characters ("Self-regulatory guidelines," 2003: 3). Since it is a voluntary system, there are no prescribed sanctions in the document for advertisers who fail to adhere to the guidelines.

The Motherhood Project developed its own code for advertisers and sent it to industry representatives in 2001. The "Mother's Code for Advertisers" includes the following six statements:

1 No advertising, marketing, or market research in schools, including high schools.
2 No targeting of advertising and marketing at children under the age of 8.
3 No product placement in movies and media programs targeted at children and adolescents.
4 No behavioral science research to develop advertising and marketing aimed at children and adolescents.
5 No advertising and marketing directed at children and adolescents that promotes an ethic of selfishness and a focus on instant gratification.
6 Good faith efforts to reduce sponsorship of gratuitously sexual and/or violent programming likely to be watched by children. ("Watch out," 2001: 28)

The advertising industry is as likely to accept this code from concerned mothers as it is to stop buying time during the Super Bowl. Unfortunately for parents and their children, the advertising industry makes too much money targeting children. That means it will continue to take advantage of almost "No Boundaries" and continue to "Just Do It."

References

Alexander, A., and K. Hoerrner (2006). Advertising, children's. In J. Ciment (ed.), *Social issues in America: An encyclopedia* (pp. 37–44) Armonk, NY: Sharpe Reference.

American Academy of Pediatrics (1995). Policy statement: Children, adolescents, and advertising. *Pediatrics* 95(2): 295–7.

Bishop, T. (2005). Advertisers raise ante on marketing to children; Report links focused trend with food products to obesity. *The Baltimore Sun* (Dec. 8): 1D.

"Carrots monster?" (2005). *USA Today* (McLean, VA) (Dec. 13): A12.

Dominick, J. R. (2007). *The dynamics of mass communications: Media in the digital age.* New York: McGraw-Hill.

Kunkel, D. (2002). Children and television advertising. In D. G. Singer and J. L. Singer (eds.), *Handbook of Children and the Media* (pp. 375–94). Thousand Oaks, CA: Sage Publications.

Kunkel, D., B. L. Wilcox, J. Cantor, E. Palmer, S. Linn, and P. Dowrick (2004). Report of the APA task force on advertising and children. <http://www.apa.org/releases/childrenads.pdf>, accessed May 5, 2006.

McNeal, J. U. (1992). *Kids as customers: A handbook of marketing to children.* New York: Lexington Books.

McNeal, J. U. (1999). *The kids market: Myths and realities.* Ithaca, NY: Paramount Marketing.

Moses, E. (2000). *The $100 billion allowance: Accessing the global teen market.* New York: John Wiley.

Pecora, N. O. (1998). *The business of children's entertainment.* New York: Guilford Press.

"Self-regulatory guidelines for children's advertising" (2003). New York: Children's Advertising Review Unit.

"Selling junk food to toddlers" (2006). *New York Times* (late edition, East Coast) (Feb. 23): A26.

"Watch out for children: A mother's statement to advertisers" (2001). New York: Institute for American Values.

Counterargument

No! Children are smarter than we think. We coddle them enough already!

J. Walker Smith

Marketers care about only one kind of person: consumers of their products. Admittedly, marketers care more about purchasers than mere users, but a person who is neither is of no interest. This is the only reason marketers are interested in children – that's where the demand for their products is found. Like it or not, kids are consumers.

Marketers didn't invent this fact. This is the reality within which marketers operate. Perhaps it could be argued that marketers should not care so much or in certain ways about particular sorts of consumers. But if so, that's for policymakers to decide. Setting the rules is not the same thing as playing the game. Marketers can hardly be blamed for competing within the rules.

Vilifying marketers as con artists preying on children is nothing but a straw man in a discussion that should center on the social and economic roles we are willing to let different people to play as well as the corollary consequences we are willing to accept. Kids are consumers because, by and large, we're okay with it. After all, parents are not shy about entrusting their children with central roles in household shopping decisions.

The 2005 Yankelovich Youth MONITOR surveyed 1,458 teens and pre-teens 6 to 17 years of age, along with a parent or guardian of each of the children interviewed. The results are a reminder of what everyone knows to be true – kids have a very big say in the decisions that shape the consumer marketplace.

- 85 percent of kids reported that they had helped their parents pick out the sneakers they wear. 90 percent of parents said that their children's preferences for sneakers are very or somewhat important in their decisions about what to buy.
- Figures are comparable for all kids' categories (respective percentages show the percent of kids who said they helped and the percent of parents who think children's preferences are very or somewhat important).

Kids' clothes: 84/96 percent. School supplies: 83/92 percent. Snack foods: 78/88 percent.

- Figures are only slightly lower for family dining decisions. Fast food restaurants: 76/84 percent. Breakfast foods: 70/88 percent. Dinner foods: 64/86 percent.
- Figures for family products show sizable participation by children, even if not the majority in some cases. Place to go for vacation: 50/79 percent. Family car: 26/38 percent. Hotel to stay at when traveling: 20/37 percent.

There is nothing unexpected in these findings. From time immemorial, parents have accommodated their children's preferences by including them in household decisions, thereby making their kids into exactly the kinds of people who affect the bottom lines of businesses. Directly and indirectly, kids influence the spending of roughly $400 billion each year. No wonder marketers target kids. Influencing the decisions of those who buy and use their products is what marketers do, and, indeed, what marketers must be allowed to do if the marketing process is to work.

Yet, as much as parents want their children to learn by getting hands-on experience as consumers – and not infrequently, by taking complete control of many household buying decisions – they don't want marketers overwhelming their kids with ads. In the Yankelovich Youth MONITOR, 77 percent of parents agree that their children are bombarded with too much advertising. But as long as marketers don't subvert their authority, parents are okay with what their kids watch – 68 percent agree that "with the right parent interaction, TV can reinforce the values [they are] teaching [their] children."

Parents are following through on their determination to teach their children how to use media and be smart consumers. From 2001 to 2005, the proportion of parents reporting that they discuss TV commercials with their children went up from one-third to just over half. 70 to 80 percent of parents talk to their children about TV shows and news stories.

In spite of the growing time and resource pressures of contemporary life, more and more parents are trying to be a buffer between their children and marketers. Parents are enforcing limits by using ads as a teaching moment. Of course, this may not be enough. Children are said to be so much more vulnerable to the importuning of marketers that they need special protections beyond what parents are able to provide.

The vulnerability and special needs of children are not in question. Marketers don't dispute any of the definitive and extensive body of

academic research demonstrating this. Indeed, children are afforded special consideration and treatment in a wide variety of realms, not the least
of which are the workplace and the criminal justice system. But when it
comes to marketing, the case for special protections is less clear.

Regulating the access of marketers to consumers based on the cognitive
abilities of consumers is a knotty challenge. It has never been the case that
a particular type of cognition is required in order to be allowed to shop.
There is no prescreening for rational over emotional thinking or for the
ability to differentiate reality versus fantasy or for holistic versus materialistic responses to ads, or, indeed, for anything. Different consumers think
and process information and advertising in different ways. Except for
outright fraud, marketers are free to engage consumers in whatever way
might boost sales.

When it comes to the machinations of advertisers, adults are no less cog-
nitively challenged than children. The literature on the cognitive incapacities of adults is just as extensive and definitive as that about children. (There
are just as many critics of advertising to adults as there are critics of advertising to children. Advertising is an easy and convenient fall guy for many
social ills.) Princeton University social psychologist Daniel Kahneman was
awarded the 2002 Nobel Prize in Economics for a lifetime of research (much
of which was completed with his late collaborator Amos Tversky) into
the innate cognitive biases that cause people to routinely reach decisions
and take actions that, technically and even economically speaking, are
illogical, irrational, suboptimal and, oftentimes, not in their own best
interests.

Academic research about bad decision-making periodically makes for best-
sellers. Arizona State University Regents' Professor of Psychology Robert
Cialdini's (2006) widely read introduction to the principles of persuasion,
now in its fifth edition, borrows more examples from advertising than from
academic experiments. In fact, his book can be found on the bookshelves
of many marketers. Not only does Cialdini dissect the ways in which perceptions can be manipulated, he counsels readers on how to protect themselves from persuasive appeals that take advantage of their mental habits
and biases. In other words, Cialdini cautions adult readers to take special
measures to protect themselves from their cognitive incapacities.

Harvard University social psychologist Daniel Gilbert (2006) recently
tackled the issue of happiness in his bestselling book. After an exhaustive,
book-long review of academic research on the numerous ways in which
cognitive processes lead people astray, Gilbert concludes that people

mistakenly believe that money brings greater happiness because people are simply no good at all at predicting what will make them happy.

David Myers, the well-known Hope College social psychologist, is the author of two widely used psychology textbooks as well as many bestselling books that address key social issues from the perspective of social psychological research. In his text on social psychology (2005), Myers does more than simply report what's known. He gives students practical suggestions about how to manage their own attitudes and behaviors. In chapter 7 of the latest eighth edition, Myers includes a section entitled "How can persuasion be resisted?" (that has a sub-section called "Inoculating children against the influence of advertising"). Like Cialdini, Myers knows that because of their innate cognitive biases, adults need as much special coaching and protection as children.

If the cognitive incapacities of children justify more restrictions on marketers, then the same restrictions must be applied to most if not all adults, too. Adults are not making voluntary decisions to practice poor consumer decision-making any more than children are doing so, nor are adults any more aware of their biases. To keep marketers from advertising to children because children's minds don't work in accordance with some preset criterion is to presume that there is only one kind of mental process that marketers should be permitted to target. If this is true, then it applies as much to adults as to children. Stricter limits on advertising to children that are justified on the basis of cognitive incapacities create a slippery slope that would shut marketing down entirely (and thus the consumer economy, too).

One of the more common criticisms of advertising to children is that it makes kids too materialistic and overly infatuated with brands. Whether or not this is true, the notion that this is bad is not a scientific critique; it is a value judgment. It's chancy to base policy on value judgments in a free market system in which the fundamental role of policy should be to safeguard the ability of different people to subscribe to different values. If advertising is required to impart a certain set of values or to induce certain types of responses in order to be permitted, then it becomes little more than an organ of the state. Besides, whatever the merits and failings of materialism – a debate with a long, quarrelsome, and wholly inconclusive intellectual history – in a highly sophisticated consumer-based economy such as America's, it is probably good for children to learn about it early and to be intimately immersed in it and deeply knowledgeable about it.

One of the more extreme recommendations about regulating advertising to children is that marketers not be allowed even to conduct research in support of marketing to kids. This idea is so excessive that it might sound too far-fetched to ever happen, but in fact once the screw begins to tighten on marketing to children everything connected with it becomes fair game, marketing knowledge no less than marketing practice. But if marketing researchers aren't allowed to study what persuades kids, then academic researchers won't be allowed to do so either. It's the knowledge itself that would be taboo, not the source of the research generating such knowledge. Limits on marketing to children will not seem reasonable and benign once they begin their inevitable snowball and start impinging on the very research collected and used by critics to justify such limits. This is the paradox inherent in trying to dictate outcomes by limiting access. Prohibitions on research run counter to basic American ideals about the free exchange of knowledge and opinions.

Of course, there is no need to fret over the difficulties of regulating advertising to children if there is no need to do so to begin with. Maybe kids are naive, but in the 2005 Yankelovich Youth MONITOR, 81 percent of the 6- to 17-year-old respondents agreed that more companies should ask kids their opinions of things. Children want a voice with marketers. Just over half feel that companies do not understand the kinds of foods kids like to eat or the kinds of clothes kids like to wear. Kids want their say as consumers.

In fact, the entire consumer marketplace is moving in the direction of greater consumer control, to the point that *Time* magazine's 2006 Person of the Year was "You" (2006/2007). What *Time*'s choice recognized was that the marketplace has now crossed a threshold such that marketers can no longer succeed without involving consumers in a collaborative, power-sharing relationship. Kids have dramatically changed the marketing landscape already through internet sites like YouTube and MySpace. Kids are now coming of age in a world in which they are expected to be in charge, and as a result, they will be even more assertive tomorrow.

Participation is the essential characteristic of every technology at the disposal of teens and pre-teens nowadays. Reinvention is the dynamic that their involvement brings to the marketplace. In a very real sense, kids are no longer at the mercy of marketers so much as marketers are at the mercy of kids. Maybe marketers are naive, but this is exactly how marketers feel these days. A. G. Lafley (2006), CEO of Procter & Gamble, the most storied consumer marketing company of all time, now speaks passionately of the modern "let-go" world in which marketers can retain control of their brands only by ceding more control to consumers.

Not only has the internet put new tools into the hands of consumers – with which children are often the most proficient – it has also opened up information to consumers that they have never had access to before. In particular, the internet has put people in touch with other people. Peer-to-peer interaction is the true essence (if not the utter genius) of the internet, giving people unprecedented fingertip access to opinions, feedback, and counsel that provide a ready counter to marketing and advertising. In particular, parents are able to use this information to their advantage in their attempts to buffer their children from marketers. But for kids no less than for their parents, consumer control and empowerment is the future of the marketplace.

The popular culture to which children are exposed nowadays is teaching them new skills and perhaps making them smarter at the same time. Science writer Steven Johnson (2005), a Distinguished Writer in Residence at New York University, contends that contemporary popular culture is far from the mind-numbing wasteland it is often made out to be. Johnson marshals research and personal experience to argue that video games, prime-time TV shows, the internet, and movies are teaching kids new ways of thinking and of processing information that have made today's children measurably smarter than yesterday's children. Marketers face an increasingly sophisticated audience of teens and pre-teens. The playing field may not be level but it is by no means tilted heavily in favor of marketers any longer.

Kids are not marketing dupes, but they are not marketing resistance masterminds either. Sometimes, kids need help. But helping kids by regulating marketers opens a Pandora's box of problems and precedents. The best way to help kids is not to impose more regulations on marketers but to change the character of demand in the marketplace. Whatever the angle of the playing field they encounter, that's how marketers play the game.

Ted Levitt (1986), the late, renowned Harvard Business School marketing authority, once wrote that "[c]onsumers don't buy products. They buy solutions to problems." This is business and marketing at its best – solving people's problems in innovative and affordable ways. One way to understand Levitt's observation is to recognize that problems constitute demand. What marketers do is respond to demand. If problems change, then demand changes. When demand changes, marketers change.

Regulations are hard to put in place and harder still to enforce. Business lobbies will fight against the imposition of stricter regulations and businesses themselves will push the envelope with ways to operate within the law while still marketing aggressively to children. This is what always happens. Despite best intentions, regulations continue to come up short in giving kids the help they need. That's why this debate about protecting children from advertising goes on and on . . . and on and on and on. There is too much faith in regulation as a panacea.

While marketers resist the yoke of regulation, they do not fight against demand. Instead, they pursue it – because that's where money is to be made. To enlist the support of marketers in the cause of improving marketing to kids, the focus must be on changing the character of demand, not on imposing more regulations.

Demand can be changed in many ways. Educating kids and parents is the most obvious way. Governmental and non-profit institutions can offer instruction and alternatives that would cause kids to be different kinds of consumers. There are successes to emulate from programs focused on things like drugs, smoking, and sexual behavior. Myers cites one notable example in which an educational program proved very effective at giving children a "more realistic understanding" of advertising.

Even greater impact can come from direct incentives, however. If there are foods or toys or activities that are better for children, then the answer is to "pay" children or their parents to consume these things. Marketers will scramble to offer more of anything that people are being "paid" to buy. Probably the best way to do this is to subsidize the preferred offerings so that they are cheaper. But however it's accomplished, the idea is to give kids a compelling reason to consume differently.

Even more important than incentives for children and their parents are incentives for marketers. These kinds of incentives change the character of demand by introducing governmental purchasing or tax policies into the picture. It's known to work. Many of the foods marketed to children are said to be unhealthy because they contain high-fructose corn syrup, a sweetener that is widely used because governmental agricultural subsidies make it the cheapest alternative for food and beverage companies to put into the products they produce and market (Maclean, 2002). Changing the ways in which governmental subsidies affect marketers' bottom lines is a much more straightforward way to get marketers to market different foods – and products of all sorts – to children.

In short, the best way to do the right thing by children is to work with marketers, not to do battle with them. More regulation guarantees a fight without guaranteeing anything for children. It's not clear that children need a lot more protection, but the best way to ensure that children get what they need is to make it profitable for marketers to provide it. If there is demand for it, marketers will do so willingly and enthusiastically. Marketers aren't so ambitious that they will try to lead demand, but if the demand is there, they will definitely go after it.

Let's stop trying to put marketers off the scent of the consumer demand coming from children. Let's be smarter and put marketers on to the new scent of a different demand coming from children so that marketers will gladly give children what they ought to have.

References

Cialdini, R. (2006). *Influence: The psychology of persuasion*, rev. edn. New York: Collins Business Essentials.

Creamer, M. (2006). A. G. Lafley tells marketers to cede control to consumers to be "In Touch." *AdAge* (Oct. 6).

Gilbert, D. (2006). *Stumbling on happiness*. New York: Alfred A. Knopf.

Grossman, L. (2006/7). *Time* Person of the Year: You. *Time* (Dec. 25, 2006/Jan. 1, 2007).

Johnson, S. (2005). *Everything bad is good for you: How today's popular culture is actually making us smarter*. New York: Riverhead Books.

Levitt, T. (1986). *The marketing imagination*, expanded edn. New York: The Free Press.

Maclean, M. (2002). When corn is king. *Christian Science Monitor* (Oct. 31).

Myers, D. G. (2005). *Social psychology*, 8th edn. New York: McGraw-Hill.

4

Political Advertising

Necessary, Necessary Evil, or Evil Necessarily?

In this chapter, Anne Johnston and Jennifer Greer make compelling arguments both for and against political advertising. Both scholars agree that political communication changed in 1952 when Dwight Eisenhower ran for President against Adlai Stevenson. With television an untested political communication outlet and some easy potential character jabs (Stevenson being divorced, for starters), the world of mud-slinging entered a new arena. Who could blame the Republicans for wanting to parade their hero on television for all the world to see? Only when the ads pre-empted *I Love Lucy* did the public say "Enough!" And, with a popular war hero like General Eisenhower, who could blame the Democrats if they wanted to use negative advertising to knock the hero down a peg or two?

Although ultimately unsuccessful, the Democrats tried hard to argue that Ike's military experience was not the same as political experience. As political scholar, Kathleen Hall Jamieson points out in her book *Packaging the Presidency* (1996), the Democrats used negative ads that pointed toward Eisenhower's political blunders, saying in one ad that Ike was "loud, firm, and [has] frequently inconsistent opinions on almost every subject under the sun" (1996: 50).

Every presidential campaign since the Eisenhower/Stevenson campaign has been criticized for being negative and nasty. Whether it was Lyndon B. Johnson's "daisy ad" that implied his opponent, Barry Goldwater, would cause a nuclear war (Hook, 2004) or George W. Bush's ads that said voting for John Kerry might increase the threat of terrorism, research indicates that political ads can impact voters' choices. Estimates for costs of political advertising during the 2008 presidential campaign have been as high as $4.5 billion (Lieberman, 2007). During the Iowa caucus alone, $1 million per day was spent on TV advertising as candidates jockeyed for top spot (Szalai, 2008).

What are Political Ads, Anyway?

The Radio and Television News Directors Foundation's "Campaigns for Sale: A Newsroom Guide to Political Advertising" defines political ads as "paid communications to the public about anything political" (1999: 9) The guide divides ads into two main categories: *express advocacy ads*, which advocate for the election or defeat of a candidate, and *issue advocacy ads*, which advocate ideas. Express advocacy ads are regulated and have some disclosure requirements (such as how much money is spent), while issue advocacy ads have fewer restrictions. The Swift Boat ads paid for by the Swift Boat Veterans for Truth to question John Kerry's war record is an example of a controversial issue advocacy ad. When you think about the costs of political advertising, it's important to realize that one reason expenditures are increasing exponentially is the increase in the number of these issue ads. Often they are created without the candidates' knowledge or approval.

Benoit (1999) argues that political advertising uses *acclaims* (reasons to vote for the candidate), *attacks* (exposing the weakness of the candidate), or *defenses* (responding to attacks in order to set the record straight). Political advertising allows for these roles in a way that the news media cannot. In the best-case scenario, it is somewhat easy to see how these three issues are important to help voters make informed decisions on the candidates that they would like to see in office. But the reality usually comes up short.

Why is Political Advertising an Ethical Issue?

Political advertisements receive more protection under the First Amendment than other advertisements. This is because the courts hold in high regard communication that contributes to "democratic governance" (Middleton and Chamberlin, 1991: 51). For better or for worse, political ads typically are considered part of this communication. Given the scope of protection, the temptation to "stretch the truth" in political advertising is strong. Some would argue that, over time, political ads have moved to a position where they have become deceptive to the point of being unethical.

Some consider political ads a necessary evil, some people consider them a necessary nuisance, and some people consider them not only unnecessary, but downright harmful. But, ultimately, you have to make up your own mind. Would we be better off if there were no political ads? How would you decide for whom to cast your vote? Would you pay attention to what the news media were reporting? Would you believe what you read? Is political communication, as we practice it now, unethical? *You decide.*

Ideas to get you thinking . . .

1 Are there ethical limits to what politicians and their supporters should be allowed to advertise during a campaign? If so, what would those limits be?
2 Imagine running a political campaign that used no negative advertising. Do you think you could win? Why or why not?
3 What areas (if any) ought to be off limits for issue advocacy advertisements?

If you'd like to read more . . .

Craig, S. C. (ed.) (2006). *The electoral challenge: Theory meets practice.* Washington, DC: CQ Press.

Kaid, L. L., and C. Holtz-Bacha (eds.) (2006). *The Sage handbook of political advertising.* Thousand Oaks, CA: Sage Publications.

Schultz, D. A. (2004). *Lights, camera, campaign! Media, politics, and political advertising.* New York: Peter Lang.

Thurber, J. A., and C. J. Nelson (eds.) (2004). *Campaigns and elections American style.* Boulder, CO: Westview Press.

Williams, A. P., and J. C. Tedesco (2006). *The internet election: Perspectives on the Web in campaign 2004.* Lanham, MD: Rowman & Littlefield.

Young, S. (2004). *The persuaders: Inside the hidden machine of political advertising.* North Melbourne: Pluto Press Australia.

References

Benoit, W. L. (1999). *Seeing spots: A functional analysis of presidential television advertisements, 1952–1996.* Westport, CT: Praeger.

"Campaigns for sale: A newsroom guide to political advertising" (1999). Washington, DC: The Radio and Television News Directors Foundation.

Hook, J. (2004). The race for the White House: Campaigns accentuate the negative. *Los Angeles Times* (Oct. 17).

Jamieson, K. H. (1996). *Packaging the Presidency*, 3rd edn. New York: Oxford University Press.

Lieberman, D. (2007). Fight is on for campaign TV ad dollars. *USA Today.* <http://www.usatoday.com/money/media/2007-08-08-political-ad-spending_N.htm/>.

Middleton, K. R., and B. F. Chamberlin (1991). *The law of public communication*, 2nd edn. White Plains, NY: Longman.

Szalai, G. (2008). Candidates sprint out of gate with political ads. *The Reporter* (Jan.15).

Argument

Political advertising serves an important role for American voters

Anne Johnston

During the 1952 presidential election, a Democratic campaign worker criticized the Republican presidential TV ads for selling their candidate like a product: "the box tops this time are ballots. Send in enough of them and you get not only the general, you also get as an extra bonus a political space cadet with built-in secret code-breaker, atomic muscles made by United States Steel and smile by Barbasol" ("Ball blasts plan," 1952: 93). Most recently, during the 2004 presidential election, newspapers criticized broadcast ads for their formulaic content: "negative ads all look and sound like trailers for a teenage horror movie; positive ones, with their stirring montages of flags, smiling old folk and white porches, look like commercials for Paxil and Wellbutrin" (Stanley, 2004: 18). Can campaign content that looks like product ads or teenage horror movies really serve voters in making decisions about who to support during an election? Some scholars and journalists would answer no to that question, saying that political ads are too short to allow for in-depth discussion of issues, are too costly and make campaigning too expensive, and are filled with manipulative images, half-truths, and emotional appeals. All of these statements could certainly be true about specific ads or certain campaigns, but political advertising can and does serve important functions in political campaigns and, yes, can serve voters in making decisions.

The Functions of Political Ads

Historically, political advertising has served several important functions for candidates and for campaigns (Devlin, 1986; Jamieson, 1996; Sabato, 1981). Political advertising can serve to rally votes for a candidate, to create enthusiasm for a candidate, and to encourage people to vote in general. Ads can help candidates define and redefine their image for voters and provide a forum for explaining issue positions. Finally, ads have helped candidates speak to the American public without the filter of news media or news coverage and to counteract any negative or nonexistent coverage the candidate has received in the media. News media sometimes concentrate their coverage on well-known candidates or frontrunners (Graber, 1993). For some candidates the only way of equalizing that coverage is to use advertising to bring their campaign vision and message to the American public. Incumbent candidates generally have an advantage in terms of media coverage, so challengers have used their ads to contrast their issue stands and their policies with those of incumbents (Kaid and Johnston, 2001).

Images and Issues in Ads

Although we sometimes think of political ads as 30 seconds of image fluff and no issue discussion, they contain both image and issue information. In fact, a study of televised broadcast ads used by presidential candidates from 1952 through 2000 found that 65 percent of the ads were dominated by issue-related concerns (Johnston and Kaid, 2002) Research has consistently shown that ads contain issue information, and the amount of ads considered issue-focused has actually increased in the last two presidential elections (Kaid, 2002, 2005). What types of issues are contained in political ads? The issues in political ads have reflected and sometimes led the discussion of the issues during a campaign. For example, some of the most frequently discussed issues, overall, during the past years of presidential campaigns have been economic concerns, taxes, international/foreign affairs, and military spending (Kaid and Johnston, 2001).

Although ads do contain issue information, most critics say that the issue information in ads is too brief and claim that it's not possible to provide an in-depth discussion of issues in 30 seconds. And they're right. Political ads are not the place where a lengthy discussion of issues can occur; nor should they be. Political ads were never designed to function as the sole source of political information. In fact, debates, conventions, and news coverage all serve to show the voters what the candidates' issue and political stands are. Political ads provide brief summaries to voters about these stands. They are information shortcuts that work only if news media cover the issues in depth and if voters look to other sources for a complete discussion of the issues. But ads do help voters learn about the issues during a campaign. Ads may help voters who don't have lots of information, but ads are most beneficial to voters who already have some basic information about the campaign, the candidates, the issues, and other political information (Valentino et al., 2004).

In addition to containing issue information, political ads also contain lots of image information. Political ads are used to help a candidate define or reshape his or her image for voters. And candidates do spend time in their ads talking about their personality characteristics. In past elections, presidential candidates have talked about their competency, their aggressiveness, their qualifications, and their honesty in their ads. (Kaid and Johnston, 2001). Although it is important for candidates to let voters know where they stand on issues, it can be just as important for candidates to address character issues in their ads. In some elections or during some campaigns, a candidate's credibility, honesty, or integrity may be an important factor in the voters' decision-making process. Sometimes candidates running for the same office have very similar issue stands. In this case it may be that a candidate's competency to run a country or lead a government will be the critical issue for voters. Political ads provide this type of information by addressing what characteristics and values are important to the candidate.

Political ads, then, contain both issue and image information for voters. The information they provide is certainly under the control of the candidates and their media advisors. But these short, candidate-controlled forms of political communication aren't the only sources of information during an election. Ads have their functions, but candidate websites, direct mail, debates, blogs, and mainstream news coverage also have their place in this campaign communication mix. Ads don't take the place of in-depth news coverage of a political campaign, and political advertising shouldn't have to substitute for good news coverage of candidates. In the past, news media have not always done as good a job of covering and analyzing candidates and their ads during an election. In 2004, local television news in states where the candidates were competing for votes devoted less time to campaign news than to campaign advertising. Almost half of the campaign stories were devoted to strategy or details of the daily horserace and less than a third of the stories focused on campaign issues. (<www.localnewsarchive.org>). Even when news organizations have provided "ad watches" or analyses of the claims and visual images used in ads, they have not always helped voters understand or become more critical about the ads (Gobetz and Chanslor, 1999; Kaid et al., 1996). Political advertising shouldn't take the place of better news coverage during an election.

Some of the concern about political ads is less about the type of information (whether issue or image) that they contain and more about the effect that the ads have on voters. Some critics believe that political ads persuade voters to change their votes or to vote a particular way because of the information received from the ad. But what are the effects of political ads? How do they affect voters in elections? And what about the special case of negative advertising?

The Effects of Political Ads

Overall, voters do learn about candidates and issues from ads, and ads do influence voters' evaluations of candidates and their feelings about candidates. But there is no strong evidence that ads can change someone's mind about a candidate or that political ads decrease voter turnout in an election (Kaid, 2006).

In the special case of negative advertising, the evidence is mixed in terms of the effects it can have. One thing we know about negative advertising is that it has been increasing in presidential broadcast ads since the earliest broadcast campaigns, and about 65 percent of ads used in presidential elections are now negative (Kaid and Johnston, 2001). But not all negative ads are attacks on a candidate's character. In fact, of the 462 negative ads used in presidential TV advertising from 1952 to 1996, 74 percent were dominated by issue concerns and attacks on issue stands. Candidates have generally used negative ads to compare and contrast what their views are as compared with their opponents' views.

But perhaps the more important question is: How do negative ads affect voters?

Voters have proven themselves to be more skeptical and cynical about the claims in negative ads than was earlier thought. Although people generally express contempt for campaigns because of negative advertising and find negative advertising less useful, they don't become more apathetic about politics because of negative advertising (Pinkleton et al., 2002). There is also contradictory evidence about the effects of negative advertising on voter turnout, with some studies showing that negative advertising may actually stimulate voter turnout (Goldstein and Freedman, 2002) and more recent studies saying negative advertising neither increases nor decreases turnout (Clinton and Lapinski, 2004).

One problem with trying to address the criticisms of negative advertising is that not all negative ads are alike. Some negative ads can be called true mudslinging ads that denigrate the opponent's character, but there are other negative ads that compare and contrast the issue stands and policy positions of one candidate with his or her opponent. And these types of negative ads can contribute to learning and debate during a political campaign. In one experiment, negative ads that compared two candidates on specific points actually increased subjects' thinking of counterarguments to the ads and stimulated voters to think of things that contradicted the ads (Meirick, 2002). Other studies have shown that voters who were more knowledgeable or sophisticated about politics were the persons who gained lots of information from negative ads (Stevens, 2005). In addition, really negative ads don't always help the candidate using them. In some cases, the sponsor of the negative ad can suffer if voters decide they don't like the ad or that the sponsor was too nasty in it. This backlash on the sponsor, coined the "boomerang effect" (Garramone, 1984), continues to be evident in research on the effects of negative advertising. In one recent experiment, for example, it was found that being overexposed to negative advertisements caused a decline in the image of the sponsor of the ad among women viewers (King and McConnell, 2003).

The research, then, on negative advertising is mixed. People don't like it, but they may actually learn useful information from it and be able to make comparisons using the information it offers. Really negative ads, ads that denigrate and sling mud at opponents, may cause a backlash on the person using the ad, reminding all of us that the American public is more discerning than journalists, scholars, and consultants give it credit for. But what negative advertising has not been shown to do is to completely reverse a voter's opinion about his or her candidate or discourage a voter from going to the polls. And negative ads can no longer hide who is sponsoring or paying for the ad. The Bipartisan Campaign Reform Act (BCRA), passed in 2002, requires that ads from political committees must have disclaimers, and that candidate ads on television must include an appearance by the candidate saying that he or she sponsored the ad.

The Costs of Political Ads

Another concern about an overall effect of political ads is that they are so expensive that they drive up the cost of a political campaign. It is certainly true that the media budget for any campaign has grown, and advertising (televised, specifically) is the biggest chunk of that budget. In the 2004 presidential election, for example, $1.6 billion was spent on television political ads (this includes spending by candidates, political parties, and independent groups) (Memmott and Drinkard, 2004). In this election new regulations governed advertising, with the 2002 BCRA changing the way federal campaigns are financed. Although the Act did raise limits for individual donations to individual candidates, it did away with unlimited donations to political parties and candidates from wealthy donors, corporations, and labor unions.

Another solution to the high cost of political ads and political campaigning is for candidates to be given free airtime. During past elections, networks have offered free time to presidential candidates to air their ads, and there have been some attempts to put into law a provision that would provide free airtime to candidates and to campaign issues. In October 2002, U.S. Senators John McCain, Russ Feingold, and Richard Durbin introduced the Political Campaign Broadcast Activity Improvement Act which would require broadcast stations to devote a certain amount of airtime to candidate-centered or issue-centered programming during an election. It also would make funding available (in the form of broadcast vouchers) for candidates and parties to use to place political ads on TV and radio during election cycles.

Revisiting the Role of Political Ads

Although it may sometimes seem like political advertising is used to sell issues and candidates like soap, political ads can be an important part of the communication mix in any political campaign. To limit or do away with them would limit the type of information available to voters during an election. Ads may encourage discussion and debate on issues and set the agenda of what is being talked about in the election, sometimes even forcing news media to cover those issues. Political ads were never meant to be the sole source of information about the candidates, or about the issues, for voters. They are source-sponsored communications about a candidate's or a group's vision of a campaign, or their stand on an issue. They are not substitutes for good news coverage and campaign analysis. They are not substitutes for political websites or blogs. They are not substitutes for voters' information-seeking. And to think that political ads should do all of that is to expect too much of political ads and expect too little of the American public or of the news media during an election.

References

"Ball blasts plan to fill airwaves with Ike spots" (1952). *Advertising Age* (Oct. 6): 93.

Clinton, J. D., and J. S. Lapinski (2004). "Targeted" advertising and voter turnout: An experimental study of the 2000 presidential election. *The Journal of Politics* 66(1): 69–96.

Devlin, L. P. (1996). An analysis of presidential television commercials, 1952–1984. In L. L. Kaid, D. Nimmo, and K. R. Sanders (eds.), *New perspectives on political advertising* (pp. 21–54). Carbondale: Southern Illinois University Press.

Garramone, G. M. (1984). Voter responses to negative political ads. *Journalism Quarterly* 61: 250–9.

Gobetz, R. H., and M. Chanslor (1999). A content analysis of CNN "Inside Politics" adwatch coverage of high-profile, nonpresidential races. In L. L. Kaid and D. G. Bystrom (eds.), *The electronic election: Perspectives on the 1996 campaign communication* (pp. 113–21). Mahwah, NJ: Lawrence Erlbaum.

Goldstein, K., and P. Freedman (2002). Campaign advertising and voter turnout: New evidence for a stimulation effect. *The Journal of Politics* 64(3): 721–40.

Graber, D. A. (1993). *Mass media and American politics*, 4th edn. Washington, DC: CQ Press.

Jamieson, K. H. (1996). The evolution of political advertising in America. In L. L. Kaid, D. Nimmo, and K. R. Sanders (eds.), *New perspectives on political advertising* (pp. 1–20). Carbondale: Southern Illinois University Press.

Johnston, A., and L. L. Kaid (2002). Image ads and issue ads in U.S. presidential advertising: Using videostyle to explore stylistic differences in televised ads from 1952 to 2000. *Journal of Communication* 52: 281–300.

Kaid, L. L. (2002). Videostyle and political advertising effects in the 2000 presidential campaign. In R. E. Denton, Jr. (ed.), *The 2000 presidential campaign: A communication perspective* (pp. 183–97). Westport, CT: Praeger.

Kaid, L. L. (2005). Videostyle in the 2004 political advertising. In R. E. Denton, Jr. (ed.), *The 2004 Presidential campaign: A communication perspective* (pp. 283–99). Lanham, MD: Rowman & Littlefield.

Kaid, L. L. (2006). Political advertising in the United States. In L. L. Kaid and C. Holtz-Bacha (eds.), *Handbook of international political advertising*. Newbury Park, CA: Sage.

Kaid, L. L., and A. Johnston (2001). *Videostyle in presidential campaigns: Style and content of televised political advertising*. Westport, CT: Praeger.

Kaid, L. L., M. S. McKinney, and J. C. Tedesco (2000). *Civic dialogue in the 1996 presidential campaign: Candidate, media, and public voices*. Cresskill, NJ: Hampton Press.

Kaid, L. L., J. C. Tedesco, and L. M. McKinnon (1996). Presidential ads as nightly news: A content analysis of 1988 and 1992 televised ad watches. *Journal of Broadcasting and Electronic Media*, 40: 297–308.

King, J. D., and J. B. McConnell (2003). The effect of negative campaign advertising on vote choice: The mediating influence of gender. *Social Science Quarterly* 84: 843–58.

Meirick, P. (2002). Cognitive responses to negative and comparative political advertising. *Journal of Advertising* 31: 49–62.

Memmott, M., and J. Drinkard (2004). Election ad battle smashes record in 2004: Group questions the value of costly campaigns to USA. *USA Today* (Nov. 24): online at <http://www.usatoday.com/news/washington/2004-11-25-election-ads_x.htm>.

Pinkleton, B. E., N. Um, and E. W. Austin (2002). An exploration of the effects of negative political advertising on political decision making. *The Journal of Politics* 31: 13–26.

Sabato, L. J. (1981). *The rise of political consultants: New ways of winning elections.* New York: Basic Books.

Stanley, A. (2004). Florida, an electoral prize, is awash in a sea of ads. *New York Times* (Oct. 29): A18.

Stevens, D. (2005). Separate and unequal effects: Information, political sophistication and negative advertising in American elections. *Political Research Quarterly* 58: 413–26.

Valentino, N. A., V. L. Hutchings, and D. Williams (2004). The impact of political advertising on knowledge, internet information seeking, and candidate preference. *Journal of Communication* 54: 337–54.

Counterargument

Political advertising has no place in the U.S. democratic system

Jennifer D. Greer

Two of the first people I "met" when I moved to Nevada in 1996 were Steve Jones and Cliff Young – and within 30 seconds of meeting them, I disliked them both. Jones and Young were running for the Nevada Supreme Court. They introduced themselves to me through television commercials. Actually, Jones introduced me to Young, telling me of Young's derogatory remarks toward women. Young introduced me to Jones; he showed me a grainy, black-and-white re-enactment of Jones and his wife in a physical battle that sent the wife, then five months pregnant, to jail. These men wanted to decide the most important legal cases in the state; how could I vote for either of them?

When I voted November 5, I was relieved to find that Nevada has a "none of these candidates" option for all offices elected statewide. I liked "none" much better than Jones and Young, so I checked that box for Supreme Court Justice Seat B. I wasn't alone – 88,839 other Nevadans shared my disgust with the candidates and their mudslinging ads. Our votes represented 21.4 percent of those who cast votes for the race and almost 2,400 voters more than the 86,472 southern Nevadans who sent Republican John Ensign to Congress that day.

Nevada is the only state with the "none of these candidates" option. "None" is a popular candidate in the Silver State. In the 1976 Republican primary for Congress, "none" won, with 47.3 percent of the vote. Ten years later, "none" won the Democratic primary for state treasurer (Erikson, 2003). Nevadans are an ornery bunch, but my guess is that candidate "none" would be just as popular with other Americans fed up with political campaigns marked by misleading, deceptive, and increasingly negative advertising.

A dislike of candidates is the least egregious of a series of harmful effects brought on by the current state of political advertising in U.S. elections. Modern campaign advertising, generally seen as beginning with the television ads in the 1952 presidential election, has had far-reaching detrimental effects on voter turnout, division of the electorate, voter knowledge about issues, and public attitudes toward elected leaders and governmental institutions.

Voter Turnout

The easiest way for voters to pick "none of these candidates," even in Nevada, is to stay home on election day, and an increasing number of those eligible to vote do just that every election cycle. According to the Federal Election Commission, 63.1 percent of the eligible voting-age population cast ballots in the 1960 presidential election. By 1996, that number was at its lowest recorded rate, 49.1 percent. In the 2004 presidential elections, a tight contest that expected to get out the vote, turnout was only 55.3 percent. Off-year elections have seen the same decline, from 47.3 percent in 1962 to 37 percent in 2002 (<www.fec.gov>).

Although this drop in political participation is the result of many factors, political advertising – especially the explosion of negative political advertising in recent decades – accounts for much of the political malaise that makes many Americans put getting their daily Starbucks fix ahead of stopping by the polls. West (2001) documented a sharp rise in negativity in presidential ads from 1952 to 2000. In 1960, only 12 percent of prominent presidential television commercials were critical; by 1988, that number was 83 percent, and 87 percent of the fall ads in 2000 were negative.

Stephen Ansolabehere and Shanto Iyengar in 1995 argued that political advertising should be blamed for at least part of this decline. In *Going Negative: How Political Advertisements Shrink and Polarize the Electorate* they tracked advertising tone and voter turnout in the 1992 Senate races. Ansolabehere and Iyengar classified 12 of the campaigns as mainly positive, meaning both candidates relied most heavily on positive political ads. Interestingly, these races were in sparsely populated states, home to only 13 percent of the U.S. electorate. In contrast, 15 states, home to 62 percent of the population, saw overwhelmingly negative Senate campaigns that year.

Turnout varied by tone of the campaign. In the positive campaigns, 57 percent of voters cast ballots. But in mixed-tone races, turnout was almost five percentage points lower, 52.4 percent, and turnout in the negative races was 49.7 percent. Even after controlling for other factors that can suppress voter turnout, Ansolabehere and Iyengar estimated the difference in turnout between the positive and negative races at 4.5 percentage points.

Similarly, positive and negative races had different rates of "ballot rolloff," a phenomenon that occurs when voters select a choice for key offices but skip voting for less important races on the ballot. In positive Senate races in 1992, 3.3 percent of those who turned out to vote for President failed to vote for any Senate candidate. In contrast, the ballot rolloff in states with negative races was 6 percent (Ansolabehere and Iyengar, 1995). Ballot rolloff, or those in effect choosing "none of these candidates" in Senate races, was almost double among voters inundated with attack ads.

The argument that exposure to negative advertising depresses voter turnout has been challenged by some researchers measuring the effects of negative political advertising on attitudes such as cynicism, apathy, and political efficacy (the feeling that your vote or other actions can make a difference) in experimental studies. Pinkleton et al. (2002) found that potential voters who saw the most negative ads held the most negative attitudes toward campaigns. Attitudes of those who saw negative ads were five times more negative toward campaigns than the attitudes of those who saw positive ads. Interestingly, though, the researchers did not find a rise in voter cynicism and voter apathy – two factors linked to lower political participation – and only found weak support that negative campaigns led to a drop in political efficacy.

But those measures were taken after only one brief experimental exposure to negative ads, which is not representative of the onslaught of negative ads voters see in each election cycle. Even Pinkleton et al. didn't rule out the possibility that negative ads reduce public affairs participation. "It also could indicate that negative advertising's effects on apathy and efficacy, as well as on cynicism, are cumulative and difficult to detect in a short-term manipulation," they concluded (2002: 23). And in the same 2002 issue of *Journal of Advertising* where that study appeared, Tedesco (2002) reported contrasting results, finding significant short-term increases in cynicism after subjects viewed a series of negative ads in a 2000 Senate race.

Ansolabehere and Iyengar pose three scenarios to explain how negative ads depress turnout:

1 Supporters of the candidates who is attacked might lose faith in their candidate but stay home because they can't bring themselves to vote for the attacker.
2 Attack ads leave voters disenchanted with both candidates, meaning attackers may unintentionally depress voter turnout among their own – as well as their opponent's – supporters.

3   Negative ads "diminish [the] power of civic duty," undermining the entire
    electoral process. Negative campaigns "may leave voters embittered toward
    the candidates and the rules of the game" (Ansolabehere and Iyengar,
    1995: 110).

Polarization of the Electorate

Not only do attack ads chip away at faith in the system, Ansolabehere and
Iyengar contend that they also polarize the public. With the increasing depend-
ency on TV spots in the 1960s, U.S. candidates no longer needed the
rank-and-file party workers to get their message out. They communicated
directly and unfiltered to voters, and many thought this would produce
more independent politicians not beholden to party leaders and special interest groups. Instead, Ansolabehere and Iyengar argue, by the mid-1990s,
Americans were left with a government "even more polarized and partisan
than ever. The parties in Congress represent two increasingly cohesive and
extreme positions. The electorate has reacted with frustration and anger"
(1995: 2).

How can advertising be blamed for this "new, ugly regime"? Because
all advertising, whether for soap or Senate candidates, reinforces people's
pre-existing attitudes and preferences. Simply put, political advertising
tells loyalists what they want to hear and already believe. Those out of the
system, a growing number of nonpartisans, simply tune out anything but
the negative. They're disgusted with politicians, elections, and government;
only negative ads resonate with them. Ansolabehere and Iyengar argue:

> Unfortunately, negative campaigning only reinforces the nonpartisans'
> disillusionment and convinces them not to participate in a tainted process.
> As a result, nonpartisans have not become the electoral force that they
> might have. Instead, political advertising has produced a party renaissance,
> even though partisans are an increasingly unrepresentative segment of the
> public. (1995: 3)

Another study in the early 1990s found that negative advertising can not
only divide us, but can make us think less of our fellow voters. Stanford
researcher Jeremy Cohen reported that voters viewing two attack ads said
they weren't affected by the commercials, but they expressed fears that
the ads would negatively affect others. Cohen saw the loss of faith in other

voters – and the legitimacy of the whole system – as a largely ignored consequence of attack ads. "Because we don't think others will react to the advertisements the way we do, the ads leave us thinking others aren't capable of self-governance," Cohen said in a press release (Cohen, 1992).

Voter Learning about Campaigns

Although proponents of political advertising argue that voters can learn from ads, even negative spots, several studies have suggested that voters see advertising as not useful, as uninformative, and as providing little helpful information in voting decisions (Ansolabehere and Iyengar 1995; Chang et al., 1998; Pinkleton et al., 2002). Some studies, including my own experiments in the 1990s on the effects of political adwatches, have found that only the less involved see increases in knowledge after watching political advertising. Because this group is the least likely to seek out political information and act on it, can ads really make much difference in voter learning? Those who already have a candidate preference show biased memory of candidate issue positions, indicating that any learning is hampered by pre-existing attitudes (An and Jin, 2004).

While some concede that voters could learn from well-crafted political ads that focus on issue rather than image and that clearly and truthfully outline a candidate's position rather than attacking an opponent, those ads are few and far between. Superficiality and distortion reign in modern political advertising, hampering any slim chance voters might have to learn from campaign spots. Political advertising reduces complex issues to soundbites, and uses imagery, catchphrases, and emotional appeals rather than information to sway voters.

Political ads don't provide true discourse in the form of give and take over issues. In political debates, candidates attack their opponent just as they do in ads, but debates also provide immediate rebuttal opportunities. Responses to political attack ads are not as swift. "By the time the respondent responds, days or even weeks have gone by. And of course, the natural reaction is to mount counter-attacks that are also immune to scrutiny. The net result for the viewer is an endless assault of shrill, demeaning finger-pointing. Congress on *Jerry Springer*" (Welke, 1999).

Learning is also hampered by the distortions and half-truths that ads are based on. Gribble contends that political commercials use tried and true manipulation techniques perfected by product advertisers for decades.

And why shouldn't they? They're produced by the same advertising agencies whose job it is to manipulate people to buy products and services. "More often than not these 'marketing messages' are composed of innuendo and exaggeration rather than factual claims about a product's virtues. . . . that perfect manipulation is exactly what pays the bills, undermining democracy in the process," (Gribble, 1994).

Attitudes Toward Elected Officials and Government

Chang et al. (1998) found that those who saw the most negative ads rated them as untruthful, and these ratings of untruthfulness were linked to negative evaluations of both the ad's sponsoring candidate and the candidate targeted in the attack. Thus, regardless of which side is attacking, negative ads can lead to at least short-term lower evaluations of both candidates. When both sides are attacking, these feelings are surely intensified.

Once elections are over, do voters simply forget the insults hurled at – or the barbs thrown by – the person who's won the office? Of course not, argues Hollihan (2001). "The loser concedes, wishes the winner well, and pledges support for the political process. Meanwhile, the winner gratefully acknowledges his or her worthy challenger and claims a mandate to govern. These attempts at post-election civility sometimes seem woefully phony and inadequate after the spiteful campaigns that have just been waged" (2001: 111). The result is a chipping away at respect for officeholders, the work they do, and the government they run. Bob Welke, writing in *Salon*, summed up this sentiment in 1999: "The result is disdain for everyone in the arena" (1999: 2). Welke, an "ad guy," argues that the current state of political advertising has destroyed the "brand" of democratic government envisioned by the Founding Fathers. "Instead of sending out messages about values, performance and quality, they [politicians] have blown the brand's goodwill bank account on sense-off coupons to get themselves elected" (1999: 2).

Once in office, incumbents worry only about protecting their individual brand; thus they are cautious as they eye re-election. Being associated with a difficult policy issue opens officeholders up to attack ads in future elections, and could dry up the special interest money they need to pay for future television commercials (Ansolabehere and Iyengar, 1995; Hollihan, 2001). "Some media observers have also suggested that fear of manipulation, in the form of being associated with difficult problems, actually deters incumbent officials from attempting corrective actions," Ansolabehere and

Iyengar argue. "The fear of being victimized by attack advertising is thus thought to contribute to irresponsible governance" (1995: 8).

Solutions

Adding up the multitude of harmful effects outlined above leads to one conclusion – political advertising must be banned from the U.S. political process. Will this guarantee a decline in voter turnout? A less polarized electorate? More informed voters? Less disdain for government and its officials? Only time will tell. But at the very least we'd stop our downward spiral. Without campaign ads, candidates would be forced to communicate to voters in more interactive and innovative ways, apathetic voters would have to seek out (and therefore demand) other forms of information about the candidates and issues, and news media, especially the broadcast industry, surely would devote more airtime to meaningful campaign discourse. Critics, including newsman Walter Cronkite, have chastised broadcasters for eagerly packing their commercial slots with campaign ads while virtually ignoring campaign discourse in news coverage. A September 7, 2000, spot check of the networks found an average of only 13 seconds of candidate discourse during each evening's newscast. A similar sample of 15 stations in the top 75 local markets found only 28 seconds on average (Texas Alliance for Better Campaigns, 2000).

In a world without political advertising, news coverage would improve. Speeches, town meetings, and televised debates likely would get much more attention from all three groups – voters, media, and the candidates themselves – just as these campaign communications did in the days before the 30-second candidate ruled. And in the era of blogs, podcasting, digital cable, and texting, candidates and voters could use new technology to interact in much more meaningful ways. Any of these, and dozens of other forums, would surely be preferable to the current alienating system – one in which the American public would rather cast a vote for the next "American Idol" than bother to exercise their democratic right to choose their leaders.

References

An, S., and H. S. Jin (2004). *Attitude strength, ad recall and candidate issue knowledge.* (Aug.). Toronto: Association for Education in Journalism and Mass Communication Convention.

Ansolabehere, S. and S. Iyengar (1995). *Going negative: How political advertisements shrink and polarize the electorate.* New York: Free Press.

Chang, W. H., J.-S. Park, and S. W. Shim (1998). Effectiveness of negative political advertising. *Web Journal of Mass Communication Research* 2: 1.

Cohen, J. (1992). Negative ads may fuel distrust of democracy. *Stanford University News Service* (Apr. 6) <http://www.stanford.edu/dept/news/relaged/920406Arc2309.html>.

Erikson, R. (2003). None of these candidates. Nevada State Library and Archives <http://dmla.clan.lib.nv.us/docs/NSLA/archives/political/none.htm>.

Gribble, P. (1994). The debate room: Political television advertisements. <http://www.etext.org/Zines/Intl_Teletimes/Teletimes_HTML/debate_room_94 02.html>.

Hollihan, T. A. (2001). *Uncivil wars.* Boston: Bedford/St Martin's.

Pinkleton, B. E., N.-H. Um, and E. W. Austin (2002). An exploration of the effects of negative political advertising on political decision making. *Journal of Advertising* 31(1): 13–25.

Tedesco, J. C. (2002). Televised political advertising effects: Evaluating responses during the 2000 Robb-Allen senatorial election. *Journal of Advertising* 31(1): 7–48.

Texas Alliance for Better Campaigns (2000). Alliance for better campaigns launches greedytv.org: Grassroots effort will target local television stations. (Sept. 14). Available at <http://www.tpj.org/docs/pressreleases/greedytv.html>.

Welke, B. (1999). Why we should get rid of political advertising – now. *Salon* (Sept. 2). Available at <http://www.salon.com/media/feature/1999/09/02/advertising/index.html>.

West, D. M. (2001). *Air wars: Television advertising in election campaigns, 1952–2000.* Washington, DC: CQ Press.

5

Tobacco Advertising
When People Do Dumb Things

Recently, I was getting ready to go out for a spell on my sailboat when I saw a sailor coming in to dock. It's good sailing manners to help bring the boat in, chat about the day's sail, etc. The skipper looked fairly shaken up and told me about an unusual encounter he had just had on the lake. He had to rescue a man in the water holding on to his 2-year-old son. The man had apparently decided it would be nice to jump in the water for a swim with his son. The problem was that he didn't think about what boats do when unattended. Of course, the obvious happened. The dad jumped in with his kid – and the boat floated away. If this weren't bad enough, the father had left his other child (a 3-year-old) *on* the boat. How dumb can a person get?

No question about it. People do idiotic things. There are the obvious actions, of course. Driving without a seatbelt. Getting drunk and getting into a car. Eating massive amounts of fried food. Avoiding vegetables. Riding a bike without a helmet. And smoking cigarettes.

As Michael Hoefges and Jef Richards, authors of the following essays, point out, the to-regulate or not-to-regulate tobacco advertising debate has been raging for a long time. What is the role of the government? To keep us safe? Or to keep us from hurting others? Clearly, there is evidence that at times the government steps in and makes laws to protect us from ourselves. We are supposed to wear a seatbelt. In many states it is against the law to ride a motorcycle without a helmet. Some states do not allow you to buy fire-crackers for fear you will blow up your neighbor. How do we know where to draw the line?

At this point, even with the scientific data that basically proves food with trans fat is bad for you, it is not against the law to eat it. It's also not against the law to advertise it. So, how far is this analogy from smoking? Yes, we know it's bad. (Okay, it's real bad.) But, can't people make up their own minds whether they want to kill themselves? (Or shorten their lives by several years? Or at the very least, develop premature wrinkles and brittle hair?)

Some people argue that adding restrictions is not going to change the amount of media exposure tobacco companies can garner, so by instigating bans, there may be a reversal effect. For example, when the voluntary ban on television commercials for cigarettes began, the tobacco industry did not fight hard against it. In fact, some would say it even encouraged it. Why? Some have argued that, with the removal of cigarette commercials, there would also be a removal of anti-cigarette commercials. And there were movies, sporting events, and other media venues available to explore. These would most likely end up on televi-sion anyway. In fact, there is some evidence that this is the case. Some researchers argue that the number of actors smoking cigarettes in movies has increased since the Master Settlement Agreement of 1998, which has been the biggest restriction of cigarette advertising and has been hailed as, perhaps, the most important development in advertising regulation (Ng and Dakake, 2002). So perhaps an all-out ban on the presence of tobacco in any kind of media is warranted.

Trying to figure out what side you come down on in the advertising and tobacco controversy pits free speech purists against health advocates, advertising haters against free market gurus. This is one of those topics that tends to get heated rather quickly. Debating the merits of regulating tobacco advertising (or arguing against it, for that matter) is a hard battle to win because the end result is problematic whichever side you take. What if a complete ban on advertising were promoted by the government because of the proven harmful effects of smoking: what would be next? High-cholesterol foods? All fast-food restaurants?

On the other hand, what if there were *no* restrictions? There is evidence that countries with fewer advertising restrictions have higher numbers of smokers – and, subsequently, higher numbers of smoking-related deaths. Of course, even with this compelling evidence it's difficult to know if the relationship is coincidental or causal.

Trying to work your way through the quagmire of the pros and cons of advertising regulation for tobacco is tricky. But, Michael Hoefges and Jef Richards do an admirable job, each laying out a compelling argument for the regulation of advertising or the protection of free speech. What's the right side? *You decide.*

Ideas to get you thinking . . .

1 Make a list of all the products you can think of that are extremely dangerous to a consumer. Do you recall any advertising for them? If so, what kinds of strategies do you think the advertisers used to get their messages across?
2 Could you come up with a "code of ethics" to decide when you might want to restrict advertising for a harmful product? What kinds of things would you put into the code?
3 Ask some young teens who smoke why they smoke. Do you think the media have a role in why they started to smoke?

If you'd like to read more . . .

Burrough, B., and J. Helyar (2003). *Barbarians at the gate: The fall of RJR Nabisco*. London: HarperCollins.

Master Settlement Agreement (1998). Available at <http://ag.ca.gov/tobacco/pdf/1msa.pdf>.

Mekemson, C., and S. A. Glantz (2002). How the tobacco industry built its relationship with Hollywood. *Tobacco Control* 11: i81–i91.

Pennock, P. E. (2007). *Advertising sin and sickness: The politics of alcohol and tobacco marketing, 1950–1990*. DeKalb: Northern Illinois University Press.

References

Ng, C., and B. Dakade (2002). Tobacco at the movies: Tobacco use in PG-13 films. <http://masspirg.org/MA.asp?id2=8330&id3=MA>.

Argument

Tobacco advertising: the strong First Amendment right to promote lawful products

R. Michael Hoefges

Banning or restricting advertising and promotion of tobacco products seems to be among the obvious public policy and legislative choices to curb harmful health-related effects and costs from cigarette smoking and other tobacco product usage. And such measures seem especially attractive as regulatory options when the specific goal becomes reducing underage use of tobacco products, including cigarette smoking. But do government restrictions on tobacco advertising and promotion run afoul of the First Amendment of the U.S. Constitution, which protects free speech rights including those of commercial speakers? Should the First Amendment even provide protection for messages that encourage people to purchase and use tobacco products when the health-related dangers and addictive nature of these products are well established medically and widely known among consumers? Answering these questions requires a detailed look at the extent to which the First Amendment provides protection for commercial speech in general and then, specifically, for tobacco product advertising. And this analysis suggests that yes, indeed, the First Amendment does and ought to protect commercial promotion for lawful goods and services including tobacco products, as socially unpopular as they may be.

In *Virginia State Board of Pharmacy v. Virginia Citizens Consumer Council, Inc.* (1976), for the first time in history, the United States Supreme Court extended First Amendment protection to commercial speech, meaning speech that does no more than propose a commercial transaction. The court in that case concluded that the role of free-flowing commercial information from advertisers and marketers to consumers is critical to the functioning of our free market economy in terms of facilitating and encouraging informed economic decisions by consumers in the aggregate. Thus, the court held in that case that, while marketers and advertisers certainly have a First Amendment right to promote lawful goods and services, consumers also have a concomitant and equally important constitutional right to receive this information and make purchase and other economic decisions based on their own-self-determined interests free from excessive and paternalistic government intervention in this communication process. Specifically in that case, the *Virginia Board of Pharmacy* court concluded that a state regulation that banned licensed pharmacists from advertising prescription drug prices was unconstitutional and needed to be struck down because consumers – especially those on fixed incomes – needed this information and would be keenly interested in knowing where to purchase their needed medications most economically.

However, it bears mention here that the *Virginia Board of Pharmacy* court did not extend First Amendment protection to commercial speech that is either false or misleading, or to speech that proposes an unlawful commercial transaction. Therefore, federal and state governments remain relatively unencumbered today to constitutionally prohibit such forms of unprotected advertising categorically on grounds of consumer protection in the marketplace. In other words the First Amendment speech clause is not synonymous with the term "buyer beware." In addition, the *Virginia Board of Pharmacy* court did not extend full and complete First Amendment protection to commercial speech for lawful goods and services even when truthful and non-misleading, but instead extended an intermediate level of protection. In other words, protected commercial speech is not *absolutely* or fully protected from all regulation under the First Amendment. What this means today is that even protected commercial speech – under some circumstances – can be constitutionally regulated under the First Amendment.

In a 1980 case, the court determined more specifically the circumstances under which government can indeed constitutionally regulate protected commercial speech (*Central Hudson Gas & Electric Corp. v. Public Service Commission*, 1980). In that case, the court held that protected commercial speech can be constitutionally regulated so long as the government can set out a substantial governmental interest for its regulation – meaning an important public policy goal – and also can demonstrate that the regulation in question will effectively serve that interest without burdening protected speech more than is reasonably necessary. In other words, to constitutionally regulate protected commercial speech, the government must have a good enough public policy goal and draft a regulatory scheme that is both effective and efficacious. What all of this means today is that advertisers have a constitutional right to promote lawful products and services in a truthful and non-misleading manner while, on the other hand, the government retains the ability to constitutionally prohibit unprotected advertising and to regulate even protected advertising within the constitutional parameters set out by the Supreme Court. In other words, the regulatory hands of the government are not completely tied by the First Amendment in terms of regulating advertising for important public policy purposes.

So what does all of this have to do with tobacco advertising? Well, specifically, government has the constitutional ability to regulate false and misleading advertising for tobacco products and the ability to constitutionally prohibit unprotected unfair business practices such as tobacco manufacturers using advertising to target underage consumers as potential purchasers of tobacco products. And, of course, the government has the constitutional ability to impose any number of direct product regulations, including age restrictions and limitations on places of purchase for tobacco products, and also may freely impose taxes on tobacco product purchases as well. And, as indicated, government can even constitutionally regulate truthful and non-misleading advertising for lawful tobacco products so long as the regulations will effectively serve a substantial governmental goal such as curbing underage tobacco usage without overly burdening the ability of tobacco advertisers and marketers to continue to advertise and promote their products to adult consumers. Needless to say, developing a constitutional regulatory scheme within all of these parameters is challenging but nonetheless the task with which the First Amendment charges legislators and regulators who have chosen to legalize tobacco products but now wish to regulate *speech* about those products.

In addition, government can – and does – constitutionally require advertisers to disclose health and other risks that ought to be disclosed before the purchase decision is made. For instance, provisions in the Federal Cigarette Advertising and Labeling Act require health warnings in all cigarette advertising and packaging (15 U.S.C. §§1333 et seq.). And, in a different context, the U.S. Supreme Court has held that advertisers do not have a First Amendment right to refuse to disclose such pertinent – "material" – information in advertising when to do so would be misleading or harmful to consumers (*Zauderer v. Office of Disciplinary Council*, 1985). Therefore, the regulatory option of reasonable disclosure requirements along with all of the other regulatory options listed above remains available without the need to strip tobacco product advertising of its constitutional protection under the First Amendment and close all channels of communication between tobacco advertisers and marketers and their adult customers. But should that be the case? If the government can indeed impose all of these regulations on a product and even ban legal sale of the product altogether – especially a harmful or "vice" product like a tobacco product – shouldn't the government have more leeway under the First Amendment to regulate advertising for such products more stringently than advertising for more socially acceptable products?

Basically, the U.S. Supreme Court has ruled "No." And, one could argue, rightly so. Why is this? Well, the First Amendment doesn't make such normative judgments and instead protects speech without regard to viewpoint, including speech that many would find repugnant and disagreeable. In fact, arguably, such is the type of speech that is most needy and indeed deserving of First Amendment protection because it's most at risk of being banned due to popular sentiment. Therefore, the First Amendment protects unpopular and dissident messages and allows each individual in society to decide in the "marketplace of ideas" whether a certain message is "good" or "bad," or agreeable or disagreeable, and then to respond accordingly.

Product advertising is similar, the court has held, and many would argue. So long as the government legalizes and allows the sale of a particular product, there is a strong constitutional right to promote that product to consumers in a truthful and non-misleading manner. In other words, there may not be a constitutional right to sell or purchase that product but once the government legalizes the product, there is a strong First Amendment right to *speak* about that product, including commercially. And, consumers have the ultimate right to decide in the context of the economic marketplace what to make of such messages, whether to purchase and use that product and, ultimately, what judgment to place on that product.

Along these lines, the U.S. Supreme Court has extended First Amendment protection to commercial speech related to harmful products and activities – so-called "vice" products and activities – such as beer (*Rubin v. Coors Brewing Co., Inc.*, 1995), liquor (*44 Liquormart, Inc. v. Rhode Island*, 1996), casino gambling (*Greater New Orleans Broadcasting Association v. United States*, 1999) and, yes, tobacco products (*Lorillard Tobacco Co. v. Reilly*, 2001). In these cases, the court specifically refused to create a "vice" product exemption under the First Amendment that would allow the government to more freely regulate the advertising for harmful products and services than for other types of products and services that might be more socially acceptable. As Supreme Court Justice John Paul Stevens wrote for the court in striking down a ban on broadcast advertising for casino gambling, "the power to prohibit or to regulate a particular *conduct* does not necessarily include the power to prohibit or regulate *speech* about that conduct" (*Greater New Orleans Broadcasting* at p. 193, emphasis added). Indeed, he pointed out, the court has clearly "rejected the argument that the power to restrict *speech* about certain socially harmful activities [is] as broad as the power to prohibit such *conduct*" (*Greater New Orleans Broadcasting* at p. 192). And in all of these cases the government had regulatory options to curb harmful social effects other than banning protected commercial speech about these products and services.

In a key case decided in 2001, the Supreme Court refused to allow the state of Massachusetts to, in effect, ban truthful and non-misleading outdoor advertising for tobacco products in metropolitan areas such as Boston (*Lorillard Tobacco Co. v. Reilly*). In a majority opinion written by Justice Sandra Day O'Connor, the court concluded that Massachusetts had established a sufficiently substantial regulatory goal of protecting children from the harms of tobacco products and that reducing the extent to which children are exposed to tobacco advertising and promotion probably would effectively serve this goal sufficiently to withstand the constitutional challenge in the case. However, the regulations operated as a virtual ban on commercial communications between tobacco advertisers and marketers, including retailers and their adult customers, and were unconstitutional for that reason, the court held. Although the regulations only prohibited outdoor tobacco advertising within 1,000 feet of locations where children are likely to be present, such as playgrounds, parks, and schools, there probably would not be any location where outdoor tobacco advertising would be permitted in densely populated metropolitan areas.

Therefore, according to the *Lorillard Tobacco* majority, the Massachusetts regulations unconstitutionally prohibited tobacco marketers and retailers from communicating with adult consumers and, for instance, could have been more narrowly tailored to focus on highly visible advertising or targeted messages with youth-oriented appeals. Instead, the regulations would even have prohibited small retailers from informing passersby that they sold tobacco products inside. In the case, Justice Clarence Thomas, in a strongly worded concurring opinion, specifically warned about the dangers of allowing restrictions on messages that some may find harmful. On this point, he wrote:

> Calls for limits on expression always are made when the specter of some threatened harm is looming. The identity of the harm may vary. People will be inspired by totalitarian dogmas and subvert the Republic. They will be

inflamed by racial demagoguery and embrace hatred and bigotry. Or they will be enticed by cigarette advertisements and choose to smoke, risking disease. It is therefore no answer for the State to say that the makers of cigarettes are doing harm: perhaps they are. But in that respect they are no different from the purveyors of other harmful products, or the advocates of harmful ideas. When the State seeks to silence them, they are all entitled to the protection of the First Amendment. (*Lorillard Tobacco Co.*, Thomas, J., concurring in part and concurring in the judgment, p. 590)

Justice Thomas raised the proverbial slippery slope and warned that allowing the Massachusetts ban on outdoor tobacco advertising to stand under the First Amendment likely would open the door to similar restrictions on such products as fast food and alcohol that also are deemed by many in society to be harmful yet are perfectly lawful.

So, given the fact that First Amendment protection for tobacco advertising has never been considered absolute and that the government retains the right to regulate, tax, and even ban tobacco products, it seems quite dangerous indeed to assert that commercial *speech* about such a lawful product – tobacco advertising – should be rendered devoid of First Amendment protection and permitted to be banned entirely by the government. And, of course, should the government decide to remove tobacco products from the list of legalized products available to the public by banning their sale, the First Amendment would no longer recognize any right to promote the sale or use of these products once criminalized. But, so long as the government has chosen to allow the legalized sale of tobacco products, the First Amendment does – and should – protect the right of marketers and advertisers to speak commercially about these products to lawful consumers in a truthful and non-misleading manner as well as the concomitant right of consumers to receive these communications. Anything less would violate the spirit and intent of free expression rights in the economic marketplace and, more broadly, in the marketplace of ideas.

If you'd like to read more . . .

Hoefges, M. (2003). Protecting tobacco advertising under the commercial speech doctrine: The constitutional impact of Lorillard Tobacco Co. *Communication Law and Policy* 8(3): 267–311.

Hoefges, M., and M. Rivera-Sanchez (2000). "Vice" advertising under the Supreme Court's commercial speech doctrine: The shifting Central Hudson analysis. *Hastings Communication and Entertainment Law Journal* 22(3/4): 345–90.

References

44 Liquormart, Inc. v. Rhode Island (1996), 517 U.S. 484.

Central Hudson Gas & Electric Corp. v. Public Service Commission of New York (1980), 447 U.S. 557.

Greater New Orleans Broadcasting Association v. United States (1999), 527 U.S. 193.

Lorillard Tobacco Co. v. Reilly (2001), 533 U.S. 525.

Rubin v. Coors Brewing Co., Inc. (1995), 514 U.S. 476.

Virginia State Board of Pharmacy v. Virginia Consumer Council, Inc. (1976), 425 U.S. 748.

Zauderer v. Office of Disciplinary Council (1985), 471 U.S. 626.

Counterargument

The fumes of truth

Jef I. Richards

Upon visiting the Hawai'i Volcanoes National Park, a visitor can hardly miss noticing the signs and brochures warning of the dangers inherent in walking on the recent lava flows from the active Kilauea volcano. Yet if you take the drive down to watch the glowing magma drop into the ocean, on any given night you also can watch sightseers trek off across the lava to get up close and personal with the deadly material. And, yes, there have been some deaths. There is something in human nature that provokes people to ignore even the most serious warnings, and even an ingrained need to tempt death. Then there are some people who simply doubt the validity of the posted warnings. Those are just some of the obstacles to an effective smoking prevention program. For nearly 50 million people in the United States alone, the warnings on cigarette packages and at the bottom of advertisements simply have not worked. Only, the failure of these warnings will result in far more fatalities.

Today the dangers of tobacco are well known by most educated people. At least some of those dangers have been known for a very long time.

A Little Background

Tobacco use reaches back at least a millennium. Native Americans treated this plant as a medicine, for everything from toothaches and asthma to the agony of childbirth (Chaloupka et al., 2001/2). Then, in 1560, the Europeans discovered it and initially saw it in the same positive light, but very quickly noticed its less admirable qualities. By the middle of the nineteenth century scientific evidence was beginning to prove that the benefits of tobacco were more imagined than real, and by early in the twentieth century medical research began showing a causal link between this plant and illness (Fritschler, 1975).

Indeed, as early as 1913 there were activists pushing for laws to restrict tobacco sales and use. One physician in 1927 noted in a British medical journal that nearly all his patients with lung cancer were regular smokers (Consumers Union, 1963). Evidence of the health dangers continued to grow in study after study. Still the cigarette manufacturers effectively denied the facts and included claims in their advertising that their cigarettes were recommended by "outstanding nose and throat specialists" (Philip Morris), that "More doctors smoke Camels than any other cigarette," that they were "Just what the doctor ordered" (L&M), or even that the product was good for your "T-Zone" (Camel), which included your throat. So in the 1950s the American Medical Association took its own action, banning tobacco ads from its publications, while a report in Congress indicated that cigarette companies had been deceiving consumers (Consumers Union, 1963).

In 1964 the U.S. Surgeon General published a report whereby the federal government officially acknowledged that smoking is a dangerous activity. The very same year the Federal Trade Commission (FTC) tried to force companies to include a warning on cigarette ads and packages, but political maneuvers in Congress stopped this from taking effect and substituted watered-down warnings on packages, with none in ads (Fritschler, 1975). The warnings finally were mandated on cigarette ads in 1972, after significant political foot-dragging.

In 1968, while debate over the warnings continued, the Federal Communications Commission (FCC) began requiring radio and television stations to allow anti-smoking commercials. According to the FCC all of the cigarette commercials being aired at that time presented only one side of the smoking "controversy," and so in "fairness" the stations were required to give away free time for the other side of the story. The more cigarette ads a station ran, the more anti-smoking ads it must run at no cost. As a result, anti-smoking commercials became commonplace from 1968 through 1970. The cigarette companies were hurt, with sales declining and no apparent way out. The more they advertised, the more they hurt their own cause. And they were prohibited by antitrust laws from getting all the cigarette companies together to agree to pull their ads off broadcast. But they devised an ingenious solution, whereby these companies lobbied Congress to pass a law forcing cigarette commercials off radio and TV (*Capital Broadcasting Co. v. Mitchell*, 1971). That happened at the start of 1971 and the warnings soon appeared in the print advertisements, so almost overnight the smoking controversy dropped from the public eye.

Concerns over tobacco did not really rise to the level of public awareness again until the end of 1985, when U.S. Surgeon General C. Everett Koop declared smoking the nation's number one cause of premature death or disability. This fueled bill after bill in Congress and efforts by many local, state, and federal officials, who tried a variety of measures to curb tobacco use, including annual proposals to put limits on the industry's massive advertising initiatives (Richards, 1996). Finally on November 23, 1998, a major step forward was accomplished when 46 states succeeded in threatening lawsuits aimed at tobacco companies, strong-arming them into signing a Master Settlement Agreement (MSA) that required they pay $206 billion, over 25 years, and restricting them from certain advertising practices. Four states already had settled for another $40 billion (Nocera, 2006). But while the MSA did manage to ban billboards and limit ads targeted at children, thanks to the negotiation process it left open the door to tobacco advertising on non-tobacco merchandise, sponsorship of events, and other creative promotional devices, as well as print advertising targeted at adults. It should be noted that a deal previously had been struck for $368.5 billion which also would have allowed for far more tobacco regulation, but Congress got involved and politics destroyed that agreement (Nocera, 2006).

It is obvious that tobacco has been a recognized killer for a long time, and numerous efforts have been made to stop its deadly effects. But politics and lobbying by tobacco sellers, above all else, have prevented policies from being adopted to save lives. After at least a century of knowing the truth, the United States – a supposedly developed and enlightened society – still allows people to die from a defective product, even though we now have an arsenal of facts to support drastic regulatory measures.

The Facts

Between 1994 and 1998, when it was quite popular as a recreational drug, 27 people in the United States died from using Ecstasy. Between 1995 and 2002 another popular party drug, GHB (gamma hydroxybutyrate), is known to have been responsible for 73 deaths (Leinwand, 2002). Both of those drugs are considered dangerous, and as a result are illegal for use by the general public. By contrast, according to data accumulated by the Centers for Disease Control (CDC), *in 2008 alone* smoking will kill about 438,000 people in the U.S. Indeed, if you add the premature deaths from illegal drugs, automobile accidents, firearms, unprotected sex, along with toxins and microbes, all together they would not equal the number of deaths from tobacco use (Mokdad et al., 2004). It was recently estimated by the World

Health Organization that *500 million* of the 5 billion alive at the beginning of the twenty-first century would die from tobacco use (Chaloupka et al., 2001/2). Yet tobacco remains legal.

Some other facts should be mentioned here. For example, the number of deaths worldwide is even more staggering, estimated at 5 million. The average smoker loses 13 to 14 years of his or her life. For every death from smoking, there are another 20 people who suffer serious illness from its use. The monetary costs include $75.5 billion in healthcare expenses and $92.4 billion in lost productivity, *per year*. And every day 3,900 children smoke their first cigarette (CDC, 2006). Many of those kids will eventually die from smoking. Clearly, there are few other dangers to life, health, and the U.S. national economy as great as the ongoing effects of this one product.

The best solution to this immense threat, without question, would be to ban tobacco use altogether. Unfortunately, that is not a practical solution at this point in time. Almost 21 percent of adults in the U.S. are smokers (CDC, 2006), and that represents a significant number of voters. Few politicians have the courage to ignore that many potential supporters, especially those in their own party. Perhaps more important is the fact that a lot of legislators and their friends smoke. A ban would hurt their own self-interests. Those friends, of course, include lobbyists. And, in addition to a well funded lobbyist machine representing the tobacco industry, the manufacturers contribute directly to some of those politicians. For example one tobacco company, Philip Morris, gave no less than $14.3 million to Republicans, alone, between 1989 and 2002 (Lazarus, 2002). Then, in addition, there are legislators who represent tobacco-growing states like Kentucky, Tennessee, and North Carolina, among others, and the onus most certainly is on them to support the livelihoods of their constituents. Stopping the sale of tobacco simply is not going to happen in the current political environment.

Given that enormous barrier, a more viable alternative is to institute limitations on the marketing of this deadly product. Admittedly, this is a half-step that will not as quickly or definitively end the dangers, but politicians have shown a willingness and ability to pass laws enacting such limits. And at the same time, by further removing tobacco from public view its consumption is bound to decrease. Research shows that after the MSA took effect manufacturers increased the cost of cigarettes, which caused a decline in sales, so they increased their advertising, which helped to offset the loss of sales (Keeler et al., 2004). In other words, advertising caused sales to go up, so by logical extension this suggests that eliminating advertising will cause sales to drop. Advertising works for tobacco as it does for other products, by building demand (Goldberg, 2003). Clearly, cigarette companies would not advertise unless they thought it helped sales. And they certainly do advertise.

Although the exact current amount is difficult to determine, in 2003 the cigarette industry spent more than $15 billion in advertising and promoting its products (CDC, 2006). This is no trivial amount, especially when you consider the fact that *all* U.S. advertising expenditures for *all* products and services, from the neighborhood barber shop to the enormous McDonald's and WalMart, from television commercials to ads on matchbooks or in telephone books, that year totaled about $245 billion. In the words of the late Senator Everett Dirksen, "A billion here, a billion there, and pretty soon it adds up to real money."

There is little question that stemming this font of persuasive appeals is the best option to begin saving millions, even hundreds of millions, of lives. The primary defense used by the tobacco industry in America is the First Amendment of the U.S. Constitution.

The Law

The First Amendment protects the right to free speech, but "speech" did not include advertising or other marketing communications until 1976. At that point the Supreme Court stepped in to declare "commercial speech," including advertising, to be protected. That did not mean, however, that it received the same amount of protection as that accorded to traditional speech categories. In fact, the court continued to embrace the notion that commercial speech must be more regulable, which led it to establish a test in the *Central Hudson* (1980) case. If a law regulating commercial speech can pass the test, it passes constitutional muster. The test has four steps:

1 Does the speech concern a lawful activity and is it not misleading?
2 Is there a substantial government interest to be served by the regulation?
3 Does the regulation directly advance that interest?
4 Is the regulation not more extensive than necessary to serve that interest?

This is the same test that is used today.

While tobacco advertising does involve a lawful activity, tobacco sales, there undoubtedly is a case that could be made that much, if not all, of it is misleading. Until the Surgeon General's warning was a required addition, the lack of health warnings would constitute a "material omission" of important information, thereby making tobacco ads misleading. And since that time the emphasis in ads on healthy activities like hiking and canoeing and volleyball deceptively implies smoking is a part of a healthy lifestyle. If the speech is misleading, the other three questions are not required in this test, because the regulation is deemed constitutional!

Even if a sufficiently strong case were not made that tobacco advertising, today, is misleading, that only means the regulation must pass the remaining three steps. The government interest is stated clearly above: saving enormous numbers of lives (not to mention lots of tax dollars). That is an easy step to pass. The third step simply asks whether the regulation will accomplish that goal of saving lives and money. So if tobacco advertising causes people to smoke, banning that advertising will save lives. Again, it's that simple. Then the last step simply asks if the ban is narrowly tailored to that purpose. In other words, does the regulation ban significantly more speech than it needs to ban? So long as the law only deals with tobacco use, whether in smoking, chewing, or other forms of ingestion, it would seem to be restricted only to the speech that contributes to the problem. Consequently, the constitutional barrier to outlawing tobacco advertising is not at all insurmountable.

Some anti-regulation advocates argue that *Lorillard Tobacco Co. v. Reilly* (2001) serves as the court's last word on tobacco advertising, and that the case declared this type of commercial speech protected under the First Amendment. They would dispute the conclusion in the previous paragraph. In that case the State of Massachusetts passed a law banning outdoor tobacco advertising near schools and requiring point-of-purchase displays for such products be at least five feet from the floor. The court in that decision, however, really only says that the regulation *in that particular situation* was not properly tailored to the government's stated interest. In other words, it failed the fourth step. In that circumstance the State of Massachusetts argued its "substantial government interest" was to protect children, and since the law also kept adults from seeing the ads, the fix did not fit the problem. The state's solution was too broad for that narrow target. In other words, if the state had built its case on a government interest of protecting *all* its citizens, the regulation would have fit that problem. Ironically, then, the state simply tried to be too modest in its regulations, protecting too few members of the endangered public. As a result, it should be easy to avoid the same result with any subsequent tobacco advertising ban.

But, again, most of the difficulty in passing and enforcing a ban on tobacco advertising remains political, rather than legal. This is evident in the latest, international, attempt to deal with this health threat.

The World Health Organization

In 1999, through the World Health Organization (WHO), 191 countries agreed to create an international treaty, the Framework Convention on Tobacco Control (FCTC). Its terms were debated over the next four years, but in 2003 the FCTC was officially adopted (Meier, 2005). The plan was for all of these countries, representing virtually all the peoples of the world, to join forces to stamp out the planet's single most preventable cause of death and disability. Among the many provisions of the treaty, it would ban or severely limit cigarette advertising while requiring much larger health warnings on cigarette packages. This might be the most significant health initiative ever taken.

Throughout the negotiations, however, the U.S. was resistant to restrictions on advertising and promotion. The Bush administration fought to include a provision allowing countries to opt out of any requirement they do not like (Lazarus, 2003). A version of that "opt out" provision was finally included in the FCTC, and its provisions have now been ratified by 133 of those countries. In spite of this, as of July 2006 President Bush still had not forwarded the treaty to the U.S. Senate for ratification (Anonymous, 2006). Congress has not rejected it, nor has a judge found it unconstitutional; it simply was stalled in the White House for more than three years (and counting). During that time about 1.5 million Americans died from tobacco-related illness.

Conclusion

The problem with tobacco is simple. It is one of the most lethal products sold on the open market, and that fact has been known for a very long time. Warning labels are not enough. Even now, 21 percent of adults smoke, and every day that nothing more drastic is done to stop this plague another 1,200 Americans die. In the U.S. the state and local governments seem far more willing to take action to stop the killing than Congress or the White House. The MSA and local laws banning smoking in restaurants and workplaces are testaments to that fact. It is time for the federal government to show it is serious about the sanctity of life, instead of merely paying lip service to the idea, and to pass laws that will curtail the promotion of this defective product. There is no legal impediment to this important step; there is only political obstruction. It is time to ratify the FCTC, and begin saving our loved ones from an early death.

References

Anonymous (2006). World conference on tobacco in Washington DC calls attention to Bush administration failure to ratify Global Tobacco Treaty. *PR Newswire US* (July 11).

Capital Broadcasting Co. v. Mitchell, 333 F. Supp. 582, 588 (D.D.C. 1971) (Wright, J. dissenting).

CDC (Centers for Disease Control) (2006). Fast facts website (Mar.): <http://www.cdc.gov/tobacco/overview/Fast_Facts.htm>.

Central Hudson Gas & Electric Corp. v. Public Service Commission of New York (1980), 447 U.S. 557.

Chaloupka, F. J., E. J. Hahn, and S. L. Emory (2001/2). Policy levers for the control of tobacco consumption. *Kentucky Law Journal* 90: 1009.

Consumers Union (1963). *The Consumers Union report on smoking and the public interest.* Mount Vernon, NY: Consumers Union.

Fritschler, A. L. (1975). *Smoking and politics: Policymaking and the federal bureaucracy*, 2nd edn. Englewood Cliffs, NJ: Prentice Hall.

Goldberg, M. E. (2003). Correlation, causation, and smoking initiation among youths. *Journal of Advertising Research* (Dec.): 431.

Keeler, T. E., T.-W. Hu, M. Ong, and H.-Y. Sung (2004). The US National Tobacco Settlement: the effects of advertising and price changes on cigarette consumption. *Applied Economics* 36: 1623.

Lazarus, D. (2002). U.S., pushed by Philip Morris, stalling global ban on tobacco ads. *San Francisco Chronicle* (Nov. 20): B1.

Lazarus, D. (2003). Bush tries to weaken tobacco treaty. *San Francisco Chronicle* (Apr. 30): A1.

Leinwand, D. (2002). "Date rape" drug GHB making inroads in nation's club scene. *USA Today* (Jan. 28): 1A.

Lorillard Tobacco Co. v. Reilly (2001), 533 U.S. 525.

Meier, B. M. (2005). Breathing life into the framework convention on tobacco control: Smoking cessation and the right to health. *Yale Journal of Health Policy, Law and Ethics* 5: 137.

Mokdad, A. H., J. S. Marks, D. F. Stroup, and J. L. Gerberding (2004). Actual causes of death in the United States, 2000. *The Journal of the American Medical Association* 291(10): 1238.

Nocera, J. (2006). If it's good for Philip Morris, can it also be good for public health? *The New York Times Magazine* (Jun. 18): 46.

Richards, J. I. (1996). Politicizing cigarette advertising. *Catholic University Law Review* 45: 1147.

6

Alcohol Advertising

A Match Made in Heaven or a Pact with the Devil?

While academics often pair alcohol advertising and tobacco advertising together in the ethical debate on advertising regulation, in reality, these two "vice" products are really worlds apart. For example, people tend to be smokers or not. Many smokers want to quit, but can't. Others who don't use cigarettes can't stand being around smoke. Many restaurants have become completely non-smoking. People tend to appreciate this – even the smokers.

Drinking, however, is a bit different. You can be a social drinker, an "at home" wine connoisseur, an occasional celebratory champagne drinker, etc. Medical reports espouse the value of a glass of red wine to keep our circulation systems healthy. Drinking can even be a bit of a religious experience. Some monks make beer in their monasteries. For example, St. Sixtus of Westveteren, a Trappist monastery in Brussels, brews a consistently top-rated (and high alcoholic content) beer to support the monastery.

The problems with advertising alcohol on television are legion. Back in 1993, Professor Joel Grube documented some of alcohol's presence on television. Beer commercials were most often present at televised sporting events. But, it's not just the association of beer and sports that's problematic. Kids are in the grandstands watching the sporting event. And they're also at home watching – often with their dads (who may very well be guzzling beer and chowing down on salty foods galore, all of which require more beer). Beer and football is bad enough. But beer and NASCAR? Whose idea was it to associate drinking and really fast cars anyway?

Then there are all the other television programs that will include beer commercials. If we think kids are only watching children-appropriate television, we're even more naive than the naysayers say we are!

And it's not just about beer advertising any more. While broadcast television has upheld its voluntary ban on advertising distilled spirits for a quarter of a century, this resolve looks to soon be a thing of the past. As the lines between cable television and network television continue to blur, it's only a matter of time. According to the Center on Alcohol Marketing and Youth, distilled spirits advertising increased nearly 6,000 percent from 2001 to 2004! That's a lot of ads.

No one really debates the problem of alcohol abuse. A July 16, 2007, article in *Time* magazine states that 7.7 percent of the U.S. population is dependent on alcohol or abuses alcohol in some way associated with irresponsible drinking (2007: 44). As both Lara Zwarun and Jason Chambers point out, there are plenty of perils that come with drinking too much.

So what does all this have to do with advertising? The argument boils down to some basic ideals that we tend to hold dear. The balance of free speech and responsibility. The belief that individuals have the power to think for themselves – and that they should exercise that power. The slippery slope that might develop if we ban alcohol advertising because someone has decided that it's an unhealthy product. What's next? Banning fried ice cream? (No one could argue that *that's* good for you!) Can advertising influence our decision to drink in the first place? Or is it all more about brand awareness and trying to grab competitors' customers? *You decide.*

Ideas to get you thinking . . .

1   Is there something different about alcohol ads? Are they more unethical than other kinds of advertisements? Why, or why not?

2 Find some magazine ads touting wine or spirits. List out the creative strategies that you see in these ads. Can you make any general observations from what you've found?
3 Compare some alcohol print ads with television ads. Does it look like the advertisers are targeting the same or different markets?

If you'd like to read more . . .

Center on Alcohol Marketing and Youth. <http://camy.org/>.
Federal Trade Commission (2003). *Alcohol marketing and advertising: A report to Congress*. Washington, DC: Federal Trade Commission.
Nakaya, A. C. (2007). *Alcohol (opposing viewpoints)*. Chicago: Greenhaven Press.
Pennock, P. E. (2007). *Advertising sin and sickness: The politics of alcohol and tobacco marketing 1950–1990*. DeKalb: Northern Illinois University Press.

References

Grube, J. W. (1993). Alcohol portrayals and alcohol advertising on television. *Alcohol Health & Research World* 17(1): 61.
Lemonick, M. D. (2007). The science of addiction. *Time* 170(3): 42–8.

Argument

Alcohol is so problematic that advertising or promoting it in any way should be banned from all televised events

Lara Zwarun

It's hard to turn on the television these days without seeing some form of advertising for alcohol. From funny beer ads that punctuate football games to brand logo decals on race cars to the beverages that characters in sitcoms and dramas themselves consume – in a very visible way, of course! – these forms of promotion are everywhere we turn.

It's easy to imagine how the alcoholic beverage industry might justify the millions of dollars it spends on these efforts. After all, alcohol is a legal product, at least for people 21 years of age and older, so why shouldn't manufacturers be allowed to advertise it like any other product?

The thing is, there are some very good reasons why not. This essay will consider them, including the problems we have with drinking in the U.S., the influence TV has on certain audiences, the messages found in much of the advertising, and the ineffectiveness of current regulation of alcohol advertising. Together, these arguments make a compelling case that *alcohol advertising can be so problematic that it has no place on television.*

What's Wrong with Drinking?

Most people would agree that nothing is inherently wrong with drinking, provided it is done responsibly. Unfortunately, this isn't always so. An estimated 7.4 percent of people are problem drinkers (Burge and Schneider, 1999), risking health, social, and legal problems that cost society an estimated $185 billion a year (NIAAA, 2006).

These issues are not confined to people over legal drinking age, either. About 10 percent of all alcoholic beverages consumed per year are drunk by people under 21 (Eigen and Noble, 1998), and 33 percent of high school seniors report they binge drink (consume five or more drinks in a row) at least once every two weeks (American Academy of Pediatrics, 2001).

Underage drinking is problematic because of both its immediate and its long-term costs: increased likelihood of automobile accidents, unplanned sex, violence (Eigen and Noble, 1996; Siegal, 1999), and alcohol abuse and addiction (Grant and Dawson, 1998). Clearly, drinking has the potential to be far from harmless. In fact, given these statistics, it is in society's best interest to promote responsible alcohol consumption, and this includes discouraging underage drinking.

But What Does Alcohol Advertising have to do with Drinking Problems?

This is a controversial issue, despite some people's claim of "Nothing." It is true that watching an alcohol ad on TV does not turn you into a robot forced to go to the nearest convenience store for a six-pack against your will. But that does not mean that alcohol advertising has no influence either. If it had no influence, do you really think the alcoholic beverage industry would spend $2 billion per year on media advertising (Strasburger and Donnerstein, 1999)?

Let's begin by considering the influence of television in general. As noted earlier, one of the most at-risk groups with respect to alcohol problems is people under legal drinking age, who also form an audience that watches plenty of television. Over 40 percent of children live in homes where the TV is on most of the time (Rideout et al., 1999), and it is estimated that teenagers see 27,000 commercials a week (Comstock and Scharrer, 1999). As a result, TV is an important source of information for young people (Van Evra, 2004), who use it to get information about sex, relationships, and, yes, drinking (Gruber and Grube, 2000) – topics they may be curious about due to their lack of personal experience with them. Of course there are other sources of information about drinking for young people, but some of these other sources – namely, their peers – get information from the media themselves.

Thus, alcohol messages on television have the ability to reach and influence viewers. In the case of advertising, this influence comes in the form of making you aware of a product and causing you to think of it in a positive way. Alcohol advertising has been proven to contribute to drinking by associating it with certain desirable if-then relationships, known as expectancies (Goldman et al., 1987), so that you want to drink because you believe *if* you do, *then* you too will achieve those same great things.

For example, if you see people who drink in commercials hanging out with attractive members of the opposite sex, you may want to drink so that you can be popular in the same way. If you see people in commercials bringing a big cooler of beer to the beach as part of a fun day, you are likely to consider bringing along your own cooler the next time you head to the beach with friends. If you see a certain alcohol's brand name all over a sold-out concert or a dramatic sporting event, you start to associate drinking with passion and excitement.

Sure, it might seem obvious that drinking a certain beer isn't going to make you and everyone around you turn into a gorgeous model with a killer social life, but isn't part of how advertising works making us abandon this logic and go with the dream? Unless you are one of the very few people who have never bought zit medicine, an abs exerciser, or a Lottery ticket, you know it is. By appealing to people's need to belong or to succeed, advertising can persuade emotionally instead of logically, in a sense telling the story of who the viewer wants to be (Comstock and Scharrer, 1999). In this way, alcohol advertising is quite influential on the decision to drink. In fact, heavy TV viewers are more at risk of alcohol use than light viewers (Strasburger, 1995), and over half of students from grades 5–12 in one study said that alcohol advertising encouraged them to drink (American Academy of Pediatrics, 2001).

Some people claim that research has never shown that alcohol advertising causes drinking, only that drinking and exposure to the ads are correlated. However, Gruber and Grube (2000) were able to demonstrate that, though drinking does not affect how much attention people pay to alcohol advertising, attention to the advertising does precede an increase in drinking.

What Does Alcohol on TV Look Like?

It's true that just being exposed to alcohol advertising is not enough to affect alcohol usage; liking and paying attention to the ad are also necessary (Gruber and Grube, 2000). So the next logical question is, do people, particularly young ones, like and pay attention to alcohol ads? The answer is, without question, yes and yes. Numerous studies have shown that young people can recall alcohol ads, identify their sponsors, and report liking them (Aitken et al., 1988; Grube, 1993; Wallack, Cassady et al., 1990).

This is not surprising given the images and messages these ads contain. A number of studies have found the following to be prevalent in alcohol advertising: physically attractive characters; themes such as enhanced sexuality, fun and excitement, humor, sociability, success, romance, and adventure; celebrity endorsers; animation; rock music; and glamorous and risky activities such as motorcycling, boating, and skiing (Breed and De Foe, 1984; Madden and Grube, 1991, 1994; Postman et al., 1988; Wallack, Grube et al., 1990; Wenner, 1991; Zwarun and Farrar, 2005). What's lacking are many messages about moderation or realistic portrayals of the negatives that can accompany drinking, from vomiting to car accidents (Zwarun and Farrar, 2005).

What this means is that young people are repeatedly exposed to very positive messages about drinking on television, in the form of commercials that suggest that drinking is cool and fun. Add to this the extensive sponsorship of sports that many alcohol brands engage in – where you can see the product's name up to 30 or 40 minutes out of every hour (Zwarun, 2006) – as well as the drinking behavior modeled by characters on many TV shows themselves (Roberts et al., 1999), and you can see that, far from discouraging underage drinking, the alcohol advertising and promotion on television actually play a key part in contributing to this serious social problem.

Is There Anything That Can Be Done?

An alcohol beverage industry executive, upon reading the preceding paragraph, might very well argue that all alcohol companies are trying to do is sell a legal product to a legal audience for legal use. They don't want kids to drink, they don't want anyone to abuse alcohol, and they aren't even trying to make anyone take up drinking: they are simply sharing brand information with existing drinkers.

To make this case, the industry follows its own self-regulatory guidelines for responsible advertising and promotion. By doing so, it is in effect saying to the government: "No need to regulate us; we are aware of the sensitive nature of our products and we are doing the right thing" (it doesn't hurt that the government would have a tough time regulating the ads anyway due to the First Amendment). However, a recent analysis of the industry's guidelines and how they are followed (Zwarun, 2006) revealed the following interesting findings:

1   *Some of the guidelines seem to serve little purpose other than to create a rule the industry can look good for following.* For example, one of the

guidelines the beer industry created for itself is to not show people consuming beer. Of course, people don't need to see beer being swallowed to understand what it is for, so it is not clear what benefit this guideline has in terms of promoting responsible drinking. Furthermore, somewhere between half and three-fourths of beer ads strongly hint at beer being consumed, by showing it being poured, held in glasses, etc., making the guideline even more ineffective.

2   *Some of the guidelines are followed in letter, but not in spirit.* Alcohol ads are not supposed to show people drinking before they do something they shouldn't do under the influence for safety reasons, like ski down a mountain or drive a motorcycle. But some ads show drinking and the potentially dangerous activity in the same ad without a specific timeline, so the activities may still be linked in viewers' minds.

3   *Some of the guidelines are too lenient.* The alcohol industry says it won't place ads in media where at least 70 percent of the audience is not over 21 (Beer Institute, 2003). But that still means that 30 percent of the people seeing the ad may be underage!

4   *There's no real penalty for violating the guidelines.* Because the guidelines are the industry's own, not only does the industry write them, it enforces them. Or not.

Thus, current self-regulation of alcohol advertising is of questionable effectiveness. In other words, the current system is not working to keep alcohol advertising from reaching a young, impressionable audience, and reaching that audience with appealing and convincing pro-drinking messages.

This is not to say that the alcoholic beverage industry doesn't have a legal *right* to advertise. As stated earlier, commercial speech is largely protected under the First Amendment, so it would be difficult for the government to design a ban on alcohol advertising that would stand up to constitutional scrutiny. However, given what is known about drinking behavior and alcohol advertising, it is fair to say that the industry has a moral *responsibility* to consider curtailing its advertising and promotional efforts. The very fact that the industry engages in self-regulation suggests that it understands that it has such a responsibility. What remains is for the industry to take an honest look at the problems with drinking in our society and at the role its advertising plays in contributing to these problems, and to fulfill its responsibility in a meaningful way. This means taking alcohol advertising and promotion off television entirely. If the government can't or won't do it for industry, industry needs to do it itself.

References

Aitken, P. P., D. R. Eadie, D. S. Leathar, R. E. J. McNeill, and A. C. Scott (1988). Television advertisements for alcoholic drinks *do* reinforce under-age drinking. *British Journal of Addiction* 83: 1399–1419.

American Academy of Pediatrics (2001). Alcohol use and abuse: A pediatric concern. *Pediatrics* 108(July): 185.

Beer Institute (2003). *Advertising and marketing code*. Washington, DC: The Beer Institute.

Breed, W., and J. R. De Foe (1984). Drinking and smoking on television, 1950–1982. *Journal of Public Health Policy* (June): 257–70.

Burge, S. K., and F. D. Schneider (1999). Alcohol-related problems: Recognition and intervention. *American Family Physician* 59(2): 361–80.

Comstock, G., and E. Scharrer (1999). *Television: What's on, who's watching, and what it means*. San Diego: Academic Press.

Eigen, L. D., and J. Noble (1998). The extent of underage drinking in the United States. *Bottom Line* (Spring): 42–5.

Eigen, L. D., and J. Noble (1996). *Drinking under age 21: Problems and solutions*. Rockville, MD: National Clearinghouse for Alcohol and Drug Information.

Goldman, M. S., S. A. Brown, and B. A. Christiansen (1987). Expectancy theory: Thinking about drinking. In H. T. Blane and K. E. Leonard (eds.), *Psychological theories of drinking and alcoholism* (pp. 181–226). New York: Guilford Press.

Grant, B. F., and D. A. Dawson (1998). Age of onset of drug use and its association with DSM-IV drug abuse and dependence: Results from the National Longitudinal Alcohol Epidemiological Survey. *Journal of Substance Abuse* 10: 163–73.

Grube, J. W. (1993). Alcohol portrayals and alcohol advertising on television: Content and effects on children and adolescents. *Alcohol Health and Research World* 17: 61–6.

Gruber, E., and J. W. Grube (2000). Adolescent sexuality and the media: A review of current knowledge and implications. *Western Journal of Medicine* 172: 210–14.

Madden, P. A., and J. W. Grube (1991). Alcohol advertising in sports and prime-time television. Atlanta, GA: Presented at the 119th Annual Meeting of the American Public Health Association, October.

Madden, P. A., and J. W. Grube (1994). The frequency and nature of alcohol and tobacco advertising in televised sports, 1990 through 1992. *American Journal of Public Health* 84: 297–9.

NIAAA (National Institute on Alcohol Abuse and Alcoholism of the National Institutes of Health) (2006). Alcoholism: Getting the facts. <http://pubs.niaaa.nih.gov/publications/GettheFacts_HTML/facts.htm>, accessed June 13, 2006.

Postman, N., C. Nystrom, L. Strate, and C. Weingartner (1988). *Myths, men, and beer: An analysis of beer commercials on broadcast television, 1987.* Falls Church, VA: AAA Foundation for Traffic Safety.

Rideout, V. J., U. G. Foehr, D. F. Roberts, and M. Brodie (1999). Kids and media @ the new millennium: A comprehensive analysis of children's media use. Unpublished report. Menlo Park, CA: Kaiser Family Foundation.

Roberts, D. F., L. Henriksen, and P. G. Christensen (1999). *Substance use in popular movies and music.* Washington, DC: Office of National Drug Control Policy.

Siegal, H. (1999). Sex while intoxicated boosts STD risk. *Sexually Transmitted Diseases* 26: 87–92.

Strasburger, V. C. (1995). *Adolescents and the media: Medical and psychological impact.* Thousand Oaks, CA: Sage.

Strasburger, V. C., and E. Donnerstein (1999). Children, adolescents, and the media: Issues and solutions. *American Academy of Pediatrics* 103: 1–15.

Van Evra, J. (2004). *Television and child development,* 3rd edn. Mahwah, NJ: Lawrence Erlbaum.

Wallack, L., D. Cassady, and J. Grube (1990). *TV beer commercials and children: Exposure, attention, beliefs, and expectations about drinking as an adult.* Washington, DC: AAA Foundation for Traffic Safety.

Wallack, L., J. W. Grube, P. A. Madden, and W. Breed (1990). Portrayals of alcohol on prime-time television. *Journal of Studies on Alcohol* 51: 428–37.

Wenner, L. A. (1991). One part alcohol, one part sport, one part dirt, stir gently: Beer commercials and television sports. In L. R. Vande Berg and L. A. Wenner (eds.), *Television criticism: Approaches and applications* (pp. 388–407). White Plains, NY: Longman.

Zwarun, L. (2006). Ten years and one Master Settlement later: The nature and frequency of alcohol and tobacco promotion in televised sports, 2000 through 2002. *American Journal of Public Health* 96(8): 1492–7.

Zwarun, L., and K. M. Farrar (2005). Doing what they say, saying what they mean: Self-regulatory compliance and depictions of drinking in alcohol commercials in televised sports. *Mass Communication and Society* 8(4): 347–71.

Counterargument

Eliminating alcohol advertising on television because underage people drink is as misguided as restricting automobile advertising because people drive too fast

Jason Chambers

The debate over the control of alcoholic beverages has a long history in the United States. Reformers and activists have engaged in various temperance movements since the nineteenth century. These movements united people across race, class, and gender lines and helped lead to the passage of the Eighteenth Amendment prohibiting the making and consumption of alcoholic beverages. As that experience proves, however, arguments about the prohibition on alcohol consumption have proven far easier to develop than to eliminate the actual practice. Since the repeal of the Eighteenth Amendment in 1933, activists have shifted their focus from limiting consumption to limiting alcohol advertising.

Now, in the twenty-first century, the fight to reduce alcoholic beverage advertising continues. But because the issue has such a contentious history there has been little middle ground for those involved in the debate. On one side are those who argue that alcohol is the "devil's brew" and that permitting its advertising leads people down the path to ruin. On the other side are those who maintain that alcohol advertising has little, if any, impact and should be permitted in any viable space. While these represent the extreme sides of the debate, an accurate picture of alcoholic beverage advertising lies somewhere between the two poles. Alcohol advertising does have an impact on awareness, and it is an important means for beverage manufacturers to maintain an identity for their brand. But, advertising is nowhere near as powerful an influence as persons within an individual's circle. Thus, rather than greater limitations on alcohol advertising, we must reinvigorate an emphasis on personal responsibility that recognizes that individuals have a choice in their behavior. Further, if that behavior is uncontrolled, it is because of their choice, not because of Spuds McKenzie sitting next to a cooler of Budweiser.

More importantly, alcohol is a legal product for consumption by adults of legal age. Therefore, its advertising should not be any more subject to governmental censorship or network blackout than is advertising for other legal products that, when used as intended, have not been conclusively shown to cause physical harm. To provide alcohol manufacturers with the legal support to sell their product, but then to prohibit them from advertising that product, is a glaring contradiction and an unfair constraint on their revenue. In fact, to extend restrictions on alcohol advertising beyond their current level will lead to even more cumbersome and ineffective regulations. This essay will demonstrate that existing guidelines on alcoholic beverage advertising are sufficient and that manufacturers of these beverages are meeting both their legal and social responsibility.

I will examine three primary areas. First, I will show the importance of alcohol advertising on consumer awareness and market share. Second, the effectiveness of current restrictions on alcohol advertising in preventing youth exposure will be analyzed. Third, I will argue that society and activists need to turn from pursuing greater regulation on alcohol companies toward developing a greater social emphasis on individual responsibility. Promoters of events, whether they are representatives from the National Football League or from the Rolling Stones, should have the opportunity to seek out sponsors they view as most relevant to their customer base. Likewise, alcohol companies should have the latitude to find events and programming to reach their target population. If they err in that choice, their customers, of their own independent will, will let them know either through not watching the event or through not buying the products of the sponsor companies. Simply put, *To recommend eliminating alcohol advertising on televised events because underage people drink is as misguided as restricting automobile advertising because people drive too fast.*

Alcohol Advertising and Brand Awareness

Alcoholic beverage manufacturers are some of the largest advertisers in the country. Collectively, in 2004 the industry spent over $915 million on advertising (CAMY, 2005c). Much of that went for television advertising, with beer and wine companies spending most of the dollars. Accordingly, alcoholic beverage companies are key supporters of televised events, especially sports. In fact, the amount spent on alcohol advertising on sports programming dwarfs that of all other program categories. For example, one survey found that spending on cable sports programs totaled $148 million; spending during movies, the second-largest category, was just over $28 million (CAMY, 2005c: 7). Thus a valuable relationship exists in which alcohol companies want brand recognition by consumers and networks and event promoters want and need the revenue these companies will pay to reach their consumer base.

More than anything else, alcoholic beverage companies are part of sports events, either through sponsorship or direct advertising. That relationship between alcohol companies and sporting events has not gone unnoticed by critics, heirs of the nineteenth-century temperance movements. For example, during the 2006 World Cup, the largest sports tournament in the world, activists requested that FIFA, the soccer governing body, prohibit alcoholic beverage advertising and sponsorship. Groups of activists from more than 40 nations supported a resolution calling on FIFA to "stop undermining the positive values of sport by putting beer ads in front of so many young soccer fans worldwide" ("Give Bud the boot," 2006). Further, they urged FIFA officials to search for new event sponsors so they could eliminate alcohol advertisements from future World Cup events.

Without question, alcohol companies have an interest in associating their products with sports and other televised events. Sports programming provides them not only with access to consumers with attractive market demographics, but also with the excitement, energy, youthful feelings, and passion that are part of athletic competition. The desirable qualities of events like the World Series, Super Bowl, NCAA basketball tournament, and NASCAR races are ones that alcohol companies covet an association with. More importantly, the large audiences these events attract are ones with the same demographics as their desired target markets. Specifically, these events attract the group alcoholic beverage companies need most – the heavy user. The top 10 percent of all alcohol drinkers are responsible for over 60 percent of all alcohol consumption. Of those users, the majority are primarily men between the ages of 19 and 39 (Woodside, 1999). Obviously, men within that bracket are also a key demographic for sports programming. So the linkage between sports and alcoholic beverage companies is an important one for both industries.

Would a reduction in alcohol advertising lead to a reduction in consumption? Most studies say that it would not. Even in studies that demonstrate a minimal impact on lowering consumption and binge drinking, the authors admit that consistent reductions would require the "complete *elimination* of *all* alcohol advertising, with restrictions on additional expenditures on other marketing techniques, or the *elimination* of *all* forms of alcohol marketing" (Saffer and Dave, 2006, emphasis added). Draconian measures like these would effectively crush the alcohol industry in the United States. In fact, most studies have found no important connection between prohibiting alcohol advertising and consumption (Bourgeois and Barnes, 1979; Calfee and Scheraga, 1994; Franke, and Wilcox, 1987; Nelson, 1999). Further, the director of the National Institute on Alcohol Abuse and Alcoholism observed that, "There is not a single study – not one study in the United States or internationally – that credibly connects advertising with an increase in alcohol use or abuse" (Alcohol Advertising, 2006{?}).

But, this is not to say that advertising has no impact on consumption. Companies like Anheuser-Busch and SABMiller (parent company of Miller Brewing) spend hundreds of millions of dollars each year on advertising, and they would not do so if their messages had no purpose or effect. What their advertising does is convey images about their brands and about the people who consume them. Specifically, in the alcohol industry a brand's image is just as important as its taste. As one executive observed, "You don't sell on taste. You've got to sell on image" (Chura, 2001). To remove a company's right to advertise for its brands would effectively force it to cede control of its image.

Although advertising has little impact on increasing the size of the total alcohol market, it is a vital factor in increasing the market share of individual firms. Meaning that Anheuser-Busch finds sales increases for Budweiser through winning market share from its competitors, not by increasing the size of the total consumer pool. Advertising is a key weapon in that battle because it allows alcohol companies to lure consumers from competitors. Thus, to remove a company's right to advertise in the most effective venues – primarily sporting and other televised events – would remove their most effective tool in the war against their competition. As a result any benefits from a ban on alcohol advertising are infinitesimal in comparison to the impact such a ban would have on the alcoholic beverage and sports industries (Saffer and Dave, 2002).

Current Regulations and Restrictions

In terms of viewers, the overwhelming majority of persons watching sporting events that contain alcohol advertising are of legal drinking age. The Center on Alcohol Marketing and Youth (CAMY) found that less than 9 percent of the televised sports viewing audience was in the youth category (Alcohol Advertising, 2006). In fact, another survey found that children between the ages of 12 and 20 were only 10 percent of the audience for *all* television shows that feature alcoholic beverage advertising (CAMY, 2004). So, should companies with a legal product face restrictions on advertising on programs in which 90 percent of the recognized audience is of legal age? No, especially when such restrictions would effectively prohibit these companies from reaching the consumers who are of legal age to buy their products. Still, despite the desirability of these programs, alcoholic beverage companies have gone even further to restrict their advertising to underage populations.

In 2003, the Distilled Spirits Council of the United States (DISCUS) and the Beer Institute, representatives of the alcohol industry, agreed to limit their advertising placements to media venues where 70 percent of the viewing audience was over 21 (CAMY, 2005a). This target percentage reflected the current demographic of the U.S. population, 70 percent of which is over 21. The industry met this goal quickly. By late 2005 surveys found that only 0.4 percent of all alcohol ads were on broadcast network programs with an audience above the 30 percent standard (CAMY, 2004). Still, even that has not been enough for anti-alcohol groups. For example, CAMY has recommended extending the viewing population limit from the current 70/30 ratio to 85/15, to further limit youth exposure. It is worth noting, however, that even with application of the most stringent media placements now under consideration, sporting events would still be acceptable marketing venues for alcohol products (CAMY, 2005a).

Alcoholic beverage companies, especially beer manufacturers, have to be especially wary of walking the tightrope between directly marketing to underage drinkers and establishing relevance in the minds of those about to reach legal drinking age. In fact, young people consume considerable quantities of beer. However, even staunch anti-alcohol advertising critics allow that "it is hard to establish the exact percentage of all beer consumed by underage persons" (Gotwals et al., 2005). In other words, we know that persons under 21 are consuming beer, but just how much beer is not clear. The common assumption is that the amount is substantial, but we must also allow that it may in fact be minimal. Further, activists acknowledge that it is "difficult to establish a clear, causal connection between beer advertising and underage drinking" (Gotwals et al., 2005). Even recognizing this, those same activists want to hold manufacturers responsible for the actions of people who misuse their products. Alcohol advertising does not encourage abuse. Certainly it encourages viewers to associate the product with friends or good times, but to do so responsibly. But even if we allow that alcohol advertising encourages a positive brand association in the minds of underage drinkers, it should be permitted on programming that has an adult audience within currently agreed-upon media target limits.

Individual Responsibility

Alcoholism, drunk driving, and criminal and sexual assaults related to alcohol consumption and binge drinking are critical problems. However, the overwhelming majority of these problems result from the use of the product outside its intended levels. The consumer and individual merchant bear much more responsibility in the abuse of alcohol and its related problems than does the manufacturer. Alcohol companies have both exercised due diligence and upheld their social responsibility by adhering to current laws and regulations. Also, they have gone above and beyond that duty by supporting programs like "We I.D." in convenience stores and with admonishments in advertisements to use designated drivers and to "drink responsibly." We will "wait for your business," Pete Coors, Chairman of Coors Brewing, told underage drinkers (CAMY, 2005b). Some companies, such as Diageo plc, have gone even further by spending 20 percent of their broadcast advertising budget on "responsibility" messages (CAMY, 2005b). The efforts of Coors, Diageo plc, and other companies have supplemented campaigns by the Department of Health and Human Services to combat underage drinking. Thus all consumers, regardless of age, have heard consistent messages about the dangers of alcohol abuse and underage drinking, and these messages and programs are sufficient to combat these issues without further restriction on alcohol advertising.

Moreover, alcohol is neither inherently good nor bad; it is the misuse of it that matters. Specifically, the message that manufacturers, activists, and especially parents should convey to young people is that the responsible consumption of alcohol is acceptable; the abuse of it and the destructive or boorish behaviors that accompany it are not. A single glass of wine or champagne is a fine way to toast an accomplishment or act as an accompaniment to dinner, while several glasses or bottles of that same beverage is a sure route to problems. Thus we should not seek to hide alcohol from adolescents because doing so will likely do more to encourage experimentation in the seemingly forbidden than it will to discourage use. Instead, alcoholic beverage manufacturers should continue to work with schools, private organizations, and the government to educate both current and future consumers on the responsible enjoyment of alcohol.

Conclusion

Activists rightfully press alcoholic beverage companies to limit their exposure to underage drinkers. The measures imposed by the government, as well as industry-based self-regulation, are powerful forces in doing so. However, these companies also have the right to market their products in an attractive way to persons who are of legal age. Companies should not face restriction on marketing in the very areas that many of their legal-age consumers frequent. Instead, those companies should continue working with government agencies and activists for ways to further refine the advertising process. But that presupposes that activists will focus on aiding those companies in perfecting their targeting of legal-age consumers, not continuing to argue for the outright ban of alcohol advertising. At some point, critics and activists must recognize that companies selling legal products have a right to advertise those products, and it is consumers who have a responsibility to use those products in the fashion that manufacturers intended.

References

Alcohol Advertising (2006). <http://www2.Potsdam.edu/handsonj/Advertising. html>, accessed on Nov. 2, 2006. {?}

Bourgeois, J., and J. Barnes (1979). Does advertising increase alcohol consumption? *Journal of Advertising Research* 19: 19–29.

Calfee, J., and C. Scheraga (1994). The influence of advertising on alcohol consumption: A literature review and an econometric analysis of four European nations, *International Journal of Advertising* 13(4): 287–310.

CAMY (Center on Alcohol Marketing and Youth) (2003). Alcohol advertising on sports television 2001 and 2002. <http://camy.org/factsheets/pdf/AlcoholAdvertisingSportsTelevision2001-2002.pdf>, accessed Nov. 2, 2006.

CAMY (2004). Alcohol advertising on television, 2001 to 2003: More of the same. (Oct. 12): 8.

CAMY (2005a). Striking a balance: Protecting youth from overexposure to alcohol ads and allowing companies to reach the adult market. (July): 5.

CAMY (2005b). Alcohol industry "responsibility" advertising on television, 2001 to 2003. (July 20): 5.

CAMY (2005c). Alcohol advertising on television, 2001–2004: The move to cable. (Dec. 12): 5.

Chura, H. (2001). Spirited sex, *Advertising Age* 28: 36.

Franke, G. and Wilcox, G. (1987). Alcoholic beverage advertising and consumption in the United States, 1964–1984, *Journal of Advertising* 16: 22–30.

"Give Bud the boot from World Cup, groups say" (2006). *Common Dreams Newswire* <http://www.commondreams.org/news2006/0622-09.htm>, accessed Nov. 2, 2006.

Gotwals, A., J. Hedlund, and G. Hacker (2005). Take a kid to a beer: How the NCAA recruits kids for the beer market. *Center for Science in the Public Interest* (Washington, DC): 9.

Nelson, J. (1999). Broadcast advertising and US demand for alcoholic beverages. *Southern Economic Journal* 65(4): 774–90.

Saffer, H., and D. Dave (2002). Alcohol consumption and alcohol advertising bans. *Applied Economics* 34(11): 1325–34.

Saffer, H., and D. Dave (2006). Alcohol advertising and alcohol consumption by adolescents. *Health Economics* 15: 635.

Woodside, A. (1999). Advertising and consumption of alcoholic beverages *Journal of Consumer Psychology* 8(2): 184.

7

Advertising and Product Placement

And Now, the Star of the Show!

When we talk about "product placements," we usually mean brand-named items (including products, packaging, signs, and corporate names) that are *intentionally* placed in movies and on television programs. In recent years the product placement "controversy" has increased in advertising circles. Yet the phenomenon is not new. Thinking back to the early days of television, advertisers sponsored entire programs, infusing their brand's name throughout the program. Kraft Television Theatre, General Electric College Bowl, and Mutual of Omaha's Wild Kingdom are only three well-known examples from the past.

Researchers D'Astous and Chartier (2000) list three reasons why advertisers might want to place their products in movies. First, watching a movie involves high attention, so the assumption is that some of that "super" attention might fall on the product. Second, movies can produce large audiences. Even if the movie isn't a box-office blockbuster, after international sales and rentals, lots of people potentially may see the product placement. With shrinking television audiences, this is becoming even more important. Third, the "natural" placement may make audience members less irritated than they sometimes are with in-your-face advertising. And a happy viewer is potentially a happy customer.

Even though there are stunning examples of tremendous products placed in movies, many of the products that we see in movies today are not even "placed." Instead, they're merely used in the movie at the discretion of the director for creative realism or some other reason. Still, the phenomenon is growing and, most likely, here to stay. In January 2005, for example, the phrase "product placement" was mentioned in the American press over 500 times (Sauer, 2005).

While some people have argued that using product placements is a form of "stealth" advertising ("slipped into" the movie so no one realizes it might be an ad) and, in turn, is unethical, others champion the approach as innovative and effective. Sometimes there is a quirky use of a name-brand product that creates almost a cult following. For example, the aliens in *Roswell* liked to sprinkle Tabasco sauce on everything. So when the WB threatened to cancel the show after the first season (1999–2000), bottles of Tabasco started showing up at the studio offices. Some reports stated that over 6,000 bottles were sent to the studio. (The campaign "Roswell Is Hot" was successful for awhile, but the quirky alien/romance show was cancelled after three seasons.) Other examples of products that, in essence, become the "hero," such as Wilson the volleyball in the movie *Castaway* or AOL's email service in *You've Got Mail*, demonstrate all the positive reasons why advertisers may be interested in getting their products a starring role in a movie or television show.

But how do you tell when the placement goes too far? Laura Petrecca wrote an article for *USA Today* (October 10, 2006) in which she questions where the ubiquity of the advertising will end. She points out that, in the 1970s, the average city dweller was exposed to 500 to 2,000 ads per day. But now that number is more like 3,000 to 5,000. This advertising clutter forces advertisers to look for creative ways to get their products noticed. That's why we see promotions in the bottom of the trays where we put our stuff when going through a security check to board an airplane, on the doors of bathroom stalls, and on shopping carts for our perusal while we check out advertised products in the grocery store. Product placement may seem fairly innocuous after being assaulted by overt advertising all day, every day. The more viewers move toward "on demand" media consumption (watching when you want), the more "traditional" commercials are in danger – and the more advertisers will look for ways to incorporate their products into movies, TV shows, music, etc.

According to Petrecca, $941 million was spent in 2005 to integrate products into television shows. Clearly this phenomenon will only increase – both for television and movies. In 2007, VW reportedly spent $40 million on product placement (High, 2007) and marketing tie-ins for its 2008 Touareg 2 car, which is the vehicle Matt Damon uses in *The Bourne Ultimatum*. Using footage from the movie, the creative team was able to create a commercial featuring the car before the public saw the movie. So rather than stealth advertising, the advertiser is trying to ensure that the movie audience will not only pay attention to the car, rather than just to Jason Bourne's wild chase-scene antics, but be *looking for* the car. Is that manipulative – or great advertising strategy?

Whether you think product placement is a good idea or not, advertising agencies have had to struggle with how to figure out adequate payment. Some have moved toward a "time on screen" approach or a "product prominence" approach, and others have tried to develop a form of gross rating points for quantifying a branded placement in order to run comparisons for different media platforms. But even with these approaches, most agree that it is difficult to control product placements in movies (and more recently on television, in video games, and even in mass-market paperback books) – let alone understand the impact that they may have. Whether or not media planners understand how to "count" product placements, it is clear that they are trying. For example, in early 2004 Nielsen documented that *American Idol* showed 3,300 instances of product placements (Gibson, 2004).

As using product placement as an effective strategy for media planning becomes more pervasive, it is inevitable that people will start to question the ethics of the practice – seeing it either as a form of privacy invasion ("I paid to see the movie once, why do I have to pay again by watching the ads in the movies?") or from a pragmatic perspective. What happens when a client purchases a placement and doesn't get the box-office numbers – or the scene gets cut because of the creative director's prerogative? What happens if the new television show flops after just a few episodes? What is the media planner going to do if a big part of the advertising strategy revolved around that television show?

Why Are Product Placements Potentially So Important?

As Charles Lubbers and Kathy McKee both mention, product placement as an advertising strategy will only become more important as Tivos and other kinds of digital recorders become more prevalent. As it becomes easier for consumers to skip commercials, advertisers will become even more creative at ways to make sure the message slips in. With estimates of nearly three-quarters (72.3 percent) of television audiences now skipping commercials (Romano, 2003) advertisers need to find a way to get their messages across – otherwise, they may withdraw from television all together. At first you might think this is a good idea, but who is going to pay for television if the advertiser won't?

As Lubbers and McKee point out, product placements are here to stay. But are they unethical? *You decide.*

Ideas to get you thinking . . .

1   Watch a favorite television show. Look carefully and see if you can find any branded products. How many did you find? Do you think the products are there because of the advertiser asked for them to be there?
2   Rent a movie with a friend and watch it for the action. After the movie, ask your friend to write down all the branded products he or she can remember. Now go back and watch the movie again, noting every time you see a product placement. Did your friend catch most of them? If not, why not? Based on this "experiment," do you think these product placements were a good idea?

If you'd like to read more . . .

Galician, M. L. (2004). *Handbook of product placement in the mass media: New strategies in marketing theory, practice, trends, and ethics.* Binghamton, NY: Haworth Press.

Lehu, J. (2007). *Branded entertainment: Product placement and brand strategy in the entertainment business.* London: Kogan Page.

Twitchell, J. (2005). *Branded nation: The marketing of Megachurch, College Inc., and Museumworld.* London: Simon & Schuster Adult Publishing Group.

References

D'Astous, A., and F. Chartier (2000). A study of factors affecting consumer evaluations and memory of product placement in movies. *Journal of Current Issues and Research in Advertising*, 22(2): 31–40.

Gibson, K. (2004). Advertising crossing over into TV show. <Cnn.com> (Sept. 13).

High, K. (2007). Is it an ad or a trailer? For VW, it's both. *Brandweek* (Aug. 1).

Neff, J. (2005). Veggie porn aside, Dove OK with fake ads. *Advertising Age* 76(8): 10.

Petrecca, L. (2006). Product placement: You can't escape it. *USA Today* (Oct. 10).

Romano, A. (2003). Cable takes to product tie-ins; sales execs, buyers agree: Placement must be subtle, well matched. *Broadcasting and Cable* 133(Jan.): 14.

Sauer, A. (2005). *Brand Channel*'s 2004 Product Placement Awards, 21 Feb. <http://Brandchannel.com>.

Argument

Product placement makes a lot of sense in today's media environment

Charles Lubbers

Recent articles within the popular and trade press offer insight into the state of product placement in the United States media but also present challenges to the legitimacy of product placement as a beneficial form of advertising. There is no form of advertising currently practiced in the United States that is free of negative aspects. However, individuals who do not believe in the use of product placement are ignoring all the positive arguments for the tactic. In this essay I will briefly describe the three major reasons I believe that product placement is an important option for advertisers: its increasing popularity; its historical foundations; and its many benefits for advertisers.

Extent of Use/Importance

A 2005 PQ Media report estimated that the product placement business is worth $4.2 billion annually. While the product placement business is clearly a small percentage of the traditional advertising market of between $250 and $300 billion in the same year, the renewed interest makes it an important area for discussion (Edwards, 2005).

In addition to the overall growth in product placement revenues, recent years have seen some examples of multi-million-dollar product placement deals. For example, Coca-Cola is reported to have paid a little less than $10 million to get their logo and products prominently featured on Fox Television's hit, *American Idol* (Edwards, 2005). However, the multi-million-dollar deals aren't limited to television. One-quarter of the production cost of $100 million for the 2002 movie *Minority Report* was covered by corporations, such as Lexus, the Gap and American Express, who wanted to have their products featured in the film (Weaver, 2002).

Another sign of the growing importance of product placements is that Nielsen Media Research now tracks product placement in network television shows during primetime. One report found that, in the fall 2005 season up to November 27, the 10 primetime network television shows with the most brand identification showed 9,019 brands. This was up from 5,821 the year before (Edwards, 2005). Nielsen Media Research also reported that the total media placements in 2005 were up 30 percent from 2004, with the greatest number of product placements in reality programs (Friedman, 2006b).

History

With all the recent "buzz" about the use of product placement and the recent growth in the percentage of advertising revenues placed in the area, it would seem that this is a new phenomenon. However, product placement has been around for a long time. It appears that the recent growth in its use is part of the reason for the current concern.

In the early days of both radio and television, programs were sponsored by businesses that had a great deal of control over the content, and it was very likely that their products would be woven into the storylines of the show. This relationship existed from the early days of radio in the 1920s and continued until the 1950s. The quiz show scandals of the late 1950s were the final blow that led to the demise of advertiser-sponsored programs (Turner, 2004). However, what disappeared was the sole-sponsored television program where the advertiser could exercise undue influence on the content of the program. Sponsorship and the placement of products continued over the years, and has experienced a great deal of growth in recent years. The following section outlines some of the major benefits for product placement, thus providing the reasons for its continued survival.

Benefits to Advertisers

One of the key rules underlining the effective use of product placements is that the products must be skillfully woven into the storyline. Clearly the placement of a product simply to generate revenue is likely to distract the audience. In fact, the movies *Wayne's World* (1992) and *Return of the Killer Tomatoes* (1988) both featured comedic sections poking fun at movies attempting to integrate unnecessary products into the storyline. Thus, the benefits discussed below are predicated on the correct use of the product placement, just as one wouldn't expect a poorly developed newspaper advertisement to be effective.

1 Compensate for advertising skipping technologies found in DVRs

In 2002 Bruce Redditt, executive vice-president at Omnicom group, noted that new technologies, such as the DVR, had allowed consumers to have "more control over their own programming, content and time" (Kim, 2002b). While less than 1 million homes had such recorders in 2002, those numbers have continued to grow. The ability of the consumer to "skip" advertisements poses great concerns for traditional media buyers. Placing products and services into the storyline of the entertainment offers a way around the technological advances.

The technological advances have forced advertisers to place more of the money in their marketing mix into options other than traditional 30-second advertisements. Chunovic (2003) noted that the new options include product placement, show ownership, interstitial content, and sponsorships.

2 Deliver message when many of the receivers' filters are off

Product placement also allows the advertiser the opportunity to deliver messages to consumers when their guard is down. Most consumers are inherently skeptical of advertising claims, but those natural filters are generally off (or at least lower) when watching entertainment programming. This is one reason why product placement is so effective, but it also explains some of the concerns consumers have about the practice.

3 Allow the development of a brand image

Many marketing campaigns are designed to "brand" a product or service. The branded product has two dimensions: the actual characteristics of the product as well as the emotional or affective characteristics the consumer associates with the product. Placing a product in an entertainment program may make it much easier for the advertiser to develop those affective dimensions. For example, a drink manufacturer may have a line of teas that is widely consumed in age groups over 40. By having those drinks consumed by younger actors in shows that draw a younger audience, the manufacturer may change the emotional dimension of the brand, even though the actual product has not been altered.

4 Less obtrusive for the viewer

One consistent complaint of media consumers is that advertisements are obtrusive and have a negative impact on the viewer's enjoyment of the entertainment programming. The integration of product placement allows for advertising revenue to be generated without the annoying breaks in the programming. Evan Fleischer, co-founder of a non-traditional marketing agency, said that product placements are less obtrusive for viewers, allowing the brand message to reach consumers in their daily lives without seeming like a hard sell (Gaffney, 2003).

5 More realistic

One of the least mentioned advantages of product placement is that it can actually create a more realistic viewing situation. Efforts to remove real products from a television show or movie can create an artificial environment that is less appealing to the audience. In short, efforts to remove brands from the scene may create such an artificial environment that is actually distracting to the viewer.

6 Use in media other than television and feature films

Product placement has been traditionally associated with television and feature films. However, one of the advantages of this form of marketing is that it can be placed in a wide variety of entertainment media, even media where traditional advertising doesn't exist.

- *Music and music videos.* In 2002 it was widely reported that the Island Def Jam Music Group was wooing potential advertisers to line up product placement deals. In fact, Kim (2002a) reported that most of the major record companies had established departments to pursue deals with advertisers. Much of the interest in incorporating product plugs into music lyrics was developed by the rap artist Busta Rhymes' successful songs featuring Courvoisier. However, product placement in videos has been more difficult for record labels. Leeds (2003) reports how music companies are using several tactics to bypass MTV's prohibition of advertising in videos. Leeds notes that rapper Ms. Jade's 2003 video for "Ching Ching" prominently features two Hummer H2s, for which the Hummer manufacturer, General Motors, paid $300,000. In an age when music sales are declining, product placement in music lyrics and videos offers advertisers another outlet for reaching consumers while providing an additional revenue stream for music companies.

- *Books.* There are examples of product placement in books, as a way of increasing interest in a brand. Rothenberg (2001) noted that Beth Ann Herman's 1989 book *Power City* contained "plugs for a Beverly Hills Maserati dealership in return for a $15,000 book party." An even more definitive example was the 2001 book by Fay Weldon, *The Bulgari Connection*, which was commissioned by Bulgari.
- *Video games – both console and internet-based.* Have you played any video games recently? If so, you've probably noticed that advertisements are now being inserted into the story lines of the more sophisticated games. Each download of play of a game allows the advertiser to bring new messages to the consumer. Change the setting for the game, and you can bring in a new set of advertisers. After all, if upscale products can be successfully placed in James Bond movies, why not the James Bond games?
- *Made-for-the-web movies.* Use of the internet for entertainment delivery will only increase. Already the consumer can download, view or play, selected films, music, and games. However, in 2001, BMW began releasing a series of eight made-for-the-web movies under the heading *The Hire.* These movies not only featured BMW vehicles performing amazing feats, but helped the company get rid of the 1980s view of the BMW as a status symbol for yuppies (Vagnoni, 2001).
- *Board games.* The release of the board game "It's Only Money" in 1989 exposed players to product placement from a variety of organizations, including Harrah's casino (Rothenberg, 2001).

7 Use in traditional media of television and film, but in new ways

Product placement has been associated with television and film for decades. While the use in these media is not new, there are at least two newer trends for the use of product placement in new ways.

- *Vintage product placement in movies.* Movies set in historical periods have always strived to create an environment that accurately reflects the surroundings at that time. A more recent development is the effort to integrate historically accurate product placements into feature films. This technique can be particularly effective because the viewer is even less likely to expect vintage product placement. An example of this trend was ESPN's television movie, *The Junction Boys*. The movie featured vintage Dr. Pepper and General Motors automobiles that would have been prominent during the movies' profile of the 1954 Texas A&M football team (Friedman and Chura, 2002).

- *Digital insertion of product images into first runs and reruns.* Friedman (2006a) reported that Marathon Ventures has negotiated deals with CBS and Fox to use technology to "virtually place products on the sets of dramas and comedies." The products were not originally in the scene, but are added through the use of computer technology. Friedman goes on to note that with virtual placement advertisers can make decisions quickly. He also notes that different products can be inserted each time the show is broadcast. In fact, Goetzl reported in 2001 that Turner Broadcasting System had reached a deal allowing it to digitally insert products into the reruns of *Law and Order* that would be run on TNT. While no specifics were reported in the deal there was some speculation that insertion opportunities would include branding the soda machine in the police station or the detectives' coffee cups.

Conclusion

In conclusion, with the right product or service, product placement may be an exceptional way to increase brand awareness and to create intention to purchase. Despite the recent controversy related to its use, product placement has been practiced in the United States for quite some time. The early practitioners realized what I hope you have come to understand, that product placement can be an effective promotional tactic. However, in the end it's the audience that will ultimately decide the fate of product placement. As long as audiences find the insertion of products into the storyline acceptable the practice will continue. However, at the point that placements are rejected by audiences because of overuse or use of a product that is too contrived, audience members will vote with their remote (Meskauskas, 2004).

References

Chunovic, L. (2003). Creating ways to beat zapping. *Electronic Media* (Jan. 13). <http://www.emonline.com/advertise/011303creating.html>.

Edwards, J. (2005). The tracker: There's less than meets the eye in TV placement economy. *Brandweek* (Dec. 19). <http://insidebrandedentertainment.com/ bep/article_display.jsp?JSESSIONID=DmqvtG62rc6TW6YqGpc07TCSjT1LpYh6 ppJqGnrkbmM6jBGzKpWY!-1723770592&vnu_content_id=1001700187>.

Friedman, W. (2006a). Putting product placement in its place: A media critique. *Media Post's TV Watch* (Jan. 3). <http://publications.mediapost.com/ index.cfm?fuseaction=Articles.showArticle&art_aid=38057>.

Friedman, W. (2006b). Product placement 500 times an episode: Too much? A media critique. *Media Post's TV Watch* (Jan. 6). <http://publications.mediapost.com/ index.cfm?fuseaction=Articles.showArticle&art_aid=38232>.

Friedman, W., and C. Chura (2002). Dr Pepper, GM get 1954-era brand visuals in ESPN TV movie. *Ad Age* (Oct. 28). <http://www.adage.com/ news.cms?newsId=36407>.

Gaffney, J. (2003). Exclusive MDN survey: Planners, TV viewers warm to product placements. *Media Post* (June 10). <http://www.mediapost.com/ dtls_dsp_news.cfm?newsID=208686>.

Goetzl, D. (2001). Product images to be inserted in "Law & Order" reruns. *Ad Age* (May 21). <http://www.adage.com/news.cms?newsId=32362>.

Kim, H. (2002a). Marketers explore product placements in music. *Ad Age* (Sept. 9). <http://www.adage.com/news.cms?newsId=35982>.

Kim, H. (2002b). The changing world of content & commerce. *Ad Age* (Oct. 7). <http://adage.com/abstract.php?article_id=35942>.

Leeds, J. (2003). Commercial tie-ins, product promos invade MTV. *LA Times* (Mar. 31). <http://www.latimes.com/business/printedition/la-fi-mtv31mar31001440,1,1465955.story?coll=la%2Dheadlines%2Dpe%2Dbusiness>.

Meskauskas, J. (2004). Can you put that there? *Media Post* (Jan. 8). <http:// www.mediapost.com/eNewsletters.cfm?Aid=233098&Nid=7338>.

Rothenberg, R. (2001). Product placement carnival rolls back into town. *Ad Age* (Sept. 10). <http://www.adage.com/news.cms?newsId=32822>.

Turner, K. J. (2004). Insinuating the product into the message : An historical context for product placement. In M. L. Galician (ed.), *Handbook of Product Placement in the Mass Media: New Strategies in Marketing Theory, Practice, Trends, and Ethics* (pp. 9–14). Binghamton, NY: Haworth Press.

Vagnoni, A. (2001). The inside story of BMW's cyber-cinema ads: A slick merger of product placement and movie-making technique. *Ad Age* (July 23). <http://www.adage.com/news.cms?newsId=32430>.

Weaver, J. (2002). Marketing to a miserable economy: A carpet bombing approach to commercials. *MSNBC.com* (Dec. 18). <http://www.msnbc.com/ news/845781.asp?0si=->.

Counterargument

More than entertainment: product placement in American media channels

Kathy Brittain McKee

"And the Oscar for best supporting performance by a product, good or service this year goes to . . ."

Unrealistic? Perhaps. But considering the economic value of product placement within films – worth some $1.26 billion and growing by about 11 percent each year (Graser, 2005) – and the prominence afforded some of the brands featured in contemporary films, such recognition may be warranted. Again, while perhaps far-fetched, perhaps an equal argument might be made for awarding an Emmy, a Tony, or a Grammy for branding, too. One study cited in Graser (2005) argues that TV placement already outpaces that in films, and placement in other media is escalating. This text describes the growth of placement, not only within films and television, but its recent use in plays, recordings, magazines, novels, video games, and even in cyberworlds such as Second Life.

Obviously, the use of paid and bartered placement is a boon for producers seeking production support. But consumers and parents may have reasons for complaint and caution. Media audiences should be wary of such arrangements for at least three reasons:

1 Reluctant or naive audiences who do not anticipate receiving commercial messages cannot avoid those embedded in the entertainment content itself.
2 Such placements may elude regulation of the advertising of products deemed harmful or dangerous for some audiences.
3 Overt and blatant placements alter the creativity of narratives and characterizations.

No-Choice Advertising

If there's one thing that may safely be argued about American media audiences it's that they want choice, and increasingly technology offers such choice. Personal recording devices, from the iPod to TiVos, allow audiences to choose what they will watch or listen to and when they will watch or listen to it. They also may allow audience members to choose to be exposed to commercial messages or not. Zipping or zapping through television commercials or arriving late enough at the movie theater to avoid the opening five to 15 minutes of commercials gives audience members an opportunity to say no. But when the brand messages are within the script or lyric, or the product itself is a game or film character, they are unavoidable. From the subtle branding found in signage shown in a film to the overt placement when the product itself advances the plot, audiences cannot escape exposure.

Perhaps most adults are savvy or cynical enough to note and discount the persuasive impact of such branding. However, choosing exposure to entertainment typically means that audiences are in a positive, receptive mode when they likely expect to be able to suspend critical consumptive judgment. Viewers have chosen a film or a television program deliberatively, seeking whatever gratifications present – and then are called to simultaneously suspend disbelief in order to immerse themselves in the involving or amusing narrative while also critically noting (and perhaps discounting) the depiction and association of the products featured within that narrative.

Such a process is certainly difficult for adults, but more challenging for children who have not yet developed sufficient media literacy to be able to decode traditional advertising, let alone branding that avoids the traditional signals of a "commercial message." The cross-promotions that often accompany film and television placement that lead to the toys within the children's meals at fast-food chains or the clothing or furnishings in their bedrooms create a seamless stream of branding that deepens its persuasive impact. Such would require a high degree of media sophistication for children to be able to discern and critically judge the worthiness of the product itself. Groups such as the National Advertising Division of the Council of Better Business Bureaus have indicated they will review product placements on children's television (Edwards, 2005).

Even more troubling may be the explosion of advertisements within video or online games where the ads may be either static or subject to dynamic placements that may change as the games are played (Gerlsbeck, 2007). Some reports estimate that the "in-game" placement may grow to become a $3 billion industry by 2011 (Bulik, 2007). While the video game itself is rated to indicate the maturity needed to view its content, there is no such rating of the amount of commercial content included.

Subtle Dangers

Such a concern is magnified when the product depicted in programming may be deemed hazardous. Products that may not be legally advertised to children, for example, may find a place within film content. The number of film characters who smoke and discuss specific brands, for example, has prompted consumer advocacy groups to argue for increased regulation (Lipman, 1989). Glamorizing alcohol use or smoking without the accompanying warning labels required in traditional advertising offers marketers a different route to reach and to persuade audience members.

Perhaps a greater danger lies in the cultural impact arising from unceasing commercialization in every venue. Imagine if Dickens were writing today: Would Oliver's plaintive request for more porridge now be branded – "More Pickwick Porridge, please?" The Warhol soup can may have been more prophetic than was realized. When virtually every cultural vehicle – from films to plays to recording to television programming – carries overt commercial imprimaturs, it contributes to a pervasive hegemony of materialism that not only overrides artistic or aesthetic values but also reduces the audience to a commodity to be bought and sold again and again. Kretchmer (2004) has noted the advent of what she calls "advertainment," which she describes as "entertainment content that mimics traditional media forms but is created solely as a vehicle to promote specific advertisers" (2004: 39). Put more simply, overt placements can turn art simply into another commodity bought and sold for profit.

Restructured Creativity

Consumers have accepted the use of branding to establish characterization; we know the stereotypes of a "Marlboro man," the "Pepsi generation" and a "NASCAR dad." Writers have used products as specific props within novels and scripts for years as one way of quickly signaling insights about settings, characters, and eras. Contemporary placement often goes beyond such characterizations, however. The posed product pitching captured with *The Truman Show* should be just that – a parody of commercialization, not what we routinely experience when we watch a film or TV program or listen to hip-hop. Numerous case studies in academic journals, trade journals, and newspapers point to the editorial decisions of producers, directors, singers, playwrights, and novelists apparently made to afford the brand its negotiated positions, and a few lawsuits illustrate what may happen when the director or producer does not follow through on the agreed product depiction (see e.g. Nitins, 2005). Obviously, some of these decisions get publicized, so that audience members and critics are aware of the push to please the sponsor. But many such decisions may be made throughout a project, from the initial idea for a project as a product vehicle to post-production edits that insert or delete brands from scenes. The impact of such overt commercial consideration on originality and creativity may be impossible to measure – but it is certainly possible to observe it on screen.

Is all product placement bad for consumers? Obviously not. Some branding is amusing, some creative, some arousing. But consumers should be aware and wary of the phenomenon – and perhaps mindful that when they pay $8 for their next movie ticket or go online to play the latest "Halo" game, they may be getting more than just entertainment.

Do we really want to hear: "The Oscar for best leading role in a film by a product, good or service goes to . . ."?

References

Bulik, B. S. (2007). In-game ads win cachet through a deal with EA. *Advertising Age* 78(30): 8.

Edwards, J. (2005). Regulators take another look at product placement. *Brandweek* 46(36): 15.

Gerlsbeck, R. (2007). Getting in the game. *Marketing* 112(17): 9.

Graser, M. (2005). Product-placement spending poised to hit $4.25 billion in '05. *Advertising Age* 76(14): 16.

Kretchmer, S. B. (2004). Advertainment: The evolution of product placement as a mass media marketing strategy. In M. Galician (ed.), *Handbook of product placement in the mass media* (pp. 37–54). Binghamton, NY: Best Business Books.

Limpan, J. (1989). Outcry over product placement worries movie ad executives. *Wall Street Journal* (7 Apr.): B5.

Nitins, T. (2005). Are we selling out our culture? The influence of product placement in filmmaking. *Screen Education* 40: 44–9.

8

Sex and Advertising

I'm Too Sexy for this Ad . . .
or Am I?

No doubt about it. Sexual content in the media has increased. Just think about any episode of *Desperate Housewives* (the housewives, their husbands – and even their children – have all been shown engaged in some kind of sexual act), *Grey's Anatomy* (where the surgeons spend as much time performing various sex acts as they do performing surgery), *Glamour* and *Seventeen* magazines (which help women learn how to improve their sex lives) and it's easy to believe that sexual portrayals in the media have increased over the years. By comparison, sex in advertising is often much more subtle than the "in-your-face" approach we see in programs and articles, for example.

It's not unusual for people to think that sex in advertising is unethical, but Tom Reichert presents another thoughtful perspective. While he admits that some use of sex in advertising may be problematic, for the right product it's a useful attention-grabbing creative device. Sounds good. But just when we think we have the answer, Kathy Forde presents another side. She argues just as persuasively as Reichert that using sex in advertising is lazy. It's an abuse of tired clichés and visual boredoms. Plus she throws in this ringer: Does an ad that uses sexual appeal tell the truth? *Ouch.*

What do we know about sex in advertising, other than it's used a lot?

There's an interesting article from the South African *Sunday Times* (November 14, 2004), where author Chris Moerdyk argues that sex doesn't sell any more, so we should be seeing less of it soon. He says that part of the reason is because of 9/11: a move back toward family values. He also argues (as Kathy Forde does) that consumers are looking for something they can trust. Maybe. But according to my TV, sex in advertising has not diminished. If anything, it has increased.

It's easy to point the finger and complain about sex in advertising, but the creators of the advertising message aren't necessarily the only ones to blame. What about the company marketing executives who create products assuming the need for sex appeal, like Procter & Gamble's creation of a deodorant body spray for pre-pubescent boys? What about magazine editors who approve storylines about improving our sexual performance? What about those of us who buy a brand of cereal because we believe it will give us the body we long for – sleek, sexy, and sensational?

No one questions that sex in advertising exists. But the question remains: Is sex in advertising ever a good idea? Read the following essays. *You decide.*

Ideas to get you thinking . . .

1 Grab a magazine, or spend an evening flipping through the TV set. Note all the ads you see. Try and determine which ones are using sex appeal. How many are there? Can you decide where the line between creativity and indecency is? Are there any "sexy" ads that have made you more interested in buying the product?
2 A lot of the controversy about sex in advertising is based on the premise that it denigrates women. Look at some ads using sex appeal. What do you think?

If you'd like to read more

Gunter, B. (2002). *Media sex: What are the issues?* Mahwah, NJ: Lawrence Erlbaum.
Reichert, T. (2003). *The erotic history of advertising.* Amherst, NY: Prometheus Books.

Reichert, T., and J. Lambiase (eds.). (2006). *Sex in consumer culture: The erotic of media and marketing.* Mahwah, NJ: Lawrence Erlbaum.

Savoir, L.A. (2007). *Sex in design.* Antwerp, Belgium: Tectum.

References

Moerdyk, C. (2004). Clothes back on as sex in advertising proves a turn-off. *Sunday Times* (South Africa) (Nov. 14): Lifestyle and Leisure, 7.

Argument

Sex in advertising: no crime here!

Tom Reichert

Introduction

Bodies in a tight embrace. A bead of perspiration trickles across a dark, well-defined abdomen. Moist lips trace their way from below the ear to the base of the neck as clothing slips to the floor. His eyes are closed as a sigh of pleasure escapes his lips. Reacting without thinking, she reaches down expectantly for . . . an Uncle Ben's microwavable rice bowl.

Did I get your attention?

Good. Once you regain your train of thought continue with me as I attempt to persuade you that sexual information in advertising (aka sex in advertising) is not the felon some make it out to be. In fact, I argue that scenes like the one just described are more often used for the types of brands most relevant to sex appeal: fragrance, fashion, beauty and personal-care products, and entertainment. And far from being a simple attention-getter, sex is used to position brands as a means to enhance attractiveness, intimacy, and romance.

Don't get me wrong. Sex in advertising isn't found under "virtue" in the dictionary. Unfortunately, there are sexual ads out there that cross the line with regard to explicitness, taste, and degradation. One need only think of Calvin Klein and his ability to spark controversy to know what I am referring to. As with most things in this world, a few bad apples cast a poor light on those who act responsibly. The same is true for sex in advertising.

Why should you listen to me? Good question. I've been researching sex in advertising for over 14 years. During that time I've co-edited two books on the promotional uses of sex in the media and I wrote a book about the history of sex in advertising. I only mention this so that you'll know I've thought a lot about the issues raised in this essay. Inherently, sex in advertising is not a bad thing. It sells products, and can do so in a healthy, respectful manner. Let me begin by defining sex in advertising and then addressing two common objections regarding its use.

Definition

First, let's be sure we're on the same page. What is sex in advertising? Like most advertising, it is a persuasive message that contains sexual information. Advertisers try to get people to think, feel, or become aware of a product or idea, and sexual information can be related to that idea in greater or lesser degrees. According to sexuality research, sexual information is that which elicits sexual thoughts and/or feelings.

In some research I conducted with Art Ramirez, we asked students to think of a sexual ad and to describe what it was about that ad that made it sexual to them. Revealing displays of desirable physiques was number one. Sexual behavior was number two. An array of supporting variables such as photographic techniques, what the model said, and the context where the action took place constituted number three. These findings in light of other research confirm that most instances of sexual information are visual images of people.

But we shouldn't forget the text. Sexual innuendo, entendre, suggestiveness, and double meaning usually involve the interplay of text and image. For example, a recent magazine ad for Harlequin books features the innocuous headline: "Has he been reading your Harlequin books?" When paired with a full-page image of an attractive couple in a heated embrace, however, the implication is that reading romance novels will get him in the mood. Now that we know what sex in advertising is, let's see if it works.

Objection 1: "Sex in advertising doesn't work"

This objection comes in several varieties. One is that sex is only used to grab attention. Some people refer to this usage as "borrowed interest." In other words, advertisers attempt to take the interest generated by sexual information and use it to generate interest for their brands. In a related sense, detractors argue that, while sex may stop traffic, it only produces – at best – a one-time sale that won't build brand value needed to sustain long-term growth.

To some degree the critics are correct. Sex information does grab attention. Sex evokes a hardwired emotional response that is linked to species survival. We can't help that our eyes and ears are drawn to it because emotional information has a way of piercing our perceptual fields by rising above other environmental information trying to get our attention. So, yes, it does grab attention. And if sex is used merely to draw attention to a product that has no relevance to sex, then long-term success is not likely.

But consider the statement: "Sex is only used to grab attention." These critics should update their thinking because research indicates that sex is used for more than attracting attention. I did some work with Jacque Lambiase and we discovered that 73 percent, almost three-quarters, of sexual ads in magazines contained a sex-related brand benefit. Common themes followed the "Buy this, get this" formula. If you buy our product: (1) you'll be more sexually attractive, (2) you'll have more or better sex, or (3) you'll just feel sexier for your own sake. Recall the commercials recently used by Unilever to introduce Axe body spray. A young man sprays it on and attractive women (some are even physicians and mothers of girlfriends) find him irresistible. Credible? Doubtful. Tongue-in-cheek. Sure. I'm convinced that the agency handling Axe found through extensive research that these appeals resonated with members of the target audience (teens and young men 14–34 years old).

Again, almost three times as many ads use sex as a selling message – in most cases as the primary reason for buying and using the brand – than solely for attention-getting purposes. Axe, Tag, and Old Spice body sprays have produced a lot of revenue for their parent companies in a relatively short period of time (Axe was introduced in 2000), and all three are positioned as sexual-attractant enhancers.

In addition, there are plenty of cases in which sexual positioning strategies have resulted in long-term success. One of those is Calvin Klein. He has successfully imbued his brand's identity with sexuality. For well over 30 years, sex in one form or another has been a mainstay in Calvin Klein fragrance, fashion, underwear, and accessories ads. The result? In 2005, products with Calvin's name generated at least $1 billion in annual revenue.

The same is true for Victoria's Secret. With its stable of supermodels clad only in panties and bras, the company has grown from three boutiques in San Francisco to the most successful and recognizable intimates brand in the United States, if not the world. Much of that success was achieved through an aggressive catalog effort and inventive promotional techniques such as Super Bowl commercials, streaming fashion shows, and primetime fashion shows on network television. These promotional efforts rarely vary from Victoria's Secret's carefully crafted sexually sophisticated image. Women who want to be associated with that image, either for their own pleasure or for that of someone else, willingly pay for it.

Many other firms have successfully used sex in advertising for sustained periods of time, and sex in advertising works in other ways beyond gaining attention and offering sex-related benefits. Suffice to say that as long as people desire to be attractive to others, and as long as people desire romance, intimacy, and love, and all the wonderful feelings they involve, advertisers can show how their products help meet those needs and desires. Whether we like it or not, products play a role in society's intimacy equation.

Objection 2: "Sex in advertising contains degrading images of women"

I agree. Advertisers need to do a better job portraying women not only in sexual ads but in all advertising. Obviously, however, not all sexual ads are degrading, and the industry, especially the Madison Avenue agencies that produce nationally visual campaigns, is improving the tone of those images.

But, first, let's look more closely at the objection because it is an important one. Essentially feminists have argued that decorative images of women – women shown as one-dimensional objects merely present to look good – influence people's attitudes and perceptions about women's contributions and roles in society. Research shows that the feminists are right. Both women and men who are exposed to these decorative images place more value on women's physical attractiveness and role as a mate, and devalue their intellect, skills, and competencies. One ad won't do it, but who sees just one ad? We see thousands of them every day. Over time, and unannounced, sexist attitudes work their way into our belief system.

How does this relate to sex in advertising? Although beefcake images have made inroads in the last 20–25 years, provocatively dressed women in suggestive poses constitute a fair portion of sexual images. In some cases women are subservient to their male counterparts. Men watch as their women strip, dance, or playfully tease them in some other manner.

As a whole, these images are unacceptable. The advertising industry is increasingly aware of the sexism inherent in these types of images, and it is cleaning up its act. In some cases, the industry is policing itself. For example, there is a very influential industry group known as Advertising Women of New York (AWNY). At their annual meeting they give out awards to advertisers who portray women in the most positive and negative ways. Several instances of sex in advertising have received the "Grand Ugly" award. These awards publicly identify particularly offensive ads (and their sponsors) that result in a lot of bad press. Several years ago Candie's won the "Grand Ugly" award for a print ad featuring Jodi Lyn O'Keefe astride a computer monitor, and Sugar Ray's Mark McGrath sitting at the keyboard. On the screen a space shuttle is shown blasting upward toward O'Keefe's crotch.

Today, ads like the one for Candie's are the exception, not the rule. In fact, many sexual ads often contain humor that pokes fun at the objectifying male characters. For those of you who are too young to remember, in 1994 a very popular Diet Coke commercial turned the tables as women ogled a shirtless male construction worker. Also note that Madison Avenue isn't the primary source of sexist ads these days. Many offending ads are placed by local businesses in newspapers and major urban alternative weeklies such as the *Dallas Observer* and *Phoenix New Times*. Last, keep in mind that sexual information isn't inherently degrading to women, or men. Sexual ads that portray couples in healthy relationships, with equal power dimensions, can capture a unique and compelling slice of life with no hint of sexism (for an example, reread this essay's first paragraph).

Conclusion

In addition to these two primary complaints, there are other concerns regarding sex in advertising. For example, some, including me, have claimed that sexual ads unfairly target teens and young people. Raging hormones, sexual discovery, and newly minted critical thinking skills can cloud judgment and make teens especially susceptible to sexual appeals that advocate brands as sexual attractants. Advertisers who are guilty of targeting young adults obviously should be held accountable. Abercrombie & Fitch have felt the heat recently as public pressure is mounting to compel them to tone down the sexual explicitness of their quarterly "magalogs."

In sum, sex in advertising can be a very effective creative strategy if:

1   it is relevant to the product it is promoting;
2   it isn't sexist; and
3   it doesn't target susceptible populations.

In other words, advertising creators – perhaps like yourself someday soon – need to be aware of these issues and act in good faith. If they don't, research by Mike LaTour has shown that consumers are more likely to boycott products sold with sexist images. Also, AWNY may feature your ad as a "Grand Ugly." I hate to imagine you trying to explain that award to your client. Last, remember that advertising's job is to tell consumers how products fulfill their needs and desires. As long as people use products to attract others (e.g., fashion, fragrance, mouthwash, cosmetics, even automobiles), what's so bad about advertising helping people get what they really want – romance, intimacy, and the affection of others? In the meantime, are you going to finish that rice bowl?

References

Lambiase, J., and T. Reichert (2003). Promises, promises: Exploring erotic rhetoric in sexually oriented advertising. In L. Scott and R. Batra (eds.), *Persuasive imagery: A consumer perspective* (pp. 247–66). Mahwah, NJ: Lawrence Erlbaum.

LaTour, M., and T. L. Henthorne (2003). Nudity and sexual appeals: Understanding the arousal process and advertising response. In T. Reichert and J. Lambiase (eds.), *Sex in advertising* (pp. 91–106). Mahwah, NJ: Lawrence Erlbaum.

Pardun, C. J., K. L. L'Engle, and J. D. Brown (2005). Linking exposure to outcomes: Early adolescents' consumption of sexual content in six media. *Mass Communication and Society* 8(2): 75–91.

Reichert, T. (2003). *The erotic history of advertising*. Amherst, NY: Prometheus.

Reichert, T., and J. Lambiase (2003). How to get "kissably close": Examining how advertisers appeal to consumers' sexual needs and desires. *Sexuality and Culture* 7(3): 120–36.

Reichert, T., and A. Ramirez (2000). Defining sexually oriented appeals in advertising: A grounded theory investigation. In S. J. Hoch and R. J. Meyer (eds.), *Advances in consumer research*, vol. 27 (pp. 267–73). Provo, UT: Association for Consumer Research.

Counterargument

Using sex in advertising is never a good idea
Kathy Roberts Forde

Advertising has infiltrated nearly every nook and cranny of public life in the United States – from ceiling tiles in restaurants peddling the services of your local realtor to virtual ads selling cars inserted behind home plate in the televised broadcast of the World Series. Ours is a society of desire, where commerce is the deep structure of our daily lives. We speak and dream in the language of commodity and consumption. Even sex – or at least the idea of sex – has become something we readily consume at the click of a mouse or turn of the page.

There's no doubt that sex sells certain products to certain people. As early as the 1890s, Duke cigarettes became the leading national brand after the company began including trading cards featuring portraits of female stars in its cigarette packs (Reichert, 2002). Today, Clairol's Herbal Essences is one of the leading brands of shampoo, largely due to an ad campaign touting the "organic" (read "orgasmic") experience the shampoo offers women (Fass, 2001). But the sexual appeal doesn't work very well for products with no plausible sexual meaning (Reichert, 2002: 254). And even when ads feature products that are popularly sexualized, such as fashion and alcohol, sexual content tends to damage brand recall, especially for men, who tend to focus on breasts and legs and neglect the product and brand (Nudd, 2005). What's more, most women don't even care for sexual ads (Nudd, 2005).

Despite the ubiquity of the sexual appeal in today's advertising landscape, most Americans believe there is too much sexual imagery in the ads they view (Dolliver, 1999). It's time to rethink the use of sex in advertising. In fact, let's get rid of the sexual appeal altogether. We're collectively exhausted with sexual messages intended to persuade us to buy this or that, usually through tired cliché or norm-shocking visuals.

We've come a long way, baby, since Virginia Slims advertisements touted smoking as a sexy and emancipated pastime for women and Herbal Essence commercials shocked us with women shampooing their hair in sexual excitement. These ads seem practically demure in our contemporary marketplace where Gucci shows off its couture in a print ad featuring an impossibly thin young woman pulling down her underpants to expose pubic hair shaved in the shape of the iconic G, while a young man kneels in front of her, grasping her thigh (Kilbourne, 2005).

It's shocking, at least when you see such an image in the pages of a glossy women's magazine rather than on replays of *Sex and the City*. But when you recover from your surprise, the overwhelming feeling is boredom. Enough already.

Ennui is hardly the only suffering caused by the glut of sex in advertising. Sexual ads contribute to serious social ills, such as unhealthy sexual attitudes, beliefs, and behavior in adolescents, teens, and young adults; the objectification of women – and men – as sexual commodities; body image problems; and disordered eating. Other possible harmful effects are harder to measure, such as the trivialization of intimacy and what Jean Kilbourne has identified as the "sexual dissatisfaction" of many Americans (2005).

Teens and Sex

A recent ground-breaking study conducted by researchers at the University of North Carolina found that the more sexual content young teens aged 12 to 14 consume in the media, the more likely they are to have had sex and to engage in sexual activity in the future (Pardun et al., 2005: 88). Sexual advertisements are but one element of a measure this study termed the "Sexual Media Diet (SMD)" – which included television and movie viewing, magazine and newspaper reading, music listening, and web surfing – but they contribute to the overall sexual content of teens' media world. It is the amount, not the kind, of sexual media teens consume that influences sexual behavior and attitudes.

In the United States today, almost half of high-school students have had sex (Centers for Disease Control, 2006: 3). Although teen pregnancy and birth rates have steadily declined in the United States since 1991, these rates are still higher than in other Western developed countries. Sexually transmitted disease and abortion rates are higher, too. Teens in all these countries are exposed to sexual media, including advertisements, that rarely depict the risks involved in sexual activity such as pregnancy and STDs. A devastating difference is that U.S. cultural attitudes have prevented more robust sex education and contraceptive programs, such as those that exist in Sweden and France, from developing. There are fewer social buffers in the United States to counteract the negative effects of sexual media messages on youth (Darroch et al., 2001).

While stronger sex education campaigns in the United States are key, we also need a less sexually charged media environment. Young people today primarily learn about sex from the media (Brown and Keller, 2000). If advertisements – especially advertisements aimed at teens and adolescents – dropped the sexual appeal, that would be one step in the direction of better public health for American youth.

Objectification

In its attempt to sell merchandise and services, advertising often represents women's bodies as sexual objects. Ads for jeans show women in underwear, focusing on breasts, rear ends, and exposed skin without a shred of denim in sight. The female body parts – not the product – are the visual subject. If you wear our jeans, the ad suggests, you, too, can have a sexy body that any man would want to see and touch. It's an age-old advertising technique. It's time-worn, too.

Today women are the major consumers in the U.S. economy – spending 88 percent of a household's disposable income – and advertising continues to offer up objectified images of female bodies that many find offensive and even stupid (Crawford, 2004). The advertising industry is simply out-of-touch with today's marketplace and the contemporary woman.

The sexual objectification of women in advertisements conditions girls and women to view themselves as objects – a phenomenon called self-objectification. This way of viewing one's own body can lead to shame, disgust, and appearance anxiety, which in turn can contribute to eating disorders, sexual dysfunction, and depression. Self-objectification appears to be activated more readily by print media such as fashion magazines, in which large numbers of objectified images of women appear in advertisements, than by television (Roberts and Gettman, 2004).

Men, too, can be adversely affected by ads objectifying women. Research has shown a relationship between male acceptance of both sex role stereotypes and violence against women and viewing of such advertisements (Lanis and Covell, 1995).

But it's not only women who are objectified in advertising these days. Men, too, have become sexual objects. The body size of men has increased substantially over time in advertising depictions, with an emphasis on large, muscular physiques (Roberts and Gettman, 2004). Sexual portrayals of men have increased, too (Reichert, Lambiase, et al., 1999). Although the effects of these "beefcake ads" are uncertain, some believe they have influenced men to body-build obsessively in a kind of "reverse anorexia" (Roberts and Gettman, 2004).

Body Image and Beauty

In a country where sales in the diet industry totaled $1.9 billion in 2004, weight is on the mind of many Americans. In 1980, 47 percent of the U.S. population was overweight; the figure has risen sharply in the past 25 years to 65 percent (Mintel Reports, 2005). High-fructose corn syrup runs through the arteries of supermarkets and the fast-food industry, conditioning our bodies to store rather than burn fat, and fast-food giants push super-sized meals and feed children in school cafeterias (Critser, 2004). Yet just as economic and social forces drive the U.S. obesity epidemic, they also drive the beauty and fashion industries, which glorify thinness and youth. We live in a culture of insanely mixed messages and competing social pressures. Simply consider the message one Carl Jr. television and internet commercial sends to women and girls. Eat this half-pound hamburger! But be sure to maintain the body of a Paris Hilton – and while you're at it, work on your seductive car-washing skills!

Advertising for the fashion and beauty industries relies on making consumers feel that they just aren't attractive or sexy enough. The ideal female body is ultra-thin, young, and without wrinkle, cellulite, or blemish – an ideal no woman can attain. And yet advertisements tell women repeatedly that if they use this face lotion, wear this bra, try this diet they can reach the ideal. For many women and girls, the idealized female bodies they see in advertisements produce body shame and appearance anxiety (Monro and Huon, 2005). For men and boys, these images provide unrealistic expectations of what their girlfriends, wives, sisters, and mothers should look like and a diminished understanding of who these women can be.

America needs major social reform to address the obesity epidemic, including public health campaigns and increased regulation of the food industry. But it also needs media depictions of bodies in a range of shapes, sizes, ages, and physical capacity. Let's replace the thin, youthful, sexy ideal in advertisements with images of real women: muscular athletes, women in wheelchairs, breast cancer survivors, women over the age of 50. Let's believe there is more to women and girls than the sex objects and stereotypes we often see in advertising. And then let's insist that advertisers believe it, too.

Eating Disorders

It is estimated that one in ten college women suffer from an eating disorder such as anorexia and bulimia, and that 15 percent of young women exhibit disordered eating. It is likely no coincidence that as eating disorder rates have climbed in recent years, the media's body ideal for women has become thinner and thinner. Although many factors contribute to eating disorders, for some women and girls the media's ultra-thin body ideal is a strong influence (Stice et al., 1994).

Eating disorders affect men and boys, too. About 10 percent of those with eating disorders in the United States are male. Whether mediated messages contribute to this problem is unclear.

The good news is that advertisers can counteract such negative messages and their results by providing more realistic images of women. Research shows that young women who view average-weight models in media depictions appear to develop resistance to the negative effects of the thin body ideal. There is hope, then, that advertisements depicting real women can lessen the prevalence of eating disorders (Fister and Smith, 2004).

Regulating Sex in Advertising

Although plenty of consumers object to sex in advertising purely on moral or religious grounds, such an argument is hard to advance in a heterogeneous society with diverse social and religious practices and beliefs. A legal argument is hard to mount, too. The Federal Trade Commission rules prohibit deceptive and unfair advertising, but regulatory law has little to say about the often irrational lifestyle claims an advertisement may make, such as the attribution of a woman's sexiness to the shampoo she uses or the jeans she wears (Preston, 1998: 73). It's important to note, too, that commercial speech enjoys substantial First Amendment protection, although less robust than that afforded political and social discourse. At present, the only realistic means for changing the advertising industry's over-reliance on the sexual appeal is through self-regulation, media regulation (the power of the media to choose the advertising it will publish), and public pressure.

Public and governmental alarm over the recently recognized obesity epidemic in the United States has resulted in increased scrutiny of food advertising directed to children. In response, the food industry has made positive changes in products and packaging aimed at children and strengthened self-regulation of its marketing techniques (Parnes, 2006). Although these efforts have only just begun, similar self-regulation in the arena of sexual advertisements (directed at all audiences) may do much to ameliorate associated public health problems and social issues.

The American Advertising Federation's ethical code dictates that advertisements should tell the truth, avoid misleading the public through omission of important facts, and adhere to public standards of good taste and decency. Does an ad that uses the sexual appeal tell the truth? Does it provide all significant facts the consumer needs to make an informed purchasing decision? Is it in keeping with current social standards of good taste? These are questions advertisers should ask themselves before using a sexual appeal. But there is another question that should be encapsulated in any ethical code of advertising. Does the message in the ad contribute substantively to documented public health concerns and social ills? If yes, the ad message is ethically suspect and needs to be revised.

Conclusion

Beyond the substantive ethical argument against many sexual advertisements, there is another argument against the use of the sexual appeal in advertising – and it is this argument that may be most persuasive. Sexualized sales messages have permeated the world of advertising to such an extent that they are just plain uninteresting and, in many cases, ineffective.

What would the media landscape look like without sex in advertising? Would the creative minds in advertising come up with better, more entertaining, more publicly useful messages? O brave new world that has such ads in it! It's a world we all deserve to see and to live in.

References

Brown, J. D., and S. N. Keller (2000). Can the mass media be healthy sex educators? *Family Planning Perspectives* 32(5): 255–6.

Centers for Disease Control (2006). *Morbidity and mortality weekly report, youth risk behavior surveillance – United States, 2005* (No. SS-5). <http://www.cdc.gov/mmwr/PDF/SS/SS5505.pdf>, accessed July 17, 2006.

Crawford, K. (2004). Ads for women are "Miss Understood." *CNN Money* (Sept. 22). <http://cnnmoney.printthis.clickability.com>, accessed 12 July, 2006.

Critser, G. (2004). *Fat land: How Americans became the fattest people in the world.* Boston: Mariner Books.

Darroch, J. E., J. J. Frost, S. Singh, and the study team (2001). *Teenage sexual and reproductive behavior in developed countries: Can more progress be made?* (Occasional Report No. 3). New York and Washington: Alan Guttmacher Institute.

Dolliver, M. (1999). Is there too much sexual imagery in advertising? *Adweek* 40(11): 22.

Fass, A. (2001). Clairol tones down a campaign in an effort to give its new hair products a separate personality. *New York Times* (Jun. 25): C8.

Fister, S. M., and G. T. Smith (2004). Media effects on expectancies: Exposure to realistic female images as a protective factor. *Psychology of Addictive Behaviors* 18(4): 394–7.

Kilbourne, J. (2005). What else does sex sell? *International Journal of Advertising* 24(1): 119–22.

Lanis, K., and K. Covell (1995). Images of women in advertisements: Effects on attitudes related to sexual aggression. *Sex Roles* 32: 639–49.

Mintel Reports (2005, April). *Weight control – U.S.* Chicago: Mintel Group. Retrieved July 11, 2006, from the Mintel database.

Monro, F., and G. Huon (2005). Media-portrayed idealized images, body shame, and appearance anxiety. *International Journal of Eating Disorders* 38(1): 85–90.

Nudd, T. (2005). Does sex really sell? *Adweek* 46(40), 14–17.

Pardun, C., K. L. L'Engle, and J. D. Brown (2005). Linking exposure to outcomes: Early adolescents' consumption of sexual content in six media. *Mass Communication and Society* 8(2): 75–91.

Parnes, L. (2006). Remarks made on January 25 at the 2006 Annual Advertising Law & Business Conference, Association of National Advertisers, Orlando, FL, from the Federal Trade Commission website. <http://www.ftc.gov/speeches/parnes/0601lydiaanaspeech.pdf>, accessed July 17, 2006.

Preston, I. L. (1998). Puffery and other "loophole" claims: How the law's "don't ask, don't tell" policy condones fraudulent falsity in advertising. *Journal of Law and Commerce* 18: 49–114.

Reichert, T. (2002). Sex in advertising research: A review of content, effects, and functions of sexual information in consumer advertising. *Annual Review of Sex Research* 13: 241–73.

Reichert, T., J. Lambiase, et al. (1999). Cheesecake and beefcake: No matter how you slice it, sexual explicitness in advertising continues to increase. *Journalism and Mass Communication Quarterly* 76(1): 7–20.

Roberts, T., and J. Y. Gettman (2004). Mere exposure: Gender differences in the negative effects of priming a state of self-objectification. *Sex Roles* 51(1/2): 17–28.

Stice, E., E. Schupak-Neuberg, H. E. Shaw, and R. I. Stein (1994). Relation of media exposure to eating disorder symptomatology: An examination of mediating mechanisms. *Journal of Abnormal Psychology* 103(4): 836–40.

9

Stereotypes in Advertising

A Code to Help Us Understand a Concept Quickly? Or a Short-Changing Way to Look at the World?

It's easy to make a list of stereotypes we see in advertising. A wife who really gets excited when she cooks a homemade meal with Hamburger Helper. A husband who can't stand shopping with this wife. An old grandpa sitting on his rocker after eating oatmeal. A wayward skateboard-steering teenager who doesn't understand why his parents won't let him drive the family car. The brainy Asian math whiz. We are certainly not at a loss for images that stereotypes help us create.

While it may be easy to say stereotyping is wrong, when an advertiser has 15 or 30 seconds to tell a story, it's more challenging to explain the importance of eating oatmeal to control cholesterol if the viewer can't quickly see that the person on screen obviously needs the product! Even if we think stereotypes are expected – even necessary – in advertising, the issue is only going to become more complicated in the future. Here's why.

First, our society is becoming more segmented, so even if stereotypes are, indeed, helpful as Marie Hardin argues, it is becoming more difficult to create a meaningful stereotype that the audience can resonate with right away. For example, consider the aging population. There are currently more than 20 million Americans who are over 50 years old. Where a generation ago, "over 50" might mean middle age – or even "over the hill" – being 50 is more complicated today. Yes, many people in their fifties are, indeed, grandparents, but some are also new parents themselves. Some are competitive athletes, some are on the "most beautiful people" list, some are college students, and some, indeed, are Florida retirees, spending their days on the golf courses around the state.

Second, it is harder than ever to get a viewer's attention when it comes to commercials. Now that TiVo and other technologies are common, as well as programming on demand, advertisers have to be more daring, more targeted, more "in your face" to get your attention for even a few seconds. It could be that the days of gentle stereotyping are over! If an advertiser is too subtle, the message is most likely to get lost.

Third, in this media-saturated world, consumers have become more sophisticated about what the media can (and can't) do. Many look suspiciously at the message advertisers provide. So if it's not authentic, the consumer may very well ignore the message. If an advertiser doesn't use a stereotype, there is probably just as much chance that audience members will criticize the advertiser for being "too real" (i.e., "the company is trying too hard") and thus the company ends up being criticized as much as (or more than) if it would have been had it just gone ahead and used the stereotype.

So, what's the right way to handle stereotypes in advertising? Do we get offended if we're "made fun of" stereotypically? Or do we decide that it's a technique to quickly grab our attention and then let us decide what to make of the message? Are all stereotypes bad? Or can a "good stereotype" ("hardworking, patriotic blue-collar employee," for example) benefit the demographic that is getting praised?

Finally, we need to wrestle with the issue of why stereotypes in advertising may be an ethical issue in the first place. How important is it for us to get the "whole picture" before we make a judgment about a person? Does it matter if we judge fictional people (characters in advertising) quickly? Some people might argue that if we don't see a person accurately – even in an advertisement – then we are setting ourselves up for treating "real" people too simplistically, and, therefore, not ethically. Or, as Jane Marcellus mentions in her essay, when we believe stereotypes, we begin to expect that people will act in a certain way, which may be short-sighted and ignore the complexity of the person. Other people would say a stereotype is only an entrance into a person's life – not a definition of it. These are tough questions. What ethical role – if any – do stereotypes have in advertising? *You decide.*

Ideas to get you thinking . . .

1   Make a list of all the stereotypes you can think of. Start with the most obvious. (Housewife, football player, grandmother, etc. . . .) Then write a one-word description of the label. Now see if a classmate or friend can match the descriptions with the stereotypes. What did you learn?
2   Watch your favorite television program. List every kind of stereotype that you come across in the show. Be as specific as possible. What did you find?
3   Flip through a magazine. Every time you come across a stereotype, make a note of it. Are there certain groups that come up more than others? Which ones?

If you'd like to read more . . .

McElya, M. (2007). *Clinging to mammy: The faithful slave in twentieth-century America.* Cambridge, MA: Harvard University Press.
Parkin, K. J. (2007). *Advertising and gender roles in modern America.* Philadelphia: University of Pennsylvania Press.
Robinson, T. E., and T. E. Robinson II (1998). *Portraying older people in advertising.* London: Taylor & Francis.

Argument

Stereotypes are the best way to give consumers a quick understanding of the creative impact of the message

Marie Hardin

The 2008 Super Bowl, like most of its predecessors, provided fodder for Monday morning chatter not so much for the game as for what took place during the timeouts: the commercials (Do you remember who played? Answer: the New York Giants and the New England Patriots). Advertising during the Super Bowl attracts more viewers than any other single time slot for television. The price tag is high: 30 seconds of airtime for the Giants–Patriots game costs upwards of $2.7 million – or $90,000 a second (Sutel, 2008).

Talk about pressure – the adage "make every second count" takes on a whole new meaning. The advertiser must create a memorable message that distinguishes the product and appeals to viewers at an emotional level – and all in front of a television audience with high expectations trained by years of great Super Bowl commercials. (For those who were around, who can forget Mean Joe Greene sharing his ice-cold Coke – and a smile – with a young fan in a famous 1980 spot?)

So, what are some practical strategies for advertisers at this level? How do they *very* quickly immerse viewers in the narrative? Without seconds to spare, they don't have time to explain everything. They need shortcuts to create characters and storylines with impact.

Stereotypes provide those much-needed shortcuts. In fact, without them, you would be hard-pressed to do much at all for a client or a consumer in 30 seconds. Using stereotypes isn't a luxury for effective advertisers – it's a necessity. Stereotypes are the best way to cut through the background and get directly to a storyline that will sell.

The Truth about Stereotypes

You may be surprised to learn that stereotypes are *essential* to advertising, especially if you've learned that they are always bad. Unfortunately, the term "stereotype" has a negative connotation because people often associate only negative generalizations about others with the term; positive generalizations, however, also are stereotypes (Sheehan, 2004). Stereotypes, simply defined, are a group's generalized and accepted beliefs about the attributes of members of another group. Thus, the idea that "children love to play" is just as much of a stereotype as "men are naturally more athletic than women." The second idea is more likely to be tagged as a "stereotype" than the first, although they both fit the definition (Sheehan, 2004).

Stereotypes perform a necessary function. They are the natural, normal "noise filters" that people use (admittedly or not) to sort through the web of social groups they encounter every day in the world around them; stereotypes are an attempt to understand differences among social groups (Schneider, 2004). Indeed, they can enrich our view of the world because they remind us that we are different from others (Schneider, 2004).

The United States is a constantly shifting kaleidoscope of ethnic, racial, and social groups. More than half of the population is made up of women, who were until less than a century ago denied the right to vote but who have in recent years started to outpace men in achieving a college education. Further, one in every three people in the U.S. is a person of color, according to 2005 Census data (Altstiel and Grow, 2006). Some states are now labeled "majority minority" by the Census, meaning that although they compose the largest single racial group, whites are outnumbered by a combination of ethnic and racial minorities including Hispanics and African Americans (Bernstein, 2005). Further, the number of Americans who are in or near retirement or who identify themselves as disabled is also growing.

It's an increasingly complex culture, making the use of stereotypes even more essential because, for anyone, it is impossible to gather a complete, up-to-date picture of other groups and individuals before interacting with them. Think about the college setting, for instance. You were thrust into classrooms where many people looked like your high-school classmates, but many didn't. You probably also encountered people on the spectrum of sexuality and ability, perhaps interacting closely with them in your classes. You also had to deal with a professor for the first time. In all of these situations, whether you realized it or not, the stereotypes you had formed helped you navigate situations. (Such as deciding, for instance, not to invite your professor to your fraternity party.)

Stereotypes are not universal, nor are they fixed. In other words, they change, and they are situated in your culture (McGarty et al., 2002; Schneider, 2004). In relationship to time and context, think about stereotypes involving people who have tattoos, for instance. There was a time (ask your parents) when the stereotype of a person with a tattoo was of someone likely associated with alcohol and drugs. Then, in the 1990s, tattoos became much more mainstream, and the stereotype evolved. They also vary by culture. For instance, ask a Brit, an American and a German what it means to be French, and you will likely get three different answers (de Mooij, 2005). Understanding the cultural context of target consumers is key to effective use of stereotypes in advertising.

Being Responsible with Stereotypes

Advertising is just one form of communication that relies on stereotypes as shortcuts to meaning (Schneider, 2004). Stereotypes are used in movies, on television, in books, and in your everyday conversation. Anytime reality has to be simplified – compressed, if you will – stereotypes are necessary for their power to convey characters and images quickly and clearly (de Mooij, 2005; Sheehan, 2004). The time and space constraints of advertising and any other commercially driven message simply cannot allow for a complete representation of people from any given social group.

Recognizing that you can't provide nuanced or comprehensive images of any group should also clue you in to the importance of using stereotypes responsibly. Depending on how they are formed and used, stereotypes can present problems. They can be used in *functional* or *dysfunctional* ways. They are *functional* when they are accepted as a natural way to guide our expectations. They are *dysfunctional* when they are used as the sole way to wholly judge individuals (de Mooij, 2005). That's where stereotypes get their negative connotation – in the tendency by some to reduce people to classes based on inferences (Sheehan, 2004). Dysfunctional use of stereotypes does, indeed, have negative consequences because it could justify the mistreatment of certain groups. For instance, if you belonged to a group that was consistently and solely presented as irresponsible, lazy, or incapable of leadership, you'd have good reason to resent the stereotype when you were turned down for jobs by people who relied on the stereotype to make hiring decisions (Sheehan, 2004).

Advertisers, then, are responsible for using stereotypes in functional ways. An example of a functional stereotype would be an understanding of the role of time to different ethnic groups. To understand that German and Spanish people generally regard notions of time and being punctual differently could come in handy; for instance, to design an ad with a story-line that involves a German character being concerned about running late for a meeting would work, but doing so with a Spanish character would not (de Mooij, 2005).

Obviously, advertisers should avoid using stereotypes in dysfunctional ways. When they do, they are often embarrassed by the resulting bad publicity and outright rejection by consumers, who see the stereotypes as outdated or offensive. One example is an ad for Snickers candy bars during the 2007 Super Bowl: The ad depicted two men pulling out their chest hair to demonstrate their "manliness" after an accidental kiss as they ate from both ends of a candy bar. Advocacy groups for lesbians and gays justifiably complained about the ad because it implied that to be a gay man automatically meant to also be effeminate, which is considered a negative trait in U.S. culture. In short, the ad used overt displays of "manliness" to judge between gay and straight men – a dysfunctional stereotype.

Smart Advertising and the Use of Stereotypes

Because stereotypes are essential to good advertising, smart advertisers spend a lot of time making sure the way they use them is effective. Dysfunctional use of stereotypes – just like bad design, poor copywriting, or ineffective placement – diminishes an ad's effectiveness. Smart (functional) use of stereo-types can make an ad funny, entertaining, and memorable.

Think about your favorite ads, and you'll find that a key reason you like them is that they combine stereotypes with storylines in imaginative and unconventional ways. For instance, one recent ad campaign used a *recursive* strategy, which involves spoofing stereotypes. If you were near a television even for a few minutes in 2007, you likely saw the ads, which used a caveman protesting the stereotype that cavemen are unsophisticated. The series of ads placed the caveman and his friends in a number of situations all spoofing the stereotype. The campaign, for Geico car insurance, became so popular that ABC requested pilot episodes for a sitcom.

Another ad, which was rated by critics as one of the most effective spots that aired during the 2007 Super Bowl, also involved an ultra-clever play on the idea of stereotypes. The Fedex spot shows an office meeting in which a worker questions the use of "ground" in the name of a Fedex service that promises fast delivery. He receives responses from a series of characters with names that truly stereotype them: a long-haired, bearded man named "Harry," a giggling woman named "Joy," and, finally, a double-chinned man named "Mr. Turkeyneck."

Effective advertisers also use multiple images of a single group instead of consistently relying on one stereotype. For instance, images of women in advertising have expanded dramatically to keep pace with their changing role in U.S. society. Advertisers recognize that the image of woman as stay-at-home mom is dysfunctional because it is out of date and could be perceived negatively; thus, stereotypes have expanded to include mothers with careers, and single women. Even images of body type have expanded, a welcome development in light of decades of unrealistically thin depictions. Examples of a range of images in a single ad can be seen in campaigns by Dove and by Nike, which include women of different sizes, shapes, and ages. By using progressive stereotypes, these advertisers expand the storyline – and, ultimately, their potential for sales. They also reflect the reality of U.S. culture and help shape the formation of more progressive stereotypes for consumers (Halter, 2000).

If you're planning on going into advertising, you'll learn a lot more about stereotypes and how you can use them more effectively and responsibly to communicate. Just as you naturally use them in your everyday decision-making and conversation, you'll find stereotypes an indispensable part of crafting ads with impact.

References

Altstiel, T., and J. Grow (2006). *Advertising strategy: Creative tactics from the outside/in.* Thousand Oaks, CA: Sage.

Bernstein, R. (2005). Texas becomes nation's newest "majority-minority" state, Census Bureau announces. *U.S. Census Bureau News* (Aug. 11). <http://www.census.gov/Presss-Release/www/releases/archives/population/005514.html>.

de Mooij, M. (2005). *Global marketing and advertising: Understanding cultural paradoxes.* Thousand Oaks, CA: Sage.

Halter, M. (2000). *Shopping for identity: The marketing of ethnicity.* New York: Schocken Books.

McGarty, C., R. Spears, and V. Y. Yzerbyt (2002). Conclusion: Stereotypes are selective, variable and contested explanations. In C. McGarty, V. Y. Yzerbyt, and R. Spears (eds.), *Stereotypes as explanations: The formation of meaningful beliefs about social groups* (pp. 186–99). Cambridge: Cambridge University Press.

Schneider, D. J. (2004). *The psychology of stereotyping.* New York: Guilford Press.

Sheehan, K. (2004). *Controversies in contemporary advertising.* Thousand Oaks, CA: Sage.

Sutel, S. (2008). Companies banking on Super Bowl ads. KansasCity.com (Jan. 27). <http://www.kansascity.com/438/story/463248.html>, accessed Jan. 28, 2008.

Counterargument

What's the harm in advertising stereotypes?

Jane Marcellus

In a television advertisement for new Scrubbing Bubbles brand automatic shower cleaner, an African American woman tells the audience about the product as four more women in maids uniforms – all, like the narrator, middle-aged and overweight – climb inside a shower stall together and scrub it clean.

In an issue of *GQ* magazine (June 2006), several ads feature young white men with windblown hair and urbane expressions. Little copy accompanies these images. In most cases there is just the brand – clothing by Calvin Klein, Nautica, Banana Republic, or Prada, or cologne labeled Polo by Ralph Lauren, john varvatos, Burberry Brit. Still more ads feature white men shooting pool, riding mountain bikes, or sitting in front of a bookshelf talking about Swiss watches.

In contrast, one of the only African American men in the magazine is found in an ad for Hennessy's "Privilège" cognac. The black man is large and bald and wears a trenchcoat. He walks down a shadowy city street at night, hands in his pockets, looking back over one shoulder. In the background are two more people – one whose race and sex are unclear but the other a young white woman who seems to eye the black man warily. "I have seen Count Basie live. I have conviction. I have given back. I have 14 countries stamped on my passport. I have never forgotten where I'm from," the man tells us. Below these words is the ambiguous question, "Are you Privilèged?"

Meanwhile, in an issue of *Teen Vogue* (June/July 2006), ads for cosmetics and clothing feature skinny young women with flawless complexions. Many wear bikinis. This makes sense in the sunscreen ad, but even ads for lipstick and cellphones feature women in swimsuits. At least they wear something. In *GQ*, women are nude. An ad for Evian bottled water shows a woman lying naked on a snow-capped mountain, strategically placed flurries hiding her breasts.

But is there anything really wrong with these images? Don't they help sell the products? They don't really hurt anybody, right?

Wrong. These images are blatant stereotypes, and they do cause harm.

"Stereotype" is a word that comes from early printing, where it had to do with using a metal plate to produce the same image over and over. Nowadays, the *Oxford English Dictionary* says, it refers to an "oversimplified idea" that is used, like those metal plates in printing, over and over again. ("Cliché," by the way, has similar roots.)

While using simple, familiar images may seem like the fastest way to communicate in the blink of time an advertiser has to capture audience attention, it is still problematic. British cultural studies theorist Stuart Hall (1997: 257) said stereotyping "reduces people to a few, simple, essential characteristics, which are represented as fixed by Nature" – a process called *essentializing*. Hall (1997: 258) said stereotyping most often occurs where one group is more powerful than another. Difference is emphasized as the less powerful group becomes "the Other" (1997: 258) and the social power of the dominant group is maintained.

The main problem with stereotypes is that we start to see the world in terms of these preconceived notions. That is what causes harm. As Walter Lippmann wrote in his classic work *Public Opinion* (1922), stereotypes are "pictures in our heads" that affect the way we look at what's around us. "For the most part we do not first see, and then define, we define first and then see. In the great blooming, buzzing confusion of the outer world we pick out what our culture has already defined for us, and we tend to perceive that which we have picked out in the form stereotyped for us by our culture" (1922: 81).

In the ads described above, women and black men are both essentialized. The drudgery of cleaning the bathroom falls *naturally* to older, dowdy women, while young women in *Teen Vogue* are *naturally* thin and flawless in order, of course, to please boys. In *GQ*, male readers are invited to gaze at the naked woman in the snow or, in the same issue, at the women lounging in swimsuits around a pool in a Caesars Palace ad. These ads are perfect illustrations of Laura Mulvey's (1992) point that the "male gaze" constructs women as sexual objects in an "erotic spectacle." According to this idea, the way men see women determines their value, so women see themselves according to how they think men will evaluate them. Both sexes see women as objects.

The black man, meanwhile, is also essentialized, for it seems *natural* in our culture for him to lurk on a city street. That's why he has to explain his background. White men, who dominate the magazine in terms of both numbers and variety of images, do not. That we see ads like these over and over again without questioning their supposedly natural assumptions is at the heart of the harm they do. In seeing such images as natural, we expect real people to play out similar roles.

One way to explain this process is through *cultivation theory*, a hypo-thesis put forth by George Gerbner (1973). Cultivation theory says that tele-vision, in particular, has such power over the way we see the world that, as Denis McQuail (1994: 365) put it, "It is not a window on or a reflection of the world but a world in itself." Over time, people see what's around them in terms of this symbolic world. For example, those who watch a lot of violent shows see the world as a violent place. And those who see a lot of ads where only women scrub bathrooms and black men look surreptitiously over their shoulders on dark city streets begin to believe that these are natural behaviors for real people in these groups. We *expect* bath-rooms to be cleaned by dowdy women. We *expect* black men to lurk.

And that hurts people. In this case, it harms real women and real black men. It harms their ability to be seen as the thinking, feeling, unique individuals they are. It harms everyone else's ability to know them. If, as Lippmann said, we define first, then see, we don't really see at all.

Is selling bathroom cleaner or cognac worth that?

But maybe you're still not convinced.

Sometimes, it helps to take a step back in time and gain a historical perspective. Let's go back to that African American woman narrating the Scrubbing Bubbles ad. Does she just happen to be black? Or does she have what Raymond Williams (1961) called "cultural ancestors" whose presence in media of the past make her presence in media now seem natural?

Go to the store (or maybe to your kitchen cabinet) and look at the image of the black woman on Aunt Jemima pancake mix. She has the bright smile, neat white collar, and pearl earrings that any professional woman today would be proud to wear to an executive job. But she used to look quite different. From the 1890s, when the product was introduced, until the mid-twentieth century, she was an overweight black woman with a rag around her head – the typical "mammy" from the ante-bellum South. In fact, the first model for Aunt Jemima actually *was* a 59-year-old former slave named Nancy Green (<http://adage.com/century/icon07.html>). In a 1919 ad that ran in *Ladies' Home Journal*, Aunt Jemima was called, paradoxically, "the cook whose cabin became more famous than Uncle Tom's" – a reference, of course, to Harriet Beecher Stowe's anti-slavery novel, *Uncle Tom's Cabin*.

Back in those unapologetically racist times, the black "mammy" who some-times spoke in dialect was common in ads for household products. The

woman in a 1928 ad for an insecticide called Flit says, "Dat little easy con-
traption do de wuk of six of dem giggling house gals in de old days" –
referring to slave times. A 1931 ad in *Forbes* magazine urges businessmen
to use "Clarinda" (another mammy with a rag on her head) along with
the new imaging process of rotogravure to sell their products. "Fresh, savory,
delightful – ten thousand such words would not tell the sales story of
freshness as vividly and dramatically as the camera and Clarinda tell it
here," says this ad, which features Chase and Sanborn coffee as an example of what "Clarinda" could sell. These types of images only changed when
people became more sensitive to racist stereotypes. Aunt Jemima was
modernized gradually, with the current Aunt Jemima introduced in 1989
(<http://adage.com/century/icon07.html>).

But have they gone away completely? If you think so, then why does it
seem natural in American culture today for bathroom cleaner (or, in
another ad, medicine for constipation) to be sold by plump black women
with "down home" plainspokenness, even if they do not wear rags around
their heads? Who are their cultural ancestors?

Other groups are also stereotyped. As Debra Merskin wrote, "Trade characters such as Aunt Jemima (pancake mix), Uncle Rastus (Cream of Wheat),
and Uncle Ben (rice) are visual reminders of the subservient occupational
positions to which Blacks often have been relegated" (Merskin 2001: 160).
In the same way, she said, "Crazy Horse Malt Liquor, Red Chief Sugar, and
Sue Bee Honey similarly remind us of an oppressive past" for Native
Americans (2001: 160). Today's images of Native Americans are heir to such
stereotypes, she said (2001: 159), for they draw on ideas of "Indianness"
that many people learned as children. In the case of African Americans,
the cultural purpose of such stereotypes, she said, was originally to help
"make Whites feel more comfortable with, and less guilty about, mainten-
ance of distinctions on the basis of race well after Reconstruction." Their
daily use had the effect of "constantly and subtly reinforcing stereotypical
beliefs" (2001: 160). The same can be said for any other group that is made
"Other."

But are such images always bad? What's wrong with putting a pretty
young Native American woman on the front of the Land O' Lakes butter
carton? What's wrong with a black man walking down a city street?
Doesn't the fact that he drinks cognac, travels, and likes Count Basie tell
us that this particular black man is an educated sophisticate?

It depends. One way to judge a stereotype is to look at the other images
around it. In the *GQ* issue, for example, we are invited to see white men

in a variety of ways, but the choice for black men is limited. Moreover, even if he is a cognac-swilling sophisticate with a penthouse apartment and a six-figure salary, the words "I have never forgotten where I'm from" imply that his past is, well, less than "Privilèged." The stereotype is invoked, even if it is subverted, while the white men's individual pasts are not in question. Is this the only way to sell cognac?

And do all five people in the Scrubbing Bubbles ad really need to be dowdy, middle-aged women? Would a greater variety of types of people not be possible? Is there no other way to sell this product?

Of course, not everyone derives the same meaning from any given advertisement. *Polysemy* refers to the idea that some people interpret media images differently from others, while *polyvalence* means they apply different values. Maybe to you, that black man in the trenchcoat would look self-assured, not frightening. Maybe the white woman across the street looking his way would seem to have something other than fear in mind. And the black woman in the Scrubbing Bubbles ad? Arguably, as the narrator, maybe you would see her as the one in power – the lady of the house in charge of white maids, rather than the head maid.

We still need to remember, however, that for these images to make any sense at all to us, they must draw on ideas rooted deep in our cultural memory. Otherwise we would not be able to interpret them. Moreover, we may not always be conscious of why an ad stereotype resonates with us. "Ads seem to seep quietly into the back room of our consciousness," said Anthony J. Cortese (1999: 27). They have the power, he said, to "try to tell us who we are and who we should be" (1999: 12).

Advertising creates an imaginary world that teaches us how to see the real world – and how to see ourselves. Because ads have so much social power, those who create them have a responsibility to do so in a way that does not reinforce unequal power structures. The ability to do that is one indication, in the twenty-first century, of a truly creative, truly responsible advertising professional.

References

Cortese, A. (1999). *Provocateur: Images of women and minorities in advertising.* Lanham, MD: Rowman & Littlefield.

Gerbner, G. (1973). Cultural indicators – the third voice. In G. Gerbner, L. Gross, and W. Melody (eds.), *Communication technology and social policy* (pp. 555–73). New York: Wiley.

Hall, S. (1997). *Representation: Cultural representation and signifying practices.* Thousand Oaks, CA: Sage.

Lippmann, W. (1922). *Public opinion.* New York: Macmillan.

McQuail, D. (1994). *Mass communication theory: An introduction.* London: Sage.

Merskin, D. (2001). Winnebagos, Cherokees, Apaches, and Dakotas: The persistence of stereotyping of American Indians in American advertising brands. *The Howard Journal of Communications* 12: 159–69.

Mulvey, L. (1992). Visual pleasure and narrative cinema. In *The sexual subject: A Screen reader in sexuality* (pp. 22–34). New York and London: Routledge.

Williams, R. (1961). *The long revolution.* New York: Columbia University Press.

10

Direct-to-Consumer Pharmaceutical Advertising

A Prescription for Everything?

You've seen these ads in magazines and on your favorite television shows. Some of them make a lot of sense. Who wouldn't believe Sally Field when she urges us to ask our doctor whether we need to swallow a pill "just once a month!" to make sure our bones stay healthy?

While it may seem as if we've been watching drug ads our whole lives, the exponential growth in expenditure on them has been phenomenal and recent (from $800 million to $2.5 billion over five years according to some experts), to create messages directly to you, the consumer. Some of this money used for advertising most likely is diverted, at least in part, from important budget items such as research and development. Before the market explosion, conventional thinking was that medicine was too complex for the patient; the only person who knew enough about the drugs you need was your own family physician. How times have changed!

In some ways, watching the growth of direct-to-consumer drug advertising is like watching advertising research happening before our very eyes. How we view direct-to-consumer advertising specifically might help us better understand what we really think about advertising in general. For example, do we think that viewing an advertisement can directly cause us to want to buy the specific product advertised? If we think this is plausible (believing the "big effects" perspective of advertising), then we might be extra concerned about the deregulation of direct-to-consumer drug advertising. Could I possibly know all the side effects of Lunestra? I thought it would just help me sleep better. But if I think advertising is that powerful I might need the government (or some other objective outsider) to regulate messages to make sure what I'm hearing is true – and won't hurt me if I decide to swallow the medicine!

However, if I tend to subscribe to the "limited effects" perspective of advertising, I'm most likely to not be all that worried about drug advertising since it's not really going to have much of an effect on me. Maybe advertising does little to directly impact my need to buy things. Maybe the advertising ultimately merely helps me to seek more information about a drug or a disease. For example, maybe I don't sleep well at night. Then I see the commercial for Lunestra and realize, "Wow, there is a drug that can help people sleep." I go to the doctor, not to ask her to order me a year's supply, but instead to tell her that I can't sleep and I've learned that there might be some way to help. She may or may not prescribe Lunestra to help me with my insomnia. But the most important thing is that I've communicated with the doctor – and I might not have if I hadn't seen the drug commercial. Or that's how the argument goes.

Even in this enormous advertising spending milieu on direct-to-consumer advertising, the government sometimes questions the practice. For example, in 2005 the Federal Drug Administration (FDA) asked Amylin Pharmaceutical Company to hold off on advertising its diabetes medication Symlin directly to consumers for one year.

The authors of the following essays each lay out reasonable and persuasive arguments for and against direct-to-consumer drug advertising. Beth Barnes sums up her essay quite clearly by stating early on that information does not always equal knowledge. So we may be taking a dangerous pill if we swallow the messages in drug advertising! Debbie Triese and Paula Rausch, however, just as persuasively argue that direct-to-consumer advertising causes consumers to seek more information; the doctor ultimately decides whether the patient needs the drug. Who's right? *You decide.*

Ideas to get you thinking . . .

1 Take a few minutes and list out all the names of drugs you've heard of. Now, think about any ads for them. Do you think the advertising has an impact on your ability to name the drug? Why, or why not?
2 Are there certain drugs that you might think are okay to advertise on television? If so, which ones would be okay? Are there other drugs that should not be advertised? Which ones? How would you argue that one kind is okay, but another kind is not?

If you'd like to read more . . .

Angell, M. (2005). *The truth about the drug companies. How they deceive us and what to do about it*. London: Random House.

Goozner, M. (2005). *The $800 million pill: The truth behind the cost of new drugs*. Berkeley, CA: University of California Press.

Newman, L. M. (ed.) (2005). *Does advertising promote substance abuse?* Farmington Hills, MI: Greenhaven Press.

Argument

Doctor knows best: why DTC advertising of prescription medications is bad for patients

Beth E. Barnes

Direct-to-consumer (DTC) pharmaceutical advertising is big business. In the United States, one of only two countries that allow DTC advertising (the other is New Zealand [Richardson and Luchsinger, 2005]), $3.45 billion was spent on this type of advertising during the March 31, 2003–March 31, 2004 period (Finlayson and Mullner, 2005). When the U.S. Food and Drug Administration (FDA) acted in 1997 to make it easier for pharmaceutical firms to advertise their products directly to consumers through television and print ads and online, the reasoning was that more information would lead to better-informed patient decisions (Kaiser, 2003). But, information does not always equal knowledge. This essay will examine reasons why DTC advertising actually hurts patients rather than helping them.

Doctor–Patient Relationships

The relationship between patients and their healthcare provider is a delicate thing, based on trust on the patient's part that his or her doctor is a highly trained professional with the expertise to diagnose and treat ailments in the most effective way possible.

To the extent that DTC advertising leads patients to second-guess their physician, this type of advertising erodes the foundation of the doctor–patient relationship. In a 1998 report, shortly after the rules for broadcast DTC ads were relaxed and DTC ads began to proliferate, the American College of Physicians (1998) reported that its members "are besieged with requests for specific products patients have seen in advertisements."

Singh and Smith (2005) found that 40 percent of the adults they surveyed reported asking about a drug they had seen advertised, and 17 percent asked to be prescribed a specific brand of drug. Hausman and Kopp (2003) surveyed Hispanic consumers and found that 40 percent had asked their doctor for a drug they had seen advertised.

A survey of members of the National Medical Association, a group for African American doctors, revealed many complaints about DTC advertising. Among the 322 doctors who responded to the survey, 76 percent said "ads make people think meds work better than they do"; 76 percent said the ads "confuse people about the relative risks and benefits of drugs"; and 65 percent said "ads cause patients to second-guess diagnoses." 54 percent of the doctors said "they feel pressured to prescribe particular drugs because of ads" (Arnold, 2007).

Bradford et al. (2006) reviewed patient visit records for practices specializing in treating osteoarthritis. They compared the visit data with advertising expenditures and placement for two osteoarthritis drugs, Celebrex and Vioxx. Their analysis showed an increase in osteoarthritis patient visits to doctors that was associated with increased advertising for the two drugs. And their results suggested that patient visits led to prescriptions: "Once patients arrived at the physician's office, it was clear that DTC advertising tended to change the rate at which COX-2 inhibitors were prescribed. . . . In summary, DTC advertising for COX-2 inhibitors appears to have affected physician practices and patients" (Bradford et al., 2006: 1376).

Patients, however well informed they might be through advertisements and websites, do not have the rigorous training of physicians. They cannot understand all the issues related to drug interactions, possible side effects, and the like. While it is the physician's ultimate responsibility to prescribe or not prescribe a specific drug, the time that must be taken to talk a patient out of a drug they have seen advertised that may not be right for them is not only costly, but has the potential to erode the patient's trust in the physician.

Quality of Information

There are also questions about the usefulness of the information provided in DTC ads and on DTC websites. As noted above, the Federal Trade Commission (FTC) relaxed the requirements for DTC ads on television in 1997. The major change that was made was to no longer require DTC television ads to include the so-called "brief summary" (Macias and Lewis, 2003/4). The brief summary is a listing of "side effects, contraindications, and effectiveness" (FDA, 2004).

Without the information included in the brief summary, patients who only see DTC television advertising are ill informed at best about the drugs advertised and may even be misinformed. While all advertising is one-sided, talking only about the possible benefits of a drug without noting any of its negative qualities provides very little in the way of useful information for making an informed decision about the medication. The potential risks are too high, the potential consequences too great, for such advertising to be the basis on which patients make decisions about which drugs are "right" for them. And yet, as the research cited above shows, many do just that.

In a content analysis of television ads for prescription medications, Frosch et al. (2007) found that the ads studied relied heavily on emotional appeals and that those emotional appeals often overrode any factual claims made in the ads. Few of the ads studied talked about the factors leading to the particular medical condition the drug was intended to treat, or about the risks associated with taking the advertised medication. Frosch et al. conclude that: "By ambiguously defining who might need or benefit from the products, DTCA implicitly focuses on convincing people that they may be at risk for a wide array of health conditions that product consumption might ameliorate, rather than providing education about who may truly benefit from the treatment" (2007: 10).

What about DTC advertising that does carry the brief summary? Who hasn't seen a magazine ad for a prescription drug where the eye-catching, image-building message is followed by a page or more of tiny type listing all the things required by the brief summary and more? The information is certainly there, but is it in a form that is likely to be used by patients? Singh and Smith found that "consumers are not comfortable with the format in which drugs are advertised, they do not feel competent to evaluate the claims made in such advertising, and they are not aware of the various avenues to get more information" (Singh and Smith, 2005: 376).

Websites are fairly well-known possible sources of additional information. Macias and Lewis (2003/4) conducted a content analysis of prescription drug websites and found mixed results as to information content. Among the 83 sites they examined, only 21 percent addressed misconceptions about the condition the drug was intended to treat, and only 23 percent indicated the drug's success rate in treating that condition. Only half the sites included information on how long treatment with the drug would last, and only 52 percent indicated how long it would be before the patient would start to see an effect once they had begun taking the drug.

Advertising messages are used to inform and persuade; sales promotion messages are used to provide an incentive to buy the product. Macias and Lewis (2003/4) found that 52 percent of the websites they analyzed offered some type of financial incentive: rebates, coupons, free samples, or value-added offers of merchandise. Only 47 percent of the sites studied offered more information (video, audio, or printed material) as an incentive. Only three out of the 83 sites offered a patient support program to prospective drug users. So consumers who turn to prescription drug websites find incomplete information combined with monetary or other incentives to use the promoted drug. That hardly seems a situation promoting informed decision-making.

At-Risk Audiences

One intended audience for many prescription drug advertisements is older consumers. They are the people most likely to suffer from many of the ailments the advertised medications claim to treat, and so the most likely to pay attention to such messages (Richardson and Luchsinger, 2005). DeLorme et al. (2006) found that senior citizens do pay attention to DTC advertising, but believe that the effects of such advertising will be greater for other people than for themselves, the classic third-person effect.

Baca et al. (2005) studied college students' reactions to DTC advertising. They found that those most interested in and potentially most influenced by DTC advertising were students who self-reported their own health status as poor; students who rated their health status as good were less interested in and less favorable toward DTC advertising.

This and other evidence that two of the groups most likely to be influenced by DTC advertising are the elderly and those in poor health should raise questions about the ethics of DTC advertising. In the United States, there is a history of both legislation (Levin, 2006) and industry self-regulation (OAAA, 2006) to try and avoid harm to disadvantaged or at-risk groups through advertising practices related to specific products; why should prescription medications be treated differently? If the most likely to be influenced are also the most vulnerable, should there not be protections put in place for those groups?

Economic Consequences

In a statement made to a Federal Trade Commission healthcare workshop, Steven D. Findlay, Director of Research for the National Institute for

Health Care Management Research and Educational Foundation, pointed out that one of the most important arguments against DTC advertising is the cost of such advertising and the impact of that cost on the price of the advertised medicines (Findlay, 2002). Findlay's analysis pointed out that a dramatic increase in health insurance and health plan coverage of prescription drugs overlapped with the loosening of restrictions on DTC advertising and the increase in those messages (Findlay, 2002).

Sales of the top 50 most heavily advertised drugs rose an aggregate 32 percent from 1999 to 2000 compared to 13.6 percent for all other drugs combined. Increases in the sales of these 50 heavily advertised drugs accounted for almost half (47.8 percent) of the overall $20.8 billion rise in spending on drugs in the retail sector from 1999 to 2000 (Findlay, 2002: 3).

Given that pattern, Findlay argued that healthcare insurers, and, by extension, the Food and Drug Administration, would need to work to make sure that consumers could continue to get appropriate medication while not overmedicating needlessly based on demand fueled by DTC advertising (Findlay, 2002).

Shin and Moon (2005) asked the direct question: "is [DTC advertising] the best way to spend nearly $3 billion on health communications to the American public?" Specifically, their concern is that: "DTC advertising for prescription drugs conveys the information that mislead[s] viewers to lean more on the drugs whose prices embed the advertising costs even when they are aware of the availability of cheaper and equally-effective alternatives" (Shin and Moon, 2005: 398–9).

Conclusion

Perhaps the person best qualified to comment on the negative aspects of DTC advertising is former FDA Commissioner David Kessler, now a faculty member in medicine at UC-San Francisco. Kessler and Dr. Douglas A. Levy (2007) summarized the situation in these words:

> consumers who make health decisions based on what they learn from television commercials ultimately take medicines they may not need, spend money on brand medicines that may be no better than alternatives, or avoid healthy behaviors because they falsely think a medicine is all they need. (Kessler and Levy, 2007: 5)

While there are certainly many benefits to increased consumer information, such information is only truly useful if it can be interpreted appropriately. Without the medical knowledge and the full range of information needed to appropriately assess a drug to know if it is indeed the right treatment in a particular situation, DTC advertising does more harm than good.

References

American College of Physicians (1998). Direct to consumer advertising for prescription drugs. (Oct. 9): 3. <http://www.acponline.org/hpp/pospaper/dtcads.htm>.

Arnold, M. (2007). Black docs warm to DTC ad benefits. *Medical Marketing and Media* 42(4): 26.

Baca, E. E., J. Holguin, Jr., and A. W. Stratemeyer (2005). Direct-to-consumer advertising and young consumers: building brand value. *Journal of Consumer Marketing* 22(7): 379–87.

Bradford, W. D., A. N. Kleit, P. J. Nietert, and T. Steyer (2006). How direct-to-consumer television advertising for osteoarthritis drugs affects physicians' prescribing behavior. *Health Affairs* 25(5): 1371–7.

DeLorme, D. E., J. Huh, and L. N. Reid (2006). Perceived effects of direct-to-consumer (DTC) prescription drug advertising on self and others: A third-person effect study of older consumers. *Journal of Advertising* 35(3): 47–65.

FDA (2004). Brief summary: disclosing risk information in consumer-directed print advertisements. U.S. Department of Health and Human Services, Food and Drug Administration, Center for Drug Evaluation and Research, Center for Biological Evaluation and Research (January).

Findlay, S. D. (2002). DTC Advertising: Is it helping or hurting? Statement before the Federal Trade Commission healthcare workshop, Sept. 10.

Finlayson, G., and R. Mullner (2005). Direct-to-consumer advertising of prescription drugs: Help or hindrance to the public's health? *Journal of Consumer Marketing* 22(7): 429–31.

Frosch, D. L., P. M. Krueger, R. C. Hornik, P. F. Cronholm, and F. K. Barg (2007). Creating demand for prescription drugs: A content analysis of television direct-to-consumer advertising. *Annals of Family Medicine* 5(1): 6–13.

Hausman, A., and S. Kopp, S. (2003). DTC advertising and its impact on patient healthcare behaviors: Report presented to FDA's 2003 DTC meeting, Oct. 1. <http://www.fda.gov/cder/ddmac/P3Hausman/>.

Kaiser Family Foundation (2003). *Impact of direct-to-consumer advertising on prescription drug spending.* (June). <http://www.kff.org/rxdrugs/6084-index.cfm>.

Kessler, D. A., and D. A. Levy (2007). Direct-to-consumer advertising: Is it too late to manage the risks? *Annals of Family Medicine* 5(1): 4–5.

Levin, P. (2006). *Tobacco.* National Association of Attorneys General. <http://www.naag.org/tobacco.php>.

Macias, W., and L. S. Lewis (2003/4). A content analysis of direct-to-consumer (DTC) prescription drug web sites. *Journal of Advertising* 32(4). Accessed through EBSCO host.

OAAA (Outdoor Advertising Association of America) (2006). The OAAA Code of Industry Principles. <http://www.oaaa.org/government/codes.asp>.

Richardson, L., and V. Luchsinger (2005). Direct-to-consumer advertising of pharmaceutical products: Issue analysis and direct-to-consumer promotion. *Journal of American Academy of Business* 7(2): 100–5.

Shin, J., and S. Moon (2005). Direct-to-consumer prescription drug advertising: concerns and evidence on consumers' benefit. *Journal of Consumer Marketing* 22(7): 397–403.

Singh, T., and D. Smith (2005). Direct-to-consumer prescription drug advertising: A study of consumer attitudes and behavioral intentions. *Journal of Consumer Marketing* 22(7): 369–78.

Counterargument

Feel empowered! Enhanced health knowledge!
Debbie Treise and Paula Rausch

Americans are increasingly talking to their health providers about the prescription medicines they see advertised for problems from indigestion to "Captain Winky doesn't salute anymore" (Treise and Rausch, in press). Results of a 2004 Harris Interactive survey found that 85 percent of the respondents had seen a direct-to-consumer (DCT) advertisement in the past 12 months (Axelrod, 2006), and studies have shown that these ads can influence perceptions not only about an advertised drug, but also about the disease it treats (Zachry et al., 2003). It is estimated that Americans who watch even average amounts of television are exposed to more than 30 hours of DTC advertising each year from this source alone (Rabin, 2004). Too much?, critics ask. A study by the National Consumers League (2003), the nation's oldest nonprofit advocacy group representing consumers, found not only that a majority believed their access to this free source of information should not be limited, but also that the ads motivated 57 percent of them to seek more information. So, it's clear that DTC advertising has the potential to be one of the most influential modes for boosting consumer empowerment and health literacy among Americans.

The Food and Drug Administration (FDA) itself has recognized the value of DTC advertising. Prescription pharmaceuticals have been marketed to the public since the 1980s. In 1997, however, the administration eased restrictions on broadcast DTC advertisements, and its rationale for doing so was simple: the more restrictive guidelines prevented consumers from obtaining product information (D'Souza et al., 2003).

These relaxed restrictions led to dramatic increases in pharmaceutical advertising expenditures, followed swiftly by an onslaught of debate and criticism. Much of the research conducted on DTC advertising since then suggests there are numerous important and unexpected benefits to consumers that go far beyond the FDA's original reasoning. Indeed, a report issued by the National Health Council in 2002 concluded:

> The preponderance of evidence indicates that most consumers and physicians, as well as the Food and Drug Administration, support DTC advertising as

long as it complies with FDA's regulations and guidelines and refers consumers to their physicians. The benefits are viewed as outweighing any
negative impacts. (NHC, 2002: 2)

Just What Are Those Benefits?

Past studies have found a bounty of benefits to consumers, including:

1 Increased awareness of and education about conditions, symptoms, and
  treatment options leading to better-informed health decision-making,
  and more involvement in and responsibility for healthcare, including
  increased prescription medication regimen compliance.
2 More constructive and informed discussions with healthcare providers.
3 Empowering consumers to come forward to discuss conditions
  thought to be too embarrassing before being addressed in DTC
  advertising.
4 DTC advertising's role in enhancing health literacy.

Each of these benefits will be addressed in turn.

1 Increased awareness of and education about disease and treatment

Several studies focusing on DTC advertising's influence on consumers and
physicians have found surprising and supportive results in terms of increased
consumer awareness of health (Aikin et al., 2004; Cline and Young, 2004;
Holmer, 2002; Treise and Rausch, in press). Indeed, a 2003 FDA study (by
Aiken), conducted with a random sample of 500 American Medical Association (AMA) physicians, found that 72 percent of the participants agreed
"somewhat" to "a great deal" that DTC advertising made their patients more
aware of possible treatments – up from 67 percent reported in NHC (2002)
– while 80 percent believed that patients understood "somewhat" to "very
well" what condition the advertised drug treated. The same FDA AMA study
found that 58 percent of the physicians agreed "somewhat" to "a great deal"
that DTC advertising made patients more involved with their healthcare.

The perceived downside of a more informed consumer is ostensibly the
increased pressure felt by physicians to prescribe the advertised medication to their patients. However, 82 percent of the physicians in the FDA

study indicated that their patients understood "somewhat" or "very well" that only doctors could decide if a certain medication was correct for them, and 91 percent said the patient did not try to influence the course of treatment if the physician felt that it would be harmful to them. It is clear, therefore, that patients believe doctors remain the ultimate gatekeepers in medication decisions. More important, only 8 percent of the surveyed doctors said they felt very pressured – indeed, 72 percent indicated they felt little or no pressure. Asked whether a patient having seen DTC advertising created a problem for their interactions, 82 percent said no (FDA, 2003). Doesn't it seems ludicrous to assume that the same doctor who does not "give in" to a patient requesting narcotics who didn't legitimately need them, would feel the need to do so with patients asking for advertised drugs for erectile dysfunction or depression?

Perhaps the clearest endorsement of a more informed consumer comes from the same FDA AMA study – 88 percent of those patients asking about a specific DTC advertised medication had the condition the drug treats. So, for the 18 percent of surveyed physicians who indicted DTC advertising for causing problems for their interactions with patients – and mostly they said the major problem they encountered was the time they spent correcting misconceptions about the drug – it seems a small sacrifice if 88 percent of the patients do indeed have the condition which the requested drug treats.

Although the reasons are unclear, DTC advertising appears to increase patient compliance with a prescribed drug regimen and to induce patients to use the medications properly (Calfee, 2002). The 2003 FDA study found that 57 percent of the physicians surveyed agreed "somewhat" or "a great deal" that DTC advertising would make patients adhere to a treatment regimen. Perhaps an explanation for that compliance can be found in the results of the NHC 2002 study indicating that about half of those using prescription drugs said the ads make them feel better about the drug's safety.

Additionally, millions of Americans have diseases of which they are unaware, such as diabetes, depression, and high cholesterol, which untreated can have devastating consequences not only for the individual, but also for their family and society (Holmer, 1999). Many of these conditions can be treated by prescription medications, often those that are advertised, which may prompt people to seek additional information about the drugs or the symptoms they treat. In a survey of more than 1,000 adults, the National Consumers League (2003) found that DTC advertising led a majority to take some resulting action, either talking to their doctor (47 percent) or seeking additional information on their own (26 percent) from various other sources, including pharmacists, books, and the internet, to find out if a drug was right for them or a family member.

2 More constructive and informed discussions with healthcare providers

Yes, DTC advertising may increase the amount of time healthcare providers spend with their patients discussing medication, but not all healthcare providers feel this is a bad thing. In fact, the NHC 2000 report confirms that, from the patient perspective, 81 percent reported getting positive responses from their doctors when they discussed drugs they had seen advertised. The National Consumers League (2003) survey found that only 2 percent of respondents said their doctors became upset when asked about an advertised medication. A study conducted in 2006 (Treise and Rausch) found that nurse practitioners, a growing group of healthcare providers, use DTC advertising to "jumpstart conversations" about health. Additionally, the 2003 FDA study indicated that 51 percent of the surveyed physicians felt DTC advertising facilitated better discussions about health, and 56 percent agreed "somewhat" to "a great deal" that DTC advertising helped patients ask better questions. Perhaps this is because patients feel less intimidated and feel more confident discussing their conditions with healthcare providers because of an increased knowledge base (Alexrod, 2006). Other studies have found DTC advertising may enhance doctor–patient relationships (Bonaccorso and Sturchio, 2002; Young and Cline, 2003). Finally, far from the negative impact suggested by some critics, 70 percent of the physicians in the FDA survey indicated either that their practice had not been impacted or had been impacted very positively by DTC advertising.

3 Destigmatizing effects

DTC advertising can be credited with removing or easing some of the fears about diseases or conditions previously felt to be too embarrassing to discuss with patients' healthcare providers:

> A lot of times patients are reluctant to come in and talk about depression.
> And they may have watched a Zoloft ad. In the ad they are describing symptoms of depression: feeling sad, decreased energy, not sleeping well, fearful,

worrying, things like that. A patient will come in and say, "You know, I've been really wrestling with some of the very same things that they've been talking about on this television commercial." So at times it gives them the freedom and permission to come in and relate to something they may have been self conscious about. The ad gives them a little bit of freedom to express that. (Treise and Rausch, in press)

4 Increasing health literacy

DTC advertising also plays a somewhat unexpected role in enhancing health literacy, which has become a national priority (U.S. Department of Health and Human Services, 2000) by facilitating the ability of health providers not only to better assess the health literacy of their patients but also to address it on an individual basis (Rausch and Treise, 2005). A 2004 Institute of Medicine study indicated that 90 million people – about half of U.S. adults – have difficulty understanding and using health information, and estimates suggest these deficiencies of health literacy cost the U.S. healthcare system $58 billion a year (Alspach, 2004). Health literacy has been shown to result in a number of benefits, including "improved self-reported health status, lower healthcare costs, increased health knowledge, shorter hospitalizations, and less frequent use of healthcare services" (Speros, 2005). Erlen suggests that "functional health illiteracy is a silent and hidden disability and a significant barrier to healthcare" (2004: 151), that can decrease a person's sense of self-worth and make them vulnerable to decisions made by others that they don't understand.

Thus, promotion of health literacy is essential, and DTC advertising affords occasions for discussion with providers at the precise times that patients are likely to be most open and responsive to these efforts. By seizing these DTC advertising opportunities, providers are not only able to better educate patients about medications, but they can also enhance patient–provider communication and patient health more generally by providing individualized health literacy training. Such endeavors can have only positive ramifications by enhancing the patient–provider relationship and also by contributing to a nation of better-informed, more satisfied, and healthier consumers. As the president of the National Consumers League said about DTC advertising: "In health care, there is a general trend toward having consumers more responsible for their own health. Now, consumers can go to their physicians with a little more information" (Holmer, 1999).

References

Aiken, K. J. (2003). Direct-to-consumer advertising of prescription drugs: Physician survey preliminary results. <http://www.fda.gov/cder/ddmac/globalsummit2003/sld001.htm>.

Aikin, K. J., J. L. Swasy, and A. C. Braman (2004). *Patient and physician attitudes and behaviors associated with DTC promotion of prescription drugs: Summary of FDA research results.* <http://www.fda.gov>, accessed May 24, 2005.

Alexrod, A. (2006). Direct-to-consumer advertising: A classic case of cognitive dissonance. <http://www.dtcperspectives.com/content.asp?id=223>, accessed September 9, 2006.

Alspach, G. (2004). Communicating health information: An epidemic of the incomprehensible. *Critical Care Nurse* 24(4): 8–13.

Bonaccorso, S. N., and J. L. Sturchio (2002). Direct to consumer advertising is medicalising normal human experience. *British Medical Journal* 324: 910–11.

Calfee, J. E. (2002). Public policy issues in direct-to-consumer advertising of prescription drugs. *Journal of Public Policy and Marketing* 21: 174–93.

Cline, R. J. W., and H. N. Young (2004). Marketing drugs, marketing healthcare relationships: A content analysis of visual cues in direct-to-consumer prescription drug advertising. *Health Communication* 16: 131–57.

D'Souza, A. O., B. T. Lively, W. Siganga, and M. H. Goodman (2003). Effects of direct-to-consumer advertising of prescription drugs: Perceptions of primary care physicians. *Journal of Pharmaceutical Marketing and Management* 15: 61–75.

Erlen, J. A. (2004). Functional health illiteracy. *Orthopaedic Nursing* 23(2): 150–3.

FDA (2003). *See* Aiken, 2003.

Holmer, A. F. (1999). Direct-to-consumer prescription drug advertising builds bridges between patients and physicians. *Journal of the American Medical Association* 281: 380–2.

Holmer, A. F. (2002). Direct-to-consumer advertising: Strengthening our health-care system. *New England Journal of Medicine* 346: 526–8.

National Consumers League (2003). *Consumers Taking Control with DTC Rx Ads* (Jan. 9). <http://www.nclnet.org/dtcpr.htm>, accessed September 26, 2006.

NHC (National Health Council) (2002). Direct-to-consumer prescription drug advertising: Overview and recommendations. <http://www.nationalhealthcouncil.org/advocacy/DTC_paper.pdf>.

Rabin, K. (2004). DTC advertising for prescription medicines: Research and reflections as the second decade ends. *Journal of Health Communication* 9: 561–2.

Rausch, P., and D. Treise (2006). Direct to consumer advertising: Enhancing patient-provider communication and health literacy. Presented at the Association for Education in Journalism and Mass Communications annual conference in San Francisco on August 3.

Speros, C. (2005). Health literacy: Concept analysis. *Journal of Advanced Nursing* 50(6): 633–40.

Treise, D. and P. Rausch (in press). The prescription pill paradox: Nurse practitioners perceptions about direct to consumer advertising. *Journal of Pharmaceutical Marketing and Management.*

U.S. Department of Heath and Human Services (2000). *Healthy people 2010: Understanding and improving health*, vol. 1. <http://www.healthypeople.gov>, accessed March 19, 2006.

Young, H. N., and R. J. W. Cline (2003). "Look George, there's another one!" The volume and characteristics of direct-to-consumer advertising in popular magazines. *Journal of Pharmaceutical Marketing and Management* 15: 7–21.

Zachry, W. M., J. E. Dalen, and J. R. Jackson (2003). Clinicians' responses to direct-to-consumer advertising of prescription medications. *Archives of Internal Medicine* 163: 1808–12.

11

Puffery and Advertising
Puff the Magic Ad Man

Of all the controversial topics that might be included in a book like this one, why puffery? It's not unusual for advertising students to be completely unfamiliar with the term – or to have any idea that puffery just may be one of the most controversial issues surrounding advertising.

Here's why. The term "puffery" refers to statements in advertising that describe claims about a product with no specific facts to back up the claim. The clincher is that these "non-facts" typically imply something about the competition. For example, this morning I heard a radio commercial for Pizza Hut, "America's Favorite Pizza." It's easy to see that this statement is an over-the-top zealous attempt to position the pizza as the Number One pizza choice in America. How would you be able to tell whether it is or isn't? It's most likely *some* American's favorite pizza. But if Pizza Hut is "America's Favorite" then that implies that Papa John's is, at best, Number Two. (Pizza and puffery have a long history together as you'll discover when you read the essays that follow!)

The question is whether these "puffy" statements (you know, they're full of hot air!), are unethical. Perhaps, they could be deemed unethical if they disparage the competition to such a point that you decide not to buy a product based on the ad. For example, perhaps you have been a big fan of Papa John's pizza, but once you hear the commercial and learn that Pizza Hut is America's favorite, you decide that Pizza Hut must taste better than Papa John's. You, therefore, decide to switch your loyalties to Pizza Hut.

This issue also may be considered unethical if it's a question of deception. Does the ad imply something that simply is not true? Perhaps there are scientific taste tests that consistently show Pizza Hut at the bottom of Americans' pizza preferences. It would seem logical that a commercial pushing the opposite might be seen as deceptive.

The Federal Trade Commission (<ftc.gov>) oversees U.S. advertising regulation and offers a three-prong test for the consumer to use to decide whether an ad might be considered deceptive. In order for the FTC to rule that an ad is considered deceptive, it must first omit or include something that would likely mislead a consumer. Second, the deception must come from the perspective of the "reasonable consumer," and, third, the deception must be material. Did the advertising cause you to purchase the product when you might not have had you known the "truth"? Put in this context, it's possible that a lot of advertising might not be considered deceptive because we consider ourselves savvy consumers. But are we?

While the FTC has ruled that puffery is "mere exaggeration," and, therefore, protected under the First Amendment, that doesn't necessarily mean it's ethical. In fact, Ivan Preston passionately argues that the opposite is true. Perhaps no scholar has written more about puffery in advertising than Professor Preston, so his argument is worth our close attention. However, not to be outdone, Bruce Vanden Bergh bravely takes on Preston and argues for the other side. He even does this with a hefty helping of his own puffery by claiming that his essay is the "best darn essay you'll ever read." How can we argue he's wrong?

The dilemma about puffery in advertising is that it brings to light the very nature of advertising – both its good side and, perhaps, its bad side. What role does advertising have in our lives? You've read earlier about the controversy of deciding whether advertising is an agent of change or a mirror of our society. You've also read about the controversy on whether advertising has a "big effect" on consumers' behavior – or a "limited effect." Now, the dilemma is more about how cynical we are toward our advertising. Are we naive consumers who expect that advertising "tells it like it is," or do we think ads are "stretching the truth" and we don't care? Who knows? Maybe someone out there in ad land really does think that Pizza Hut is America's favorite. Just how accurate do we expect our advertising to be? Read these essays. *You decide.*

Ideas to get you thinking . . .

1 Flip through a magazine. Note all the ads that have the following words in the head-lines: "Best," "Better," "Great," and "Good." Do you think these ads are deceptive? Why, or why not?

2 Look for some magazine ads that you believe are deceptive. (Weight loss ads are a great place to start!) List out the reasons you think these ads might be deceptive. Now, list reasons that these ads might not be considered deceptive. Which do you think make the stronger arguments?

If you'd like to read more . . .

Hausman, C. (1999). *Lies we live by: Defeating double-talk and deception in advertising, politics, and the media.* London: Taylor & Francis.

Preston, I. L. (1996). *The great American blow-up: Puffery in advertising and selling,* rev. edn. Madison: University of Wisconsin Press.

Richards, J. I. (1990). A "new and improved" view of puffery. *Journal of Public Policy and Marketing* 9: 73–84.

Argument

Puffery is never worth the deception

Ivan Preston

A critic of puffery always gets off to a slow start with students thinking of making their careers in advertising. They admire the field and believe puffery does it no harm. Many in fact call it the essence of what the business is doing. It wouldn't be advertising if it did no puffing.

That's one reason why I feel that ad students need to accomplish some "unlearning" before they proceed with learning. The biggest unlearning comes because they were first exposed to advertising practically as infants, and experienced it for years before reaching even high school, much less college. Over those years, who could blame them for thinking that advertising's role was to entertain them by providing all that fun and excitement, great sights of all sorts, fascinating people, laughs, music and other sounds, action, amazing graphic effects, on and on?

The first unlearning, then, was when they came to appreciate that such things typically are no end in themselves to those paying for them, but merely the means to the real end. They are subgoals used to help achieve the goal of persuading people to buy products or services, or ideas. Such knowledge goes a long way toward learning the field in the necessary sophisticated way.

The question of puffery comes up later when students have gained that more mature appreciation, from which they readily see puffery as a useful form of sales persuasion. Its particular job is to express the confidence and enthusiasm that aid success in selling. It employs terms stating a superior evaluation of the product, exaggeratedly at times, through such claims as good, better, best, amazing, extraordinary, and various fanciful things such as "There's a smile in every Hershey bar."

Students also learn that the law, while prohibiting false claims about advertised items, exempts puffery from such charges because it is not factual. Facts are objective because they are about the object, the advertised item, which can be examined to determine the claim's truth or falsity. Opinions, however, known as puffery in the marketplace, are subjective because they are in the subject, which is the speaker. They apply only to that one person or organization and not to the parties being addressed, who of course may choose their own opinions. Since such statements are not about the object that the consumer is deciding about, they are not considered capable of being true or false about the object.

The regulators, therefore, say there is no risk of consumers being deceived by puffs because they know they need not accept other people's opinions, and so take them to mean nothing factually and do not use them in making their decisions. Advertisers, naturally, are happy to take the same position. Given all this, why wouldn't advertisers, and students too, see puffery as completely helpful to themselves and to the buying public?

For anyone who accepts that as the last word on puffery, let's move back to the unlearning mode. While an assumption of helpfulness, or at least lack of harmfulness, may well be appropriate for some puffs, you can never know it's correct for any particular puff unless you see evidence of consumers' actual responses to it. What you *can* know for sure, and it's one of the most major pieces of knowledge of how communication works, is that if there is one message explicitly stated, and, say, one hundred people exposed to it and interpreting its contents, their conclusions will almost surely create at least two perceived messages. Indeed, they will often create quite a few more than two, and in theory conceivably as many as the full hundred, a different one for each and every receiver of that message.

What needs to be unlearned, then, is the belief of advertising's regulators that they can know consumers' interpretations of a puff or any message merely from what they think those interpretations must be or ought to be. The regulators think that's sufficient, but they are wrong! They are well educated in the law, to be sure, but not in communication.

What messages consumers see being conveyed will be those they find sensible in their own individual contexts, and such perceptions probably won't be the same when the individual contexts obviously vary. Thus with puffery there is no reason to expect all consumers to take puffs to mean nothing factually.

Certainly some puffs may mean plenty factually. It can happen because of the difference between explicit and implied messages. What's *explicit* is what the message literally states, meaning its exact wording. What's *implied* is what message receivers see the message to be telling them, even though not literally stating it, which we cannot know from looking solely at the message but only from seeing what the person reports. Among the possible results of this difference is that content that explicitly is opinion can be factually implied. A puff, then, can absolutely imply factual content, and so be capable of being true or false, and so be subject to legal prosecution if the implied fact is false.

An old saying is that "I believe such-and-such" implies "I believe such-and-such because . . ." to the listener. That is, every opinion implies that the speaker has a factual basis for believing it. How else can speakers know about the object for sale, which is something beyond themselves, unless they look beyond themselves, which in turn means going beyond their personal opinion?

I'm not prejudging that every puff implies a false fact. The point, rather, is that a variety of things can happen, which is contrary to the law's position that consumers always take puffery to mean nothing factual about the advertised item either explicitly or impliedly. I'm not calling all puffery deceptive, but rather saying that not all puffery is non-deceptive. That's one of those naughty double negatives, but it reflects the situation precisely: the government says all puffs are non-deceptive, but I believe that is not true.

Any individual puff could certainly be non-deceptive both explicitly or implicitly, and in that case there would be no basis for blocking its use. Or a puff could imply something factually truthful to consumers, which again should create no problem. Consumers also might see implied a true or false fact about something other than the product, which is another way of being OK because they see it as telling them nothing about the product.

For other puffs, however, consumers might see a false fact implied about the product, which gets us into the problem area. They might know of the falsity, in which case they might discount the claim or otherwise be skeptical about dealing with the seller. Or they might not know of the falsity, in which case they could be deceived if they rely on it in making their purchasing decision.

Even worse, consumers might see and rely on a fact that the speaker knew was false when stated (or should have known via expertise that typical consumers don't have). The law generally considers that to be a much worse situation, calling for harsher penalties, because, while falsities may be made innocently, the speaker deliberately stated one while knowing that people could rely on it and be hurt.

All of these effects of puffery can occur, but the law says only one can. The reason why the law so decides is not fully clear, but it may result from a reluctance to acknowledge how the marketplace now differs from its earlier form. When claims were first examined for falsity several hundred years ago, sellers and buyers generally were familiar with the object and had the same degree of competence in judging it. They thus were assumed to be approximately equal in assessing claims; both were experts.

Over time buyers became less so, with sellers coming to be corporations equipped with immense experience and expertise, but consumers remaining the same individual persons as before. Today the buyer's opportunity to draw appropriate conclusions is often nowhere near the seller's. Yet the law declines to abandon its traditional way of judging puffery, saying equality is all consumers need to take care of themselves.

What, then, is the probability of puffery being impliedly false and thus potentially damaging? Puffs are out there by the hundreds, but surveys of interpretations of them are not conducted by regulators or advertisers, at least not publicly (unsurprisingly, from their position discussed above), and are far too expensive for individuals to do. Some research by academics has shown that people take puffs to imply facts, but the regulators have ignored it. So until the regulators decide to obtain real observations rather than just make assumptions, the best way to make good determinations is simply not available.

However, some less direct approaches exist and are helpful. We know that advertisers who have been puffed against have objected, mostly by going to law courts or the ad industry's informal courts. They have usually not been successful, but they have expressed their concern that puffery takes business away from them. Other indirect evidence exists in knowing that advertisers can use puffery with immunity from prosecution no matter what results it produces. They may be outright liars if they wish to be, and given human nature it does not seem inappropriate to suggest that some are. We also know that puffs typically make explicit or implied comparisons to competitors, often in product categories where comparisons are difficult because of so little difference from one brand to another. Thus it seems natural that such a competitive tool would be used frequently to imply more of a difference than actually exists.

Probably the best argument that can be made for the existence of implied false facts is that puffs are rarely accompanied by any fact basis that might establish their truth. That is a telling point because fact claims are typically more likely than mere expressions of opinion to establish value and thus be persuasive at selling. Consider the difference between "This toothbrush has been rated the best in the world by all of the panels of experts that have rated toothbrushes," accompanied by identification of the experts and their qualifications, as contrasted to a claim that merely says "This toothbrush is the best in the world."

The latter merely implies what the former says explicitly, and communication professionals would not settle for weakly implying the supporting facts when they could use the more effective communication device of stating them explicitly. Ad people are too smart to fail to use the best means to persuade, unless of course they could get in trouble for doing so. This strongly suggests that when puffs are found unaccompanied by supporting facts, none exist. That in turn suggests that speakers know there is no basis for making the puffery claim, and thus that the claim they imply of believing the puff is false.

But what does any of this mean to advertisers if they aren't caught? Let's consider the annual survey by the Gallup poll of the "honesty and ethical standards" of people working in various fields, which sometimes surveys about 25 fields, sometimes 40 or more. The ratings are very high, high, average, low, or very low, and the scores used are the sum of the first two categories. "Advertising executives" have typically scored around 10 percent. That has placed them well behind the more general category of "business executives," and typically next to last in the whole list, ahead only of "car salesmen."

The surveys do not ask why people respond as they do, and various reasons could exist. However, it is obvious that the existence of the puffery rule gives consumers an objective factual basis for thinking that ads are often deceptive, and for distrusting them. Thus I have no hesitancy in concluding that puffery is the source of a lot of the credibility problem that Gallup exposes.

It's odd to realize that sellers in this way are working against themselves: while they ought to want consumers to trust them, they readily take actions that instead encourage distrust. The problem reaches throughout the whole business, because it means that when ad people go to work they walk into a culture that includes permission to lie. The puffery rule is an enabler for falsity. And that's for more falsity than just puffs, because it's a lot easier to accelerate into more serious lies from that base than it would be if the base point permitted no lying.

Thus the topic of puffery is way larger than just puffery because it affects all claims. The opportunity to puff with immunity may encourage greater levels of lying, and it may lead to the consuming public being discontent with various other aspects of advertising.

Anytime consumers reject a claim, they are eroding their own trust in the marketplace, and they will do that more readily when they see the market as having a base point that includes lying. There's a good side to skepticism, of course, with sellers, consumer advocates, and regulators too, arguing that consumers should take care of themselves. I'm sure we all agree that anyone who knows how to do that is better off for it.

There seems to be less tendency, however, to acknowledge any down side to skepticism, which can make shopping unsatisfactory even if people don't get fooled. We shouldn't let the idea of encouraging consumers to distrust obscure the fact that we actually *need* to trust a great deal in the market. So the more we feel forced to distrust, even if it helps in the short term, the more we may feel in the long term that the market is a place we don't enjoy visiting.

So, students of advertising, if you use puffery in your selling you may deceive people, and you may pay a price for it. But when you don't deceive them, you may also pay a price. Why claim to be the best when you can do better? Seek out methods of persuasion that won't hurt your effort either way, and may even make you look more creative!

Counterargument

This is the best darn essay on puffery you will ever read

Bruce G. Vanden Bergh

If you are reading this far, I hope I have enticed you into reading my essay on why puffery is a good thing in the marketplace and why it should continue to be considered a non-actionable statement in the eyes of most state and federal regulators when it comes to regulating advertising claims. That is pretty much the intent of puffery in advertising, to break through the clutter of the marketplace and make you aware of something that might be of interest to you. Puffery, as such, is a form of boasting that no reasonable consumer would take seriously. Puffery also is part of daily life in that we all exaggerate at some time or another. Parents boast about their kids, fishermen exaggerate the size of the fish they catch, and politicians make more fuss over their accomplishments than usually is warranted. Do we take these claims literally? We typically do not take these exaggerations seriously.

You're Entitled to Your Opinion

Let me give you two advertising claims to see if you can tell which one might be considered an opinion (and therefore puffery) and which one might be implying a verifiable fact, and therefore could be considered a deceptive claim if it is not true. Papa John's Pizza, a few years ago, used the trademarked slogan, "Better Ingredients. Better Pizza," in its advertising to support its use of fresh ingredients in its pizzas (Duncan, 2006). Mueller's used the phrase, "America's Favorite Pasta," in its promotional materials and on its packaging for its brand of dried pasta (Hoffman, 2004).

Think about it for a moment. You all have a fair amount of experience as consumers in the marketplace. The courts ruled that Mueller's claim was puffery. The decision was based on the conclusion that the words "America's" and "favorite" were not specific, measurable claims, and therefore cannot be interpreted as fact. The words are vague and do not imply that Mueller's is a leader in sales nor a national brand, but that it may be well liked and admired (Hoffman, 2004).

Papa John's Pizza's claim is potentially problematic in that it might imply that competitors do not use fresh ingredients in their pizzas. And, if so, this fact could be verified by investigation to see if indeed Papa John's ingredients are fresher and tastier than the competitions' (Pizza Hut in this case) ingredients (Duncan, 2006). Pizza Hut's lawyers claimed that they had scientific evidence proving that the ingredients did not affect the pizza's taste. Papa John's initially lost the case, but it was later overturned because the federal appeals court said that the jurors were never asked if they thought consumers relied on the "Better ingredients" claim when buying pizza. The ruling seemed to come down to the use of the words "best" versus "better." "Best" is puffery while "better" could imply that the competition is worse than you are (Duncan, 2006).

The more important issue here is: did you take either of these claims at face value? My guess is that you did not because you recognize the claims as exaggerations that are the opinion of the advertisers. Also, we expect advertisers to think highly of their products and brands. I would not want to buy something from a company that did not think that its products were among the best on the market in some way, shape, or form. I expect an advertiser to present his or her brands in their best light.

How Consumers Know it's Puffery

If the courts take the stance that puffery is subjective boasting upon which no reasonable consumer would rely, what makes people reasonable consumers? Consumers are savvier than the critics of the use of puffery will admit. The focus in the argument against the use of puffery is typically on the advertising claim itself and some objective, measurable standard against which the claim can be compared. This assumes that the important knowledge we must possess is about the product in question and perhaps competitors' products. The more knowledgeable you are about your purchase, the more reasonable you might be considered. And the less likely it is that you will take puffery as fact.

Consumers have more knowledge about what goes on in the marketplace than just their knowledge of brands and products. Consumers have knowledge about how persuasion takes place, and they use this knowledge to cope with all those advertisements and salespeople they run into on a daily basis. This persuasion knowledge has been organized by Friestad and Wright (1994) into a model that they call the Persuasion Knowledge Model (PKM). The PKM has three components to it based on the three types of persuasion knowledge we acquire as a result of our experience as consumers. The three components are agent knowledge, topic knowledge, and persuasion knowledge. We use these types of knowledge to identify cues about the nature of the persuasion attempt taking place and to evaluate the intent and veracity of a message (Wyre, 2001).

Our knowledge of the agent (i.e., advertiser) includes our beliefs about the traits, competencies, and motives of the advertiser. We use our beliefs about the advertiser to evaluate the claims in an advertising message. We are more likely to be persuaded by ads from companies we have faith in and that have good products or services than we are by ads from companies we do not trust. This knowledge helps us to differentiate between boasting and opinion done in good faith to make us aware of a product versus the same done only with intent to sell us something. Think of all those automobile dealer ads. You do not trust them because you have a lot of knowledge about that type of agent or advertiser that informs you in advance that their claims are less than entirely accurate or truthful. You are, in this case, a reasonable consumer. You are not easily deceived.

Most discussions of puffery focus on what the PKM calls topic knowledge. Topic knowledge is what you know about the topic of an advertising message. This is your knowledge or beliefs about products, services, political candidates, or social issues. Obviously, the more you know about a purchase, candidate, or issue and the other sides of a persuasive argument, the better you will be at counter-arguing and coping with persuasion.

Regarding puffery, if you know the factual basis for a claim and what the competition offers, you will be able to evaluate it as implying fact or just boasting. This level of persuasion knowledge varies from situation to situation. Persuasion knowledge is the broadest and most varied type of knowledge. It can include a person's beliefs about how persuasion occurs, how advertising tactics tap into consumer psychological processes, beliefs about the effectiveness and appropriateness of tactics, and beliefs about one's ability to cope with advertising (Wyre, 2001).

Let's go back to the Papa John's Pizza situation. Most of us have eaten a lot of pizza in our lifetime. We have beliefs about who makes the best pizza so we can judge Papa John's claims against our topic knowledge for pizza. We are not in the dark about pizza ingredients. If Papa John's pizza does not come even close to the claims, we simply will not continue to believe the advertising or buy the pizza. In situations where consumers are not all that knowledgeable about a product, they are not without alternative methods for evaluating an ad. That is because consumers also have additional persuasion knowledge about the appropriateness of advertisers' tactics in different situations. We can evaluate to what extent we believe Papa John's claim to use better ingredients is literally true or just puffery.

Persuasion knowledge about advertising tactics is an often overlooked area when it comes to discussions about puffery. Consumers have a lot of experience with persuasion in different situations, from commercials on television to the behavior of car salespeople. Based on these experiences, consumers are able to assess the intent of an ad or salesperson based on the tactics employed. We all have opinions on what is appropriate for and what can be expected from different forms of communication. Our expectations for most advertising are that it will be entertaining and somewhat informative. Once we recognize the stylistic form of a message, we evaluate the content. We might expect, for example, for a news program to be more informative than entertaining, while advertising might be expected to be more entertaining and persuasive than informative. This is how we cope with our cluttered media and purchase environment.

Puffery or exaggeration is a time-honored tactic in advertising. Puffery is so widely recognized that it is a fairly regular target for advertising parodies. If you watch *Saturday Night Live* (*SNL*) or read *Mad* magazine, you are familiar with these spoof ads that poke fun at advertising's tendency to puff things up. One such *SNL* parody makes fun of how banks exaggerate services they have that every other bank in the world has, such as the ability to provide change. The commercials for CitiWide Change bank enumerate all the ways it can provide change, complete with testimonials from satisfied customers. One such customer had wrinkled-up dollar bills that she could not use in vending machines so she came to CitiWide to get new, crisp bills.

The easy recognition of puffery by consumers also opens up the opportunity to use exaggeration or puffery as an actual advertising strategy or tactic. The ongoing print and TV campaign for Altoids takes puffery and exaggeration to a whole new level. I recommend to the reader the gallery of ads at the Altoids website (<http://www.altoids.com/index.do>) for an enjoyable journey through puffery in advertising. The Altoids ads work and make us laugh because we know puffery when we see it and it can be used to entertain us. The fact that we get the Altoids jokes tells you that we all can recognize puffery and do not take it seriously. It is part of our persuasion knowledge base.

While product or topic and agent knowledge might vary from situation to situation, knowledge of ad tactics is more universal. The reasonable consumer does exist, and he or she is very skeptical about advertising. In fact, the reasonable consumer is a very important self-regulatory component of the free marketplace. Armed with substantial knowledge about persuasion, he or she is not deceived by such a common advertising tactic as puffery. It is expected.

Puffery versus Dry Facts

Okay, let's consider a world without puffery. Let's say that the Uniform Commercial Code that most states follow is amended to say that all claims an advertiser makes are part of a contractual agreement between buyer and seller. This would mean that all ad claims would be presumed to be equal and, therefore, would be relied on equally by consumers. This means that you and I would give as much credence to a claim that said a product relieved symptoms of the common cold as we would to a claim that said a battery would keep going and going and going. We know that certain over-the-counter drugs can provide some relief from the symptoms of a cold. While we know that batteries cannot last forever, we would take the exaggeration as actually meaning the battery will last for a reasonably long time. A "long time" is vague so the battery claim is really puffery.

Take all the puffery out of advertising and you also take out all the fun and entertainment value of advertising. You cannot sell products and services with just fact-based claims. Exaggeration is not so much aimed at persuading you to buy something or to agree with a particular argument as it is aimed at achieving that first step in the process, which is to gain your attention. And in a cluttered media environment inhabited by savvy consumers you better be entertaining. You better stand apart. Sometimes that means puffing up your product, sometimes it means poking fun at those who use puffery, and at other times, it means using understatement to stand out from the puffery.

How boring would it be if all advertisers were reduced to using only fact-based claims? What about all those low-involvement products that are about vague or general things like fun and excitement? How do you sell psychological benefits that often are in the mind of the consumer as much as they are in the physical attributes of the product? How do you build brands that are a combination of tangible and intangible benefits?

Think about all the product innovations technology has provided us. As great as the Apple iPod is as a new product, without some creative advertising it would not be as popular a product as it has become. And isn't all that dancing around by those silhouettes on colored backgrounds puffery? I see a lot of iPods around, but not much crazy dancing. The iPod is about music and fun. The music part is tangible, while the fun part is a little vague and in the ear and mind of the listener.

So, What Do You Think?

Have I delivered on my promise that this would be the best darn essay on puffery you will ever read? Well, that depends. How many articles on puffery have you read? If you have not read too many, then maybe my essay is pretty good. Plus, the puffery in the headline says more about me than it does about the essay. It says that I have a pretty high opinion of myself and that I am confident that I can write a good essay. You have other clues here with which to evaluate this essay. You have read a lot of articles, chapters in texts, and other materials during your college education, so you have many points of comparison. Additionally, you have your own expert opinion upon which to make an evaluation of that opening statement. You are a reasonable consumer.

At the end of the day, I would rather deal with puffery in advertising than have the state and federal regulators do that for me. The free marketplace has an exceptional capacity for weeding out dishonest advertisers and supporting the honest ones. You can only fool a consumer once. Once fooled, consumers will simply stop buying an advertiser's products.

Sure, many of us have spent a sleepless night watching those infomercials thinking that the products look really good. For those who have purchased a product based on these commercials, we have found out that in some cases the sales pitch was all puffery. These episodes make for good and funny dinner conversation. We might even go back and do it again. However, whether or not we continue to be drawn into these sales pitches, most of us know the game. And, most of us take responsibility for the purchases we make. That is because most people are reasonable consumers. Puffers beware.

Recommended Reading

Friestad, M., and P. Wright (1994). The persuasion knowledge model: How people cope with persuasion attempts. *Journal of Consumer Research* 21(June): 1–31.

Hoffman, D. A. (2006). The best puffery article ever. *Iowa Law Review*, 91(July): 1395–1448.

Preston, I. L. (1996). *The great American blow-up: Puffery in advertising and selling*, rev. edn. Madison: University of Wisconsin Press.

Preston, I. L. (2000). Advertising Educational Foundation must-read list. <http://www.aef.com/on_campus/classroom/must_read/data/33/:pf_printable?>, accessed July 4, 2006.

Richards, J. I. (1997). Advertising regulation by the FTC: Bibliography. <http://advertising.utexas.edu/research/biblio/FTC.html>, accessed July 4, 2006.

Richards, J. I. (1990). A "new and improved" view of puffery. *Journal of Public Policy and Marketing* 9: 73–84.

References

Duncan, A. (2006). Better pizza? Bigger lawsuit. <http://advertising.about.com/od/foodrelatedadnews/a/papajohns.htm>, accessed July 17, 2006.

Friestad, M., and P. Wright (1994). The persuasion knowledge model: How people cope with persuasion attempts. *Journal of Consumer Research* 21(June): 1–31.

Hoffman, I. (2004). Advertising slogans: Fact vs. puffing. <http://www.ivanhoffman.com/slogans2,html>, accessed July 4, 2006.

Wyre, K. (2001). What does "folk wisdom" about deceptiveness in advertising say about consumers' willingness to buy? The case of DRTV. Unpublished doctoral dissertation, Michigan State University, East Lansing.

12

Advertising and Social Responsibility

Being Good is Always a Good Idea – Right?

In the previous chapters, many of the topics might have elicited a strong negative reaction to advertising. After all, it's not overly difficult to imagine the evils of tobacco advertising. I mean, what kind of company wants to advertise a product that has absolutely no inherent value in it?

If tobacco advertising can represent the extreme "vice" on the advertising pendulum, we could just as easily say that social responsibility is the extreme "good" side of advertising. Or can we? Part of the controversy rests with whether we can trust the motives of a company to do good. For example, according to public health educators Sebrie and Glantz (2007), youth smoking preven- tion programs advocated by tobacco companies may be a part of a company's corporate social responsibility package, but the programs have not worked. In other words, why not promote something that inherently fights your "vice" product – especially if you know it's not going to hurt your bottom line?

In her essay, Debra Merskin takes a more positive approach toward social responsibility. She comments on several well-known "feel good" ad campaigns that tout what the company is doing to help the environment, fight cancer, feed hungry children in Darfur. Given recent celebrities' new-found interest in social issues (think Angelina Jolie and George Clooney, for example), we are most likely going to see even more companies adopting a social respons- ibility approach to their advertising. What could possibly be wrong with that? As Peggy Kreshel points out, potentially, a lot. Just for starters, why would we think an institution would do anything without an ulterior motive? Companies exist for the bottom line. Maybe ultimately that doesn't matter – especially if we save the planet in the meantime. But we should at least pause and think about what is happening when companies use social responsibility as an advert- ising strategy.

As Merskin and Kreshel each make their arguments, it's interesting to note that they both quote from Milton Friedman, a Nobel prizewinning economist who has aggressively promoted his views of a free-market economy through- out his many writings. Debra Merskin discusses Friedman from the point of view that if good is done in the interest of generating a profit, there is no prob- lem with that. Peggy Kreshel, however, looks to Friedman's idea that the socially responsible company is one that increases its profits as a warning to doubt the "good heart" of any company. This is an excellent example that demon- strates there are always two ways of looking at a controversy. But, which is the right way? *You decide.*

Ideas to get you thinking . . .

1 Try and find a magazine ad that uses social responsibility as its creative strategy. Identify what "social good" the company is selling and then do some research and see if you can verify what the company is claiming. To get started, you might go online and look at the company's homepage, read the annual report, or do a news- paper search with Lexis/Nexis.

2 Should all companies practice social responsibility? If so, should they advertise the good they are doing? Think of some companies that often are thought of negatively. (You might start with oil companies.) Think of a socially responsible act this com- pany could do. Try to write an ad about it.

If you'd like to read more . . .

Friedman, M., and R. D. Friedman (1990). *Free to choose: A personal statement.* Orlando, FL: Harcourt.

Kotler, D., and N. Lee (2004). *Corporate social responsibility: Doing the most for your company and your cause.* Hoboken, NJ: John Wiley.

Loger, F. C. (1995). *Ben & Jerry's: The inside school.* London: Crown Publishing.

Michelli, J. A. (2006). *The Starbucks experience: 5 principles for turning ordinary into extraordinary.* New York: McGraw-Hill.

Sisodia, R., D. Wolfe, and J. Sheth (2007). *Firms of endearment: How world-class companies profit from passion and purpose.* Upper Saddle River, NJ: Pearson.

References

Sebrie, E. M., and S. A. Glantz (2007). Tobacco industry "youth smoking prevention" programs to undermine meaningful tobacco control in Latin America. *American Journal of Public Health* 97(8), 1357–67.

Argument

Companies are wise – and ethical – to use "social responsibility" as a creative strategy

Debra Merskin

"We see a dream of the sea," says the headline for a recent Microsoft ad touting its teaming up with Boys and Girls Clubs of America to connect kids with technology. The copy tells us the company has established more than 2,700 computer learning centers, which help more than 1 million children. The double-page, four-color ad shows a happy African American girl sitting at her computer gazing out the window, upon which an aquarium scene is painted. The white drawing on the window makes it look as if she is wearing a deep-sea diving helmet. Another "brown" child walks by, toting his backpack, looking longingly in. Above the logo is the statement, "Your potential. Our passion." Microsoft Corporation and founder Bill Gates give millions of dollars every year to causes. They also spend millions of dollars each year telling consumers about their generosity.

In this essay, I briefly describe the foundations of social responsibility (SR) as a corporate and creative strategy, provide examples of this approach, discuss the benefits to advertisers and to consumers, and finally articulate three reasons why SR is a smart, ethical, and effective creative strategy for advertisers to use. I argue that SR is smart and ethnical if three conditions are met: (1) the advertiser is truthfully and actively engaged in the cause/concern represented; (2) there is a clear and associative relationship between said cause and the advertised product; and (3) the ads educate and inform consumer citizens about a social issues, concerns, and needs. Presenting the SR position of the company therefore rises above motivation for purely economic gain, and avoids the charge that it is "the maximization of personal wealth or other forms of self interest is not socially responsible and is unethical" (Clark, 1993: 307).

What is Social Responsibility?

What you stand for is even more important than what you stand in. (Kenneth Cole, 2003)

Organizations, be they government, corporate, religious, or educational, are obligated to act in an ethical manner when it comes to performing responsibilities. States, for example, have a responsibility to ensure the democratic rights of citizens. Corporations are not only responsible for the wellbeing of employees, but also to the society that supports them. Social responsibility is a "multidimensional" concept that goes beyond respecting people, places, and things, to recognizing and appreciating the "interdependence and connectedness with others and our environment" (Berman and La Farge, 1993: 7). Defined as "the alignment of business operations with social values," SR involves "integrating the interests of stakeholders – all of those affected by a company's conduct – into the company's business policies and actions" (Coors and Winegarden, 2005: 10). However, not everyone agrees with this approach.

In 1962 the influential libertarian economist Milton Friedman said that if good is done in the interest of generating a profit, fine, but that businesses have no obligations to society, only to stockholders. While Friedman did not approve of fraudulent or deceptive practices, he felt that, by providing jobs for communities, corporations were generating goodwill, and, as a result, more profits. Today, however, consumers are increasingly following the money corporations make and are increasingly aware of the impact these companies have on environments and local economies.

SR, as a creative strategy, made its official foray into advertising in the 1980s. In 1983 American Express launched a campaign to help restore the decaying Statue of Liberty and pledged money every time a consumer signed up and was given a new card, bought traveler's checks, or purchased an Express travel package worth $500 or more. Cardholder charges rose 30 percent and the company donated $1.7 million to the Statue of Liberty Ellis Island Foundation. The company spent $4 million advertising its involvement and pledge (Wiegner, 1985: 248).

Jerry Welsh, marketing executive at American Express Travel Related Services, declared, in 1985, "social responsibility is a good marketing hook" (in Wiegner, 1985: 248). Welsh was not referring to philanthropy, nor to public service advertising, but instead to a growing consumer consciousness about the importance of doing business with corporations that do good in terms of employee wellbeing, impact on the environment, and concerns with social issues. He found social consciousness a surprising survivor of the 1970s "me generation's" narcissism and hyper-individuality. Similar efforts came from General Foods, which in partnership with

Pacific Bell launched a "Pop into a Park" campaign to encourage year-round state park use. The same year, General Foods' Tang sponsored a March Across America for Mothers Against Drunk Drivers, donating 10 cent coupons and guaranteeing a contribution of not less than $100,000.

Kenneth Cole (2003), in his autobiography *Footnotes*, states that the atmosphere in the U.S. was changing – economic downturns, high unemployment – and people were responding. "A pervasive consciousness, a sense of activism . . . was sweeping the United States. The idea that we could collectively impact these tragedies was mobilizing everyone" (2003: 142). Cole and other corporations joined the growing commercial consciousness by aligning with social causes and activism, and made this apparent in their advertising.

Social Responsibility as a Creative Strategy

At first glance, SR and advertising creative strategy might seem mutually exclusive. However, if applied clearly and honestly, companies whose products have a perceived relationship with quality-of-life issues and concerns of consumers can use this approach to their advantage when reinforcing corporate image, to establish "reason to buy" for a particular product or service, and to give back to the world from which they earn their profits. Tinic (1997: 4) posits that advertising can be regarded as a "significant site of cultural production" and thereby become a location for public discourse around meaning, social values, and corporate goals. More simply said, "advertising which typically aims to sell a product by associating it with a resonant image, identity, lifestyle or ethos, is a form of persuasive communication that can be effectively harnessed for explicitly prosocial purposes" (Stadler, 2004: 592). Thereby, the brand becomes an active agent in the process.

Sometimes a company's involvement with social issues and the promotion of these activities in advertising are obviously linked. Companies such as women's clothier J. Jill's Compassion Fund (<jjill.com>), established in June 2002, has given out more than $700,000 in grants, and donated more than $1.2 million to related causes. The Massachusetts-based national women's clothing retailer targets organizations that help poor and homeless women.

An example of an unsuccessful use of the SR strategy was the $100 million advertising campaign by the Philip Morris Companies (now the Altria Group) publicizing their charitable giving. Not only can this do "long-term damage to an image or brand," which would be "perceived as exploiting a tragedy," Cliff Sloan, former President and CCO of the Sloan Group, says, "It's just not appropriate to plant your flag in a fresh wound" (in Elliott, 2005: 9).

The Spectrum of SR

Does the "do good," or at least "do no harm," approach work when combined with advertising? Obviously, the objective of any advertising campaign is to increase something – sales, awareness, market share, or brand image. Many corporations have used social responsibility as a creative strategy, particularly corporate social responsibility (CSR). Some of the more effective and ethical companies include Kenneth Cole, Tom's of Maine, Ben & Jerry's, and Starbucks, all of whom use a variety of media and methods in their advertising tactics. These and other companies have often eschewed the use of traditional or conventional advertising, instead relying on word of mouth, collateral materials (on recycled paper), and product placement to present a consistent message built around corporate images as a socially responsible agent.

Kenneth Cole (kennethcole.com)

Kenneth Cole, the founder and the corporation, is known for their attention to social issues and particular concern for AIDS awareness. "Advertising is an opportunity to introduce your point of view, as well as to define the nature of the relationship you'd like to have with the customer. And it can even be a chance to say something important." Cole's company, Kenneth Cole Productions, has often focused on AIDS awareness and prevention. In 1986 Cole's first ad promoting AIDS awareness was "For the Future of Our Children." Photographed by Annie Leibovitz, it featured supermodels Christie Brinkley, Beverly Johnson, Andie MacDowell, and Kelly Emberg, among others, holding children and babies. In 1992 another Cole ad only had the copy, "If we told you a shoe could help find a cure for AIDS, would you buy it?" This ad announced a month-long campaign in which 15 percent of every shoe purchase price would go to AIDS research. Cole campaigns also target women's right to choose, pro-gay liberation ("Shoes shouldn't have to stay in the closet either"), and shoes for the homeless.

Reebok (rbk.com)

Athletic shoe and apparel maker Reebok stepped up to the corporate responsibility plate in May 2007 when it launched the Reebok Global Corporate Citizenship Program. Reebok employees, retailers, consumers, artists, and athletes participate in this extension of the company's Human Rights Program. For example, Reebok 4 Real is a program designed to empower by recognizing and rewarding individual achievement among global youth with scholarships. The program has two components: the Human Rights Student Advocate Program and the Community and Education Program.

The Human Rights Student Advocate Program pairs Reebok employees with high-school students, offers grant opportunities to schools, and encourages mentorships with employees and students in community relations work. The Community and Education Program connects athletes and artists with committed students. Reebok donates supplies and equipment to high-achieving students and their schools. Red Sox batter David Ortiz kicked off the May campaign, surprising students at Jeremy Burke High School. Ortiz challenged them to write an essay answering the question: "How would a scholarship help you fulfill your potential inside the classroom and out in the community?" Reebok employees judged the essays and selected a boy and a girl as winners. In December 2007 Baron Davis launched the second scholarship competition. The winning students will each receive a $2,500 scholarship.

Tom's of Maine (tomsofmaine.com)

Founded in 1970 in Kennebunk, Maine, by Tom and Kate Chappel, Tom's of Maine, a natural personal and home care company, makes "products without artificial preservatives, sweeteners, or dyes and without animal testing or animal ingredients." Close identification with consumers is part of their corporate philosophy: "Tom's of Maine will become the trusted partner in natural care among consumers with whom we share common values."

Tom's of Maine's advertising promotes all-natural ingredients, environmentally sensitive packaging and, with clean, clear graphics with exaggerated image proportions of the fruit, herb, or mineral, the ads focus on messages of purity and trust. Advertising for Tom's appears in publications such as *Yoga Journal*, *Prevention*, and *Natural Health Magazine*, the latter of which provided complimentary copy touting the ingredients and benefits of Tom's mouthwash:

> Tom's of Maine Natural Anticavity Fluoride Mouthwash is alcohol free and contains the antioxidant green tea along with aloe vera juice and chamomile to soothe the mouth – all of which makes it ideal for sensitive sorts. ("A sweeter smile")

The company website states the credo: "We believe our company can be profitable and successful while acting in a socially and environmentally responsible manner."

Ben & Jerry's (benandjerrys.com)

Ben Cohen and Jerry Greenfield went into business together in Burlington, Vermont, in 1978. Their ice-cream business was built on an SR premise, including in their products "only fresh Vermont cream & milk, & the best & biggest chunks of nuts, fruits, candies & cookies." Distinctive products. with names such as Chunky Monkey, Cherry Garcia, Sorbet Volcano, and Phish Food, connect with consumers' sense of the past and the present, and this style is reinforced by graphics and designs on product containers. In 1992 Ben & Jerry's made the following public statement of upholding its values:

> Affirming our belief that business has a responsibility to the environment and should uphold a set of aspirational principles. Whether it is in sourcing ingredients, supporting non-profit organizations, or using our ice cream to help better the environment, we think it's important to lead with our values.

The company's strong graphic identity consistently presents a happy, black and white bovine standing in a green field, white, fluffy clouds frolicking above. The company has used advertising not only to promote products, but also to speak out on issues. A full-page ad in the January 19, 2005, edition of the *Washington Post* (timed to the presidential inauguration) carried the headline "Put red and blue aside. Think green," and was designed to bring attention to uniting America, particularly around concerns for the environment. The copy reads "there are a million issues about which we could disagree. But, as we move into the next four years, let us ponder one inarguable fact: when you remove the red and blue from our map, what you're left with is one shared environment." The ad invites readers to visit the website <www.lickglobalwarming.com>.

Ben & Jerry's ice-cream cartons are also used to carry the company message of commitment to SR. A container of "Fossil Fuel" ice cream, for example, carries the statement: "We oppose recombinant Bovine Growth Hormones," and a pledge from family farmers who supply milk and cream to the corporation. Outdoor advertising, cinema ads, and free taste-testing promotions are also a part of the creative strategy that effectively links the brand with environmental SR.

Starbucks (starbucks.com)

Founded in 1971, Seattle-based Starbucks identified early and often the importance of promoting its products in a way that highlighted the importance of the process of procurement. Each year, Starbucks produces *Beyond the Cup*, an annual report of the company's social responsibility, which describes the company's social, "environmental and economic impacts in the communities" in which it does business. Its "Guiding Principles," include building community, a commitment to youth, a supplier diversity plan, and sustaining coffee communities.

Howard Schultz, Starbucks founder and chair, established the Starbucks Foundation in 1997. The Make Your Mark campaign matches volunteer hours with cash contributions to designated nonprofit organizations ($10 per hour, up to $1,000 per project). In 2005 the company contributed more than $1.4 million to such organizations.

A full-page, two-color ad in the *New York Times* describes Starbucks' commitment to Fair Trade coffee beans. The headline for the all-text ad, "Small Coffee Farms Don't Grow Small Coffee," appears over a background of an exterior, pale green wall, and a cornice featuring the Starbucks logo. Notably, the copy about the company's commitment appears above the logo as a way of visually demonstrating purpose over profits. The ad invites readers to visit Starbucks website, "To learn more about what we value," at <www.whatmakescoffeegood.com>, where viewers can "follow the bean" from picking to grinding, accompanied by the ambient sounds of a busy Starbucks store.

Conclusion

How do corporations benefit by taking the SR approach in their advertising? Certainly having employees who are committed to corporate causes is good for morale and corporate image. Sherry Southern, a VP at

Starbucks, said she targeted the company in her job search because "I really wanted to work at a company that treats its employees with respect and as part of the solution instead of the opposite" (in Weber, 2005: ¶7). A 2003 study by Stanford University and the University of California, Santa Barbara, of 800 MBA students at 11 top North American and European business schools found 94 percent would accept as much as 14 percent lower salary to work for environmentally friendly, employee-concerned, socially responsible corporations (Weber, 2005).

Out of respect for people who purchase their products, I argue, corporations, particularly those that avow socially responsible practices and use this position as an advertising creative strategy, must acknowledge their debt to the people who work for them, to the people who support them, and follow through with participation and performance, i.e. walk the walk of the talk they profess.

Despite protests by ice-cream lovers, investors, lagging stock prices, and slowed sales led to Ben & Jerry's sale to Unilever in 2000. The ice-cream company with a corporate conscience became another unit in Unilever's portfolio. Odwalla, who was picked up by Coca-Cola, picked up Fresh Samantha. Nike bought Converse. Stonyfield Farms sold to Dannon. Estée Lauder bought Aveda, and L'Oreal picked up Body Shop. Tom's of Maine became a subsidiary of Colgate-Palmolive. Will it make a difference in philosophy and advertising strategy and ethics that these once-upon-a-time alternative, natural companies are now part of multinational conglomerates? If, as Tom's of Maine founder Tom Chappell says, 25 percent of Americans are interested in buying their products from SR companies, and it was the growth that made them attractive to the big companies, that is a good thing. Coors and Winegarden (2005: 11) remind us, "Just because the advertising comes in the form of social responsibility does not make it any less like advertising." Yet SR, grounded in ethical fundamentals, is a creative strategy from which we all can benefit. SR as a creative strategy is ethical if the company legitimately supports the causes it clamors around, has a connection to the product, and is truthful in its statements. Consumers benefit by receiving complete information and can spend their dollars with companies who share their opinions, beliefs, and ideals.

References

"A sweeter smile" (2006). *Natural Health* (March): 28.
<BenandJerrys.com>, accessed June 11, 2006.

Berman, S., and P. La Farge (1993). *Promising practices in teaching social responsibility*. New York: State University of New York Press.

Clark, C. R. (1993). Social responsibility ethics: Doing right, doing good, doing well. *Ethics & Behavior* 3(3/4): 303–27.

Cole, K. (2003). *Footnotes*. New York: Simon & Schuster.

Coors, A. C., and W. Winegarden (2005). Corporate responsibility – or good advertising? *Regulation* (Spring): 10–11.

Elliott, S. (2005). The delicate task of showing corporate concern for the tsunami victims, without seeming promotional. *New York Times* (Jan. 4): 9.

Friedman, M. (1962/2002). *Capitalism and Freedom*. Chicago: University of Chicago Press.

<jjill.com>, accessed June 5, 2006.

<kennethcole.com>, accessed June 11, 2006.

O'Rourke, D. (2006). Selling out or buying in? *The Boston Globe* (Apr. 5): A15.

Stadler, J. (2004). AIDS ads: Make a commercial, make a difference? Corporate social responsibility and the media. *Continuum: Journal of Media & Cultural Studies* 18: 591–610.

<starbucks.com>, accessed June 11, 2006.

Tinic, S. (1997). United colors and untied meanings: Benetton and the commodification of social issues. *Journal of Communication* 47: 3–25.

<tomsofmaine.com>, accessed June 11, 2006.

Weber, G. (2005). The recruiting payoff of social responsibility. *Workforce Management* (Jan.). <http://www.workforce.com/section/06/article/23/93/45.html>, accessed June 12, 2006.

Wiegner, K. K. (1985). A cause on every carton? *Forbes* (Nov. 18): 248–9.

<workingassets.com>, accessed June 11, 2006.

Counterargument

The adoption of social responsibility through cause-related marketing as a business strategy is unethical

Peggy Kreshel

Prologue

My job is to make Red a well-known-enough brand so that 10 years from now people will think of it like the Nike swoosh. I want to create a brand marketers feel they must have or they will lose business. (Bobby Shriver, Red CEO, quoted in Kingston, 2007)

In January 2006, rock star and activist Bono introduced the global brand Red, to benefit the Global Fund to Fight AIDS, Tuberculosis and Malaria. Other celebrities, perhaps most notably Oprah Winfrey and Chris Rock, joined Bono in championing the campaign, which involves joining with "iconic names to pump out some cool, co-branded products" to market Red-themed specialty products.[1] Shoppers contribute by buying products ranging from Red Gap Empowe(RED) T-shirts, to Red MOTORAZR V3 Phones and Red iPod nanos, to Red mud-cloth Converse sneakers. A portion of the revenue from the sale of these products goes to the Global Fund.

The campaign is an ambitious one that was "designed to get people used to the idea of an entirely new fundraising model" (Shriver, 2007). Bringing together a globally recognized cause, corporate vendors/"partners" with highly marketable brands, high-profile celebrities, and consumers already immersed in an increasingly commercialized culture who rarely question how buying "stuff" translates into the alleviation of human suffering on "faraway" continents, Red is the first cause-marketing effort to allow brands as well as the cause to make a profit. Bono claims the commercial imperative is essential to maintaining a revenue stream for the Global Fund. However, critics are uncomfortable with the lack of transparency in the administrative aspects of the campaign and with the underlying mix of charity and consumption. One of the most recognized of the critics, a San Francisco-based site (<buylesscrap.org>), parodies the Red campaign, invites consumers to "join . . . in rejecting the ti(red) notion that shopping is a reasonable response to human suffering," urges direct donation to charity as "the most efficient way to support a cause," and provides direct-donation links to over 50 charities.

Also on the site, in a letter to Red's CEO, Bobby Shriver, Ben Davis, a San Francisco marketing executive and co-creator of the site, lauds RED as "an extraordinary and innovative endeavor" which "has the potential to do amazing good." Alluding to questions about the "effectiveness of RED's business model,"[2] he urges Shriver to adapt that model by providing administrative transparency (that is, disclosing publicly the actual amount donated to the cause), making it clear how much money goes to the Global Fund with each purchase, and making it easy to donate to the fund without purchase. In that letter, Davis concludes:

> The immediate implementation of these steps would . . . help establish a set of best practices for future cause-related marketing efforts. . . . This would create an even greater and lasting positive legacy for Red. (<buylesscrap.org>)

Amid ongoing controversy, the rapidity with which the Red campaign, has become a highly visible, widely recognized component of American, and indeed global, culture, is noteworthy. Shriver reported that, in just over a year, the Global Fund had netted $28 million from the Red effort (Panepento, 2007), "five times the amount the Global Fund has received from the private sector since its inception in 2001" (Kingston, 2007).

Introduction

The Red campaign emerged at the intersection of a number of trends in culture, and more particularly in business culture. Among these are:

- Increased recognition of corporate social responsibility and the apparent establishment of a corporate social norm to do good (Kotler and Lee, 2005).
- Transformation in the conceptualization of corporate philanthropy from giving as an obligation to giving as a strategy (Kotler and Lee, 2005; Smith, 1994; White, 2007).
- Evolution and growth of cause-related marketing initiatives as a strategic approach to demonstrating corporate social responsibility and to the attainment of corporate objectives.

• Consumer acceptance of the injection of commercial logic and the corporation as a plausible approach to social problems.

Corporations undertake a variety of initiatives in the name of corporate social responsibility and good corporate citizenship; cause-related marketing is but one.

In this essay I will argue that the adoption of social responsibility through the use of cause-related marketing as a business strategy is unethical. In making my argument, I begin with a brief history of the evolution of corporate social responsibility and the emergence of cause-related marketing as a business strategy in that conceptual context. As a part of that historical account, I highlight some early, widely recognized and influential critiques of the concept of social responsibility as it applies to business. While these critiques are no longer defensible in their purest form, being as they are products of particular historical circumstances, they do provide a valuable starting point from which I develop my argument in the section which follows. Interspersed throughout that section are "snapshots" drawn from a health/disease-related cause, breast cancer, to illustrate the bases of my argument as well as to provide evidence of its veracity. In a concluding section, I provide a brief summary and pose a series of questions to bring to the forefront precisely that which has gone unexamined in "a nation that shops to save the world" (Copeland, 2007).

Changes in the Social Contract: The Evolution of Corporate Social Responsibility[3]

> For more than two centuries, the social contract has undergone cycles of definition and redefinition. This has occurred not through formal acts of government, but through evolving norms and expectations of the purpose of business in society. (White, 2007: 19)

The trend toward increased recognition and adoption of corporate social responsibility as a philosophy and a set of practices, as well as the controversies, comforts, and discomforts surrounding it, are best understood in the context of the changing social contract. Indeed, the concept of a social contract has been appearing more and more frequently in recent discussions about the role of business in society (see, e.g., Mendonca and Miller, 2007; Smith, 1994; White, 2007). In this section, I first clarify that concept and then overview the evolution of corporate social responsibility in the "cycle of definition and redefinition" of that contract.

The social contract is a complex philosophical theory (it has its various underpinnings in the work of Thomas Hobbes, John Locke, and Jean-Jacques Rousseau) about how groups of people maintain social order. That is, in a vastly oversimplified sense, it's about how societies are structured so that we "get along." White (2007) writes that the social contract was a precursor to the ideas of democracy,

> wherein ultimate power resides with citizens who willingly delegate certain authority to the state so that individuals might fruitfully participate in a social arrangement that enhances the shared prospects among all participants prospects in a shared community. (2007: 4)

It is noteworthy here that early formulations of the social contract didn't include corporations, but were about the relationships between individuals and between individuals and the government. Public health, education, welfare, and safety were just that – public goods; providing them was a government function. Corporate intervention was a rarity.

Corporations gradually became actors in this contract only as they expanded in scope and complexity. Corporations were granted many of the privileges and protections of "natural persons." Correspondingly, White writes:

> as the scale of corporations grew, their readiness to exercise political influence to reconstitute their position and form increased in parallel. This . . . laid the foundation for what would evolve into the uncontested pre-eminence of capital in defining the corporation's obligation to society. (2007: 6)

The social contract evolved, then, to include the relationship between business, government, and society; the responsibility of business was to create shareholder profit.

> According to an unspoken ethic, society was well served when each of its three sectors – business, government, and nonprofit – was permitted to do what it did best without intruding in the affairs of the others. (Smith, 1994)

When government began to issue rules directed at corporate behavior (e.g., limits on resource use, pollution, etc.), corporations were forced to divert a part of their economic resources to compliance and away from share-holder profit. This "signaled at least a temporary weakening in the grip of shareholder primacy as the paramount principle in defining the bound-aries in the social contract between business and society" (White, 2007: 8). The expectations of these corporate social obligations deeply divided the business community.

> By pursuing his own interest [an individual] frequently promotes that of the society more effectually than when he really intends to promote it. I have never known much good done by those who affected to trade for the public good. (Adam Smith, *The Wealth of Nations*)

Theodore Levitt, an economist and later a professor at the Harvard Business School, wrote in a *Harvard Business Review* article, "The Dangers of Social Responsibility": "The governing rule in industry should be that something is good only if it pays. . . . This is the rule of capitalism" (1958).

Economist Milton Friedman, made precisely that argument in a *New York Times* article titled "The Social Responsibility of Business is to Increase its Profits" (1970). Friedman, like Levitt, believed in Adam Smith's notion of "the invisible hand" guiding the marketplace," that social good would come from the pursuit of profit. Friedman argued that if a corporate executive assumes a "social responsibility" in his capacity as a businessman, he acts in a way other than in the best interests of his employers.[4] This social respons-ibility doctrine would suggest, for example, that the businessman:

> refrain from increasing the price of the product in order to contribute to the social objective of preventing inflation, even though a price increase would be in the best interests of the corporation. Or that he is to make expendi-tures on reducing pollution beyond the amount that is in the best interests of the corporation or that is required by law in order to contribute to the social objective of improving the environment. Or that, at the expense of corporate profits, he is to hire "hardcore" unemployed instead of better qualified available workmen to contribute to the social objective of reduc-ing poverty. (1970: 17)

Identifying social responsibility as unethical in the sense that "the corpor-ate executive would be spending someone else's money for a general social interest," and "fundamentally subversive" in a free society, Friedman concluded with the oft-quoted "Friedman doctrine" that there is one and only one social responsibility of business – to use its resources and engage in activities designed to increase its profits so long as it stays within the rules of the game, which is to say, engages in open and free competition without deception and fraud. (1970: 17)

As the quotation which opened this section suggests, the cycle of definition and redefinition of the social contract – the relationships between business, government, and society – has been the result of changes in norms and expectations. The contract continues to evolve. Concerns about global economic stability; the emergence of what White (2007) calls civil society organizations (which range from transnational humanitarian organizations to advocacy groups to scientific organizations, focus on a wide diversity of issues, and employ a variety of tactics) as parties in the social contract; the escalation of unresolved social perils: poverty, disease, global warming, health-care; and the erosion of public trust in corporations – only 28 percent of Americans indicated in a recent poll that they trusted corporations and corporate executives "to do what is right" (Mendonca and Miller, 2007) – have all contributed to current discomforts with the "way we get along."

Today, the stark position advocated by Levitt and Friedman decades ago clearly is no longer defensible. Yankelovich identified a "shift in moral values" from the unenlightened self-interest which characterized the 1970s, "winning for yourself; I win you lose," to enlightened self-interest, when you "make a profit by meeting a need, by fulfilling a social function" (Mendonca and Miller, 2007). Similarly Rotzoll et al. wrote that "businesses have apparently been sufficiently institutionalized in a 'responsibility' ethic to support company activities that seem to have no directly self-interested 'bottom-line'" (1996: 35). Still, writers in the business press vigorously debate the notion that profit-seeking will advance public good. For example, one writer in *The Economist* suggested that, today, every corporate strategy must pass two tests: (1) Will it enhance long-term profit? (2) Does it serve the public good? The challenge is to determine a strategy that can do both, and to recognize the tension that emerges when attempting to arrive at that strategy (Mendonca and Miller, 2007).

Once, corporations were somewhat reluctant to link themselves with a cause, concerned that consumers would view corporate involvement as exploiting that cause for commercial gain. But, over the past 20 years, societal expectations about businesses' role in society have changed dramatically; consumers appear not only to expect corporate involvement in social concerns, but to reward it. According to the 2007 Cone Cause Evolution Survey (<coneinc.com>), nine out of ten Americans say "companies should support causes that are consistent with their responsible business practices." Additionally, the results of the survey indicate that consumers will reward companies they view to be good citizens in a number of ways, including switching brands, deciding which companies they want doing business in their communities, choosing where to work, holding a positive image of the company, and recommending products or services to others. In response, "doing well by doing good" has become the mantra of many in the business community.

In *Corporate Social Responsibility: Doing the Most Good for Your Company and Your Cause*, Kotler and Lee write that "An underlying assumption of this book is that most for-profit corporations will do some good, for some cause, at least some of the time" (2005: 2). They distinguish six types of corporate social initiative, some of which are marketing-related (cause promotions, cause-related marketing, and corporate social marketing), and others which fall outside the marketing arena (corporate philanthropy, community volunteering, and socially responsible business practices). Certainly a case can be made for maintaining ethical integrity in corporate operations, community volunteering, and any number of social initiatives. What of cause-related marketing?

In the section that follows, I briefly introduce cause-related marketing, outlining the dimensions it has assumed in our culture and in our business culture.

Cause-Related Marketing: Getting Consumers (Citizens?) Involved

Cause-related marketing refers to corporate social initiatives that depend upon consumer participation. It first appeared on the scene some 25 years ago (1983), when American Express undertook to help in the restoration of the Statue of Liberty for its 100-year anniversary in 1986. American Express donated 1 cent for each dollar cardholders charged to their card, plus it made an additional donation for each new-card application. At the conclusion of the effort, American Express donated $1.7 million to the Statue of Liberty Ellis Island Foundation, and saw a 27 percent increase in card usage, and a 10 percent increase in new card applications (Kotler and Lee, 2005; Schoenberg, 2007).

Today, cause-related marketing initiatives are diverse; the degree and nature of consumer involvement varies; the relationships developed in the process are often both intricate and complex. In some instances, consumers simply are asked to purchase a product; a percentage of sales, though in many cases the percentage remains unspecified, goes to the cause. In their "Save Lids to Save Lives" program, Yoplait Yogurt promised to donate 10 cents for each pink lid they received between September 1 and December 31, 2007 to Susan G. Komen for the Cure (<yoplait.com>).[5] In other cases, companies create items particularly to raise money for a cause. Simmons Jewelry Company created a rough diamond and malachite green bracelet, donating "50 percent of net profits" from the sale of the bracelet, to the Diamond Empowerment fund, a nonprofit international organization dedicated to support education programs in Africa.[6] Something of a "hybrid" of these two approaches to cause-related marketing, actor Paul Newman developed Newman's Own, a line of all-natural food products ranging from popcorn to salad dressing to lemonade. He "donates all his profits and royalties after taxes for educational and charitable purposes" (<newmansown.com>). In other instances, consumers are asked to buy a symbol of their support of a cause – breast cancer's looped pink ribbon, a red dress pin for heart disease, a royal blue bracelet for prostate cancer – "wearable proof . . . a visible declaration of concern" (Walker, 2004). The Nike/Lance Armstrong "Live Strong" yellow silicone bracelets introduced in 2004 quickly became a widely recognized "charitable must-have" (Walker, 2004). Extreme, fitness-based, fundraising events such as the Leukemia and Lymphoma Society's Team-in-Training, the Susan G. Komen Race for a Cure, and Avon's Two-Day Walk for Breast Cancer have become so commonplace that a writer in the *New York Times* (Sweeney, 2005) recently identified them as "the latest trend in fitness." In these events, charitable foundations link with corporate sponsors to provide endurance training programs for individuals who participate in long-distance bike rides, walks, marathons, etc. to raise money for a cause.

The Dangers of Cause-Related Marketing: Underlying Ethical Problems

Cause-related marketing's case has never been clearer or more compelling. More people are becoming increasingly civic-minded; supporting causes by purchasing products that promote them is a simple way to express this disposition. Simplicity is the key. That's why cause-related marketing provides so much money for charitable causes; it's simply more convenient for con-sumers than other forms of fundraising. (Glenn, 2003: 18)

There is little doubt that corporate cause-related marketing fits almost seamlessly in America's consumer culture, and perhaps even comfortably. Individuals routinely create their identities and announce their allegiances (as well as their generosity): buying, charging, even cooking for a cause; sporting yellow bracelets, pink ribbons, red iPods, and rough diamond and malachite bracelets; walking, running, and cycling for a cause. Indeed, cause-related marketing initiatives are so much a part of the business and cul-tural landscape that they proceed virtually unnoticed.

One day soon marketers will drop the prefix "cause-related" and see campaigns that stir the consumer's conscience as plain, simple marketing – unremarkable and barely worthy of comment. (Glenn, 2003: 18)

Are cause-related marketing campaigns "unremarkable and barely worthy of comment?" It is precisely the normalization, the almost-unconscious participation in an increasingly commodified philanthropy, that underlies my belief that corporate adoption of cause-related marketing as a business strategy is unethical. The "good deeds" achieved through cause-related marketing efforts are touted regularly through public relations efforts, and there is no doubt some truth in observations like that which opened this section. The industry, in fact, has constructed cause-related marketing as a "win-win-win, [providing] consumers an opportunity to contribute for free to their favorite charities" (Kotler and Lee, 2005: 23). Yet such cele-bratory assessments are simply snapshots of isolated campaigns, essentially micro-sites of success. At the risk of being cliched, in looking at the trees, we fail to recognize the forest of which they are a part. Such assessments naturalize the perception of consumption as a route to social benevolence, camouflage demands placed upon causes and transformations which occur as causes construct themselves to better fit the commercial logic inherent in cause-related marketing, and leave critical dimensions of the emerging social contract unexamined.

My argument arises out of three broad characteristics inherent in the cause-related marketing enterprise:

• The injection of profit-motivated strategic considerations into what might be called the "public sphere," arenas never intended to be part of a market-based model.

- The blatant appeal to conspicuous consumption as an avenue to "building a better world," and the reconstruction of activism from a political act to an act of "buying more stuff."
- The resultant commodification of social, philanthropic causes.

The repercussions of what is essentially the transformation of "cause" to "marketable product" are numerous, far-reaching, and I believe, undemocratic. It is these repercussions that have led me to view the corporate adoption of cause-related marketing as a business strategy as an unethical practice.

Injection of profit-motivated strategic considerations. My concern with regard to profit-motivated strategies entering into the realm of social issues is by no means a new one. For example, although Levitt (1958) was firmly grounded in the belief that self-interest (pursuit of the profit motive) would result in public good (a view I do not share) he voiced a concern similar to mine in his essay "The Dangers of Social Responsibility." He noted there that

> at bottom [a corporation's] outlook will always remain narrowly materialistic. What we have, then, is the frightening spectacle of a powerful economic functional group whose future and perception are shaped in a tight materialistic context of money and things but which imposes its narrow ideas about a broad spectrum of unrelated noneconomic subjects on the mass of man and society. Even if its outlook were the purest kind of good will, that would not recommend the corporation as an arbiter of our lives. (1958: 44)

In short, responding to calls for corporate social responsibility, he was pointing out the danger of corporate logic, with its "tight materialistic context of money and things," overwhelming the public sphere. This is an important warning. Today, frequently camouflaged in headlines of "dollars raised" and annual reports on corporate social responsibility is the simple fact that corporate decision-makers, motivated primarily by the needs and objectives of the corporation rather than by social welfare, regularly make decisions about the relative importance of social needs in achieving/ maintaining public welfare. What's a more vital concern? Environmental sustainability? Education? Healthcare? Where should resources be allocated? To AIDS? To providing clean drinking water to the rural villages of Guatemala? To the preservation of the rainforest?

Kotler and Lee (2005) may have unwittingly provided insight into how these decisions are made when they identified "tough questions" to ask when choosing a social issue. These questions are:

Consider the case for breast cancer philanthropy

Samantha King has written that "breast cancer research and education remains a – if not *the* – favorite issue for corporations seeking to attract female consumers" (2004: 476). This suggests that corporations have made strategic decisions to "partner" with the cause. Why might this be so?

- According to Amy Langer, director of the National Alliance of Breast Cancer Organizations, one reason is that, with breast cancer, "there was no concern that you might actually turn off your audience because of the life style or sexual connotations that AIDS has. . . . that gives corporations a certain freedom and a certain relief in supporting the cause" (in Ehrenreich, 2001: 48).
- Another reason might be the name recognition and of course, the pink ribbon. Bartlette (2007) wrote: "Everywhere you look, there are pink ribbons. And why not? The pink ribbon is the poster child for corporate cause-related marketing: it boosts the public image of the company and increases profits."

- How does this support our business goals"
- How big a social problem is this?
- Isn't the government or someone else handling this?
- What will our stockholders think of our involvement in this issue?
- Is this something our employees can get excited about?
- Won't this encourage others involved in this cause to approach us (bug us) for funds?
- How do we know this isn't the "cause du jour"?
- Will this cause backfire on us and create a scandal?
- Is this something our competitors are involved in and own already? (2005: 19)

Is this an ethical process of making decisions with regard to public welfare? Recent research (Bonini et al., 2007) shows that consumers and corporate leaders prioritize concerns differently. Is this decision-making process democratic?

The "danger" in this situation is compounded by the fact that corporate decision-makers frequently have little or no competence or expertise of note on which to base decisions which in themselves may have far-reaching and long-term implications. Again, decisions regarding resource allocation in some of the most vital arenas of public welfare – health, environment, education – are made by marketing professionals and corporate executives focused on corporate needs and objectives, rather than by professionals in the relevant areas.

The lack of competence or expertise is further amplified by the fact that the decision to "partner" with a particular group involved in a cause is, at the same time, a decision to advocate a particular solution to the problem: "This is the way the problem should be solved." What is the best way to approach a health-related problem? Awareness? Early detection? Treatment availability? Research to find a cure? Research to find the cause? Do corporate decision-makers have the knowledge base and experience to weigh the efficacy of these approaches to solving the social problem? For that matter, do consumers stop to consider the solution they are supporting when they purchase a Red iPod or a yellow silicone bracelet?

In the cause-related marketing scenario, nonprofits might view corporate involvement as "an opportunity to leverage big business to address complex social issues. What advertisers see is an ability to leverage desired demographics . . . in furtherance of commercial advertising" (Koulish, 2007).

Susan G. Komen for the Cure

Nancy Brinker, founder of Susan G. Komen for the Cure, is "widely credited with turning [breast cancer] into a marketable product with which consumers, corporations and politicians are eager to associate" (King, 2004: 475).

"The Komen Foundation's focus on early detection and cure-oriented science has helped it win generous sponsorship from pharmaceutical companies . . . and mammography equipment and film manufacturers." (King, 2006: 37)

Certainly everyone wants to find a cure, but "feminists even more ardently demand to know the cause or causes of the disease." The fact that the disease is increasing in industrialized nations suggests the possibility of environmental factors. But "[feminist] emphasis on ecological factors . . . is not shared by groups such as Komen and the American Cancer Society. *Breast cancer would hardly be the darling of corporate America if its complexion changed from pink to green*" (Ehrenreich, 2001: 47–8).

The realization that a decision to support one cause over another, one solution over another, may be the result of no greater urgency than the corporate need to appear beneficent to a particular target market certainly gives one pause. Is this an ethical decision-making process?

The breast cancer "audience"

"It is the very blandness of breast cancer, at least in mainstream perceptions, that make it an attractive object of corporate charity and a way for companies to brand themselves friends of the middle-aged female market." (Ehrenreich, 2001: 48)

"Breast cancer provides a way of doing something for women, without being feminist." (Cindy Pearson, Director of the National Women's Health Network, in Ehrenreich, 2001)

As the number of cause-related marketing efforts escalates, the ramifications of the commercial imperative become visible in other troubling ways. In the midst of what one author (Panepento, 2007) writing in the *Chronicle of Philanthropy* identifies as "cause clutter," relationships between nonprofits and corporations become increasingly complex. Corporations seek associations with "well-known" causes and negotiate to establish initiatives that will "stand out." It is not uncommon to read in the trade press of a corporation's desire to "own a cause" (see for example the list from Kotler and Lee, 2005, above). This is typically accomplished through some spectacular event, being "the first," or creating a particularly newsworthy initiative. Panepento (2007) writes that "charities, lured by the possibility of earning millions of dollars for their organizations, are signing [licensing] deals that grant companies the right to create specialty products bearing their name." To be sure, charities receive royalties on product sales, but again, corporate decisions are likely to be based on corporate needs; name recognition of the charity is likely to trump any social welfare criteria.

In this "marketplace," charities are put in the unfortunate situation of having to construct their cause as a commodity in order to enhance its promotional attractiveness to potential "corporate partners." This is no easy task, especially as agreements with those partners increase in complexity. The necessary research and negotiation take time and resources, both of which are frequently in short supply. "Suddenly," McAllister points out, "the supposedly noncommercialized not-for-profit organization becomes in essence a commercial entity" (1996: 214).

Finally, in aligning themselves with particular causes, and with particular participants in those causes, corporations are actively attempting to shape their own public image, but at the same, though perhaps unwittingly, they shape public perceptions of the cause – its "definition," its characteristics, its parameters, and its relative importance.

The story of AstraZeneca*

National Breast Cancer Awareness Month (NBCAM) was founded in 1985 by Zeneca (now AstraZeneca), a multinational pharmaceutical corporation and then subsidiary of Imperial Chemical Industries. AstraZeneca is the manufacturer of tamoxifen, the best-selling breast cancer drug, and until corporate reorganization in 2000 was under the auspices of Imperial Chemical, a leading producer of the carcinogenic herbicide acetochlor, as well as numerous chlorine and petroleum-based products that have been linked to breast cancer.

AstraZeneca's interest in promoting mammography and thereby raising detection rates and increasing sales of tamoxifen is a story widely circulated in activist circles and progressive media but almost entirely ignored in mainstream discourse. And, not surprisingly, AstraZeneca and its allies in National Breast Cancer Awareness Month, such as the American Cancer Society, continue to carefully avoid environmental issues, or indeed reference to prevention in general.

* This account is drawn verbatim from: King, 2006: xx–xxi.

Philanthropy and consumption: who knew striving for social justice was so easy?

- Join us in rejecting the tired notion that shopping is a reasonable response to human suffering. (<buylesscrap.com>)
- Who knew that striving for social justice had become so easy? (Ravisankar, 2007)
- What other disease can we cure by shopping? (Bartlette, 2007)

- But is the rise of philanthropic fashionistas decked out in Red T-shirts and iPods really the best way to save a child dying of AIDS in Africa? (Frazier, 2007)
- Do you have to suffer and sacrifice to make the world a better place? Or can you just buy more cool stuff? (Schoenberg, 2007)
- . . . where corporate consumerism is behind a mask of charity, it might be better to find solace in nothingness. We should put some serious thought about how doing less will be beneficial. Less consumption, less use of resources and less environmental degradation are related to one another and are necessary if we are ever to conceptualize and implement a model of sustainability. (Ravisankar, 2007)

The blatant appeal to conspicuous consumption inherent in the recent Red campaign has reignited a critical conversation about the linkage between consumption and charity inherent in cause-related marketing. Amid already virulent concerns about the ramifications of overconsumption – exploitation and depletion of resources, environmental degradation, growing social inequities, intractable global poverty, concerns of sustainability, escalating energy consumption, lack of clean drinking water, air pollution – "the mix of conspicuous consumption and messianic benevolence" (Marketing Week, 2007) is indefensible to many.

This conversation is important insofar as it calls our attention to the often unnoticed commercialization of everyday life. I will not elaborate on that issue here. Instead, I'd like to suggest that in focusing narrowly upon the obvious, another equally troubling dimension has been left out of this discourse: the redefinition of activism, the relinquishment of political voice.

Activism is typically viewed as an intentional action, intended to bring about social or political change. Activism can take any number of forms: well-organized movements, boycotts, demonstrations, protests and marches, civil disobedience, letter writing. In the historical sense, activism incorporates dimensions of dissent, critical questioning, and demand for change. Activism is a political act pursued by individuals and groups in their role as citizens. Increasingly, "buying more stuff" has replaced political activity; we are addressed as consumers rather than as citizens; we are asked to buy to "make a difference," rather than to question. Unfortunately, immersed as we are in a consumption culture, we too rarely notice.

It should not surprise anyone that rampant, unadulterated consumerism has become intertwined with charity and relief work. In our society, it has gotten to the point where one's identity is defined by consumption. Before, you could go to the mall, buy some commodity and bask in an illusory sense of contentment. Now, in addition to these things, you can feel like you have done your part for the world. (Ravisankar, 2007)

Conclusion

Politics and social causes are the stuff of society's public sphere, but the public sphere is being overwhelmed by the corporate logic of cause-related marketing. (Koulish, 2007)

In this essay I have argued that cause-related marketing as a business strategy is at its very foundations unethical. At the heart of my argument is the belief that Adam Smith had it wrong – corporations' self-interested pursuit of profit will not result in public good. In Levitt's words, even if the corporation's "outlook were the purest kind of good will, that would not recommend the corporation as an arbiter of our lives" (1958: 44). The injection of profit-motivated corporate strategies into the public sphere has created a marketplace in which social causes are constructed as commodities, in which social causes are essentially "bought and sold" primarily to meet corporate objectives rather than to advance public welfare. This is not ethical. This is not democratic.

- Should corporations, which by definition in our capitalist economy are profit-motivated enterprises, be primary decision-makers in identifying what is most important for our social welfare?
- Are corporate decisions in the public arena informed by knowledge, expertise, and competence beyond that of marketing?
- Upon what criteria are those decisions being made?
- Are corporations interested in public welfare, or only in the welfare of those (as texts in the field tell us) who have resources to spend and are willing to spend them?
- Should social causes be constructed, marketed, and sold like dishwashing detergent, breakfast cereal, and automobiles?

Then, too, in the midst of silicone bracelets of every hue; pink ribbons; Red iPods; charging, running, riding, and cooking for a cause, what has become of activism? What does it mean to be politically active?

What we have witnessed over the past two decades is the emergence of a corporatized public sphere in which political sentiments and critical energies are largely expressed through the purchase of products, the donation of money to "good" causes or participation in volunteer activities. And, as the belief that America's survival depends on publicly celebrated, personal, consumer-based acts of generosity has attained hegemonic status, it becomes ever more difficult to think critically about such philanthropy and volunteerism and their place in US culture. (King, 2004: 489–90)

Still, we must think critically. For in the midst of celebratory success stories, cultural spectaculars, and a buoyant trade press, any suggestion that cause-related marketing as a business strategy is at its very foundations unethical may seem rather extraordinary. And yet, if we examine what goes on behind the curtain of the seeming normality of consuming for a cause, and if we ask and answer the difficult questions, perhaps it doesn't seem so extraordinary after all.

Notes

1   The quote is from Bobby Shriver, RED campaign CEO, quoted in Conlin 2006. Corporate partners at the time of the Red launch included Gap, Apple, Motorola, Giorgio Armani, Converse, and American Express (UK). Red continues to talk with prospective vendors; vendors are required to state how much they will donate for each product sold, and to sign five-year contracts. They are not allowed to charge premium prices for Red products. According to recent estimates, 15 companies are now a part of the Red stable of partners (Panepento, 2007).

2   Though somewhat controversial from the outset, the maelstrom of public debate seems to have begun in earnest with the publication of an *Advertising Age* article titled "Costly Red Campaign reaps meager $18M; Bono & Co spend up to $100 mil on marketing, incur watchdog's wrath" (March 5, 2007). In that article, Mya Frazier notes that "The disproportionate ratio between the marketing outlay and the money raised is drawing concern among nonprofit watchdogs, cause-marketing experts and even executives in the ad business" (1). Shriver and Richard Feachem of the Global Fund adamantly denied the veracity of Frazier's account, which they deemed to be "caustically critical" in separate letters to the editor of *Advertising Age* (<joinred.com>).

3   A large part of this discussion is based upon White's (2007) occasional paper written for Business of Social Responsibility, a company that assists business in "achieving success in ways that demonstrate respect for ethical values, people, communities and the environment" (<www.bsr.org>).

4   I use the masculine pronoun here only because Friedman did so in his article.
5   Yoplait will make a contribution of up to $1.5 million with a guarantee of $500,000.
6   According to the advertisement for this promotion, "you will be supporting the education initiatives that develop and empower people in African nations where diamonds are a natural resource."

Websites

Business for Social Responsibility	bsr.org
Buy Less	buylesscrap.org
Cause Marketing Forum	causemarketingforum.com
Cone Inc.	coneinc.com
Susan G. Komen Cancer Foundation	komen.org
Newmans Own	newmansown.com
Red campaign	joinred.com
Yoplait Yogurt	yoplait.com

References

Bartlette, D. R. (2007). Pink ribbons or green dollar signs? A look at the breast cancer business. *Arkansas Traveler* via the University Wire (April).

Bonini, S. M. J., K. McKillop, and L. T. Mendonca (2007). The trust gap between consumers and corporations. *McKinsey Quarterly* 2. <http://www.mckinseyquarterly.com>.

Conlin, M. (2006). Shop (in the name of love). *Business Week* (Oct. 2): 9.

Copeland, L. (2007). High-water marketing. *Washington Post* (Feb. 18): D1.

Ehrenreich, B. (2001). Welcome to Cancerland: A mammogram leads to a cult of pink kitsch. *Harper's Magazine* (Nov.): 43–53.

Frazier, M. (2007). Costly red campaign reaps meager $18m; Bono & Co. spend up to $100 mil on marketing, incur watchdog's wrath. *Advertising Age* (Mar. 5): 1.

Friedman, M. (1970). The social responsibility of business is to increase its profits. *New York Times Magazine* (Sept. 30).

Glenn, M. (2003). There's a simple rationale behind ties with causes. *Marketing(UK)* (Mar. 20): 18.

King, S. (2004). Pink Ribbons Inc.: Breast cancer activism and the politics of philanthropy. *International Journal of Qualitative Studies in Education* 17(4): 473–92.

King, S. (2006). *Pink Ribbons, Inc.: Breast cancer and the politics of philanthropy.* Minneapolis: University of Minnesota Press.

Kingston, A. (2007). The trouble with buying for a cause. *Maclean's* (Mar. 26): 40.

Kotler, P., and N. Lee (2005). *Corporate social responsibility: Doing the most good for your company and your cause.* Hoboken, NJ: John Wiley.

Koulish, R. (2007). Turning to corporate America to save the world. *Baltimore Sun* (July 22): 19A.

Levitt, T. (1958). The dangers of social responsibility. *Harvard Business Review* (Sept./Oct.): 41–50.

Marketing Week (2007). Charity: Paved with good intentions. (Mar. 15): 24.

McAllister, M. P. (1996). *The commercialization of American culture: New advertising, control and democracy.* Thousand Oaks, CA: Sage.

Mendonca, L., and M. Miller (2007). Exploring business's social contract: An interview with Daniel Yankelovich. *McKinsey Quarterly* 2. <http://www.mckinseyquarterly.com>.

Panepento, P. (2007). Courting consumer dollars. *The Chronicle of Philanthropy* 19(19): 21.

Ravisankar, R. (2007). Consume(r ed)ucation. *Ohio State University Lantern* via the University Wire (March 26).

Reason Magazine (2005). Rethinking the social responsibility of business: A Reason debate. <http://www.com/news/printer/32239.html>, accessed 7/8/07.

Rotzoll, K. B., and J. E. Haefner, with S. R. Hall (1996). *Advertising in contemporary society: Perspectives toward understanding.* Urbana: University of Illinois Press.

Schoenberg, N. (2007). BUY(LESS) targets cause-related marketing. *Chicago Tribune* (Mar. 23).

Shriver, B. (2007). Letter to the editor of Advertising Age in response to Mya Frazier article. <http://www.joinred.com>.

Smith, C. (1994). The new corporate philanthropy. *Harvard Business Review* (May/June): 105–16.

Sweeney, C. (2005). The latest in fitness: Millions for charity. *New York Times* (July 7): E1.

Walker, R. (2004). Live strong bracelet. *New York Times Magazine* (Aug. 29).

White, A. L. (2007). Is it time to rewrite the social contract? *Business for Social Responsibility* occasional paper. <http://www.bsr.org>.

Index